WORLD CUP FEVER

Also by Simon Kuper

Football Against the Enemy

Ajax, The Dutch, The War

Soccernomics (with Stefan Szymanski)

Football Men

Barça

Impossible City: Paris in the Twenty-First Century

*Good Chaps: How Corrupt Politicians Broke Our Law
and Institutions - And What We Can Do About It*

Chums: How a Tiny Caste of Oxford Tories Took Over the UK

*The Happy Traitor: Spies, Lies and Exile in Russia:
The Extraordinary Story of George Blake*

WORLD CUP FEVER

A Footballing Journey in Nine Tournaments

SIMON KUPER

London, 3/10/25

To Mark,

Simon Kuper

Profile Books

First published in Great Britain in 2025 by
Profile Books Ltd
29 Cloth Fair
London
EC1A 7JQ

www.profilebooks.com

1 3 5 7 9 10 8 6 4 2

Typeset in Sabon by MacGuru Ltd
Printed and bound in Great Britain by
CPI Group (UK) Ltd, Croydon CR0 4YY

A CIP catalogue record for this book is available from the British Library.

Our product safety representative in the EU is Authorised
Rep Compliance Ltd., Ground Floor, 71 Lower Baggot Street,
Dublin, D02 P593, Ireland. www.arccompliance.com

ISBN 978 1 80522 410 5
eISBN 978 1 80522 413 6
Export ISBN 978 1 80522 411 2
Audio 978 1 80522 636 9

For Leo and Joey, even though they support France

Contents

1

The World Cup Diaries

One evening in June 1990, when I was a twenty-year-old university student, my friend Bryn walked into the college bar. 'If you had tickets to the World Cup,' he asked, 'would you go?'

I didn't think it was a very difficult question.

'I can get match tickets,' Bryn explained, 'but if I bugger off to Italy in the middle of term, I'll get into trouble.'

I said, 'If I had tickets to the World Cup, I'd also get tickets for my friends.'

'Oh, that's not a problem,' said Bryn. 'I can get as many tickets as I want.'

It was all thanks to Mars. The food company was sponsoring the tournament and had thousands of match tickets for business associates, but few of them wanted to go. If they were American or Asian, they probably didn't care about football. If they were European, they tended to be put off by visions of British hooligans sacking the Italian peninsula. (Margaret Thatcher, the prime minister, had encouraged the English FA to 'consider very carefully' withdrawing from the tournament.) And so some guy at Mars – the dad of a friend of Bryn's – had been stuck with stacks of spare tickets.

A few days later, Bryn, our friend Henry and I were chugging to Dover in Bryn's battered car. We crossed the Channel by boat, and spent twenty-four hours in an increasingly smelly railway carriage having the sorts of conversations that bumptious twenty-year-old male students had in the days before PlayStation: about girls, politics, and the World Cup.

Though we had only the dimmest awareness of it, globalisation

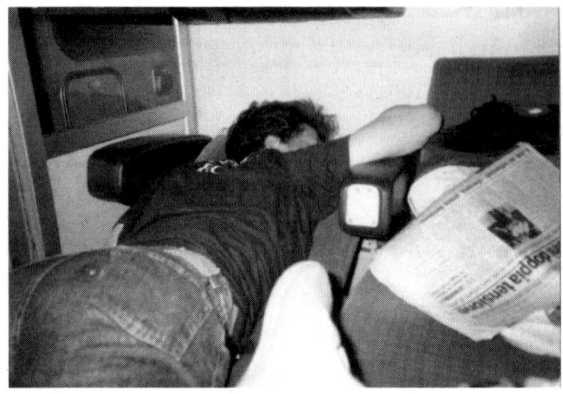

had just begun to accelerate. The Berlin Wall had fallen seven months earlier, China was opening up, and new technologies were connecting the world: cheap flights, high-speed trains, cable TV and – coming soon – the internet. The new era would change the World Cup, as I would discover over the next three decades.

The three of us were busy resolving the Bulgarian governmental crisis when our train chugged out of France and stopped at an Italian border post in the middle of nowhere. We waved our stiff-backed blue British passports at the two border guards. They studied them, and spotted that Bryn was born in Liverpool – the city at that point associated with the Heysel disaster, which five years earlier had killed dozens of Italians at the Liverpool-Juventus European Cup final. The guards conferred with each other and then told us, in broken English: 'You cannot enter Italy.'

'What?' we said.

'You might be hooligans,' they pointed out.

We pulled our IDs out of our pockets, but nothing could sway them. As a last resort we waved our library cards. 'Studenti di *Oxford* Università!' we shouted.

The border officials conferred. On a pretty weak sociological basis, they decided that if we were Oxford students, we probably weren't hooligans. It was an early lesson in the benefits of institution-dropping. They waved us back onto the train and into Italy. That's how professional the security operation for the 1990 World Cup was.

I know we arrived in Milan on the evening of 8 June, because the opening match between Diego Maradona's Argentina and Cameroon had just finished in the San Siro, and though an Argentinian victory was a foregone conclusion, we didn't yet know the score. We walked from the station into town behind a lone Cameroonian fan wrapped in his country's flag. Every passing car tooted at him in tribute. We realised that Cameroon had beaten the world champions.

Our friend's father bought us dinner in a real restaurant in Milan, then went off on a business trip. We stayed in his flat for free, and never saw him again. We had tickets for Colombia-United Arab Emirates in Bologna, Czechoslovakia-USA in Florence, and Scotland-Costa Rica in Genoa.

Inside the stadiums, we saw that Mars's business associates weren't the only people to have snubbed the World Cup. Leafing through my photographs of the tournament today, I'm struck by the underpopulated stands. My first World Cup was a village fête.

The amateurish feel extended to some of the teams, too. A few of the American players we saw beaten 5-0 by Czechoslovakia in Florence were college students, as were a large chunk of their followers. And Cameroon's thirty-eight-year-old forward Roger Milla, who scored four goals at Italia '90, had been playing for a waiters' team on the island of Reunion in the Indian Ocean.

*My first World Cup game:
Colombia-United Arab Emirates, Bologna,
9 June 1990*

Our tempers frayed on the journey home, and my friend Henry insists to this day that I chucked his untouched KFC meal into a bin at Dover, but that can't be right.

I have been to every men's World Cup since – nine in all as I write this, in 2025. That ranks me fairly high on the leader board. Even the man who created the World Cup, Jules Rimet, a guiding spirit of this book, only saw five tournaments. In Qatar in 2022, FIFA and the international sports press association AIPS held a ceremony for the seventy-odd journalists who had attended at least eight World Cups. The doyen was eighty-eight-year-old Argentinian radio commentator Enrique Macaya Márquez, who had covered seventeen tournaments since his first in Sweden in 1958. I'm not a member of AIPS, so I wasn't invited to the ceremony; I later watched the video of each journalist being handed a miniature World Cup trophy by the beaming Brazilian great Ronaldo. One of the recipients was Grant Wahl. Within a fortnight, I would watch him die of a ruptured aneurysm in the stands at Argentina-Holland.

I wrote this book partly to share the experience of being at a men's World Cup. (I should say straight away that the book doesn't cover the women's World Cup, a whole different story

that somebody else should tell.) The tournament occupies the thoughts of billions of people, and produces images that many will remember all their lives, but most fans never get to attend it. Much of this book recounts fragments of my journeys around World Cups since 1990. Some of my best moments at these tournaments have been far from the stadium, in exotic places that I'll never see again, from the Amazon to the battlefield at Stalingrad. Nick Hornby wrote that he had measured out his life in Arsenal fixtures. I have done the same with World Cups.

In my office in Paris (the city where I live, thanks largely to the 1998 tournament), I have a bookshelf lined with over 200 journalistic notebooks spanning most of my career – A6 hardcover books that you can slip inside a jacket and carry around.

These notebooks are the primary sources of this book. Sometimes I jotted down something from an interview, or a vignette I saw or overheard, not for the next day's paper, but hoping it might come in handy decades later. For this book, I also pillaged the

articles I pumped out during World Cups. I have written up my experiences using hindsight, trying to evoke what it felt like that day, but also knowing what we know now.

What's it like to be at a World Cup? And what's it like to play in one? I asked winners from Maradona to Kylian Mbappé (and some losers with lifelong regrets). The day after you win the thing, says Didier Deschamps, the victorious French captain in 1998, you wake up, and you still have the same first name, the same surname, but you now also have two more words that will attach to you forever: 'World champion.'

Even if you don't win, an inspired moment or an immortal blunder at a World Cup can fix your reputation forever. One day, that match, perhaps played when you were a twenty-year-old who thought life lay ahead of you, might be the opening line of your obituary. I've tried to evoke certain on-field moments, but I haven't recounted long-gone games. There's nothing deader, for a writer, than a dead football match. I'm sorry, but you really did have to be there.

Football is never just football, and that's especially true of World Cups. In fact, many people love the World Cup despite the football. What gives the tournament its impact? What do we all get out of it? And what does the World Cup tell us about our changing world?

Each new World Cup becomes the biggest media event in history, judged by numbers of TV hours consumed and clicks generated. The tournament is a global carnival that dramatises the role of luck in human affairs, teaches us the psychology of biting, and offers us a peek into the collective Uruguayan soul, all while giving glimpses of undying genius and inspiring a worldwide conversation. For the host country, the World Cup is usually a voyage of self-discovery. Autocrats from Mussolini to Putin have tried to get in on the action.

Since Italia '90, the World Cup's geography has changed. My first five tournaments, from 1990 through to 2006, were played in the developed world, mostly in countries familiar to the tournament's founder, Jules Rimet, so Part One of this book recounts the period when old established countries did the hosting. Two hosts in this period, Italy in 1990 and France in 1998, had staged World Cups during Rimet's reign as president of FIFA from 1921 to 1954. Another host, Germany, had been an obsession of his since his years in the trenches of the First World War. The US, host of the 1994 tournament, might have seemed a new territory, but in fact an American team played in the very first World Cup, in 1930. The biggest departure from the historical norm during my first five World Cups, the 2002 tournament in Japan and South Korea, at least took place in countries that had joined FIFA during Rimet's era.

Part Two, 'New Worlds', captures the move to unexplored territories from 2010 to 2022. FIFA's choice of Russia and Qatar as hosts for 2018 and 2022 prefigured shifts in global power beyond football. Each World Cup since 2010 has dramatised certain themes of the modern world. For South Africa in 2010 and Brazil in 2014, for instance, it was the issue of multinational capitalism invading the 'Global South'.

The book takes a deep dive into the South African World Cup, the tournament with which I have the strongest personal connection due to my family history. In fact, my account of that tournament starts more than a century before kick-off, and ends in 2024. Every World Cup is a much longer story than the one-month tournament itself, but only in South Africa have I tried to tell it from beginning to end.

Brazil in 2014 hoped to showcase *jogo bonito*, its ancestral style of football that had attempted to resist globalisation. In Russia in 2018, the theme was the rise of autocrats. Qatar in 2022 dramatised migration and the might of fossil-fuel states. As I write in 2025, the 2026 World Cup risks becoming a publicity vehicle for Donald Trump. World Cups don't change the world, but they do illuminate it.

PART ONE
IN JULES RIMET'S WORLD

2

Finding Jules Rimet

One beautiful autumn morning I cycled from my flat in Paris to a municipal cemetery in the suburb of Bagneux. I was looking for the grave of Jules Rimet. Bagneux was a surprisingly unglamorous place for him to be buried; when he died in 1956, he had served as FIFA's president for thirty-three years, and the World Cup trophy had already been named after him.

Although I was armed with a map of the cemetery's celebrity graves, it took me half an hour to find the Rimet family's. Nobody seemed to have tended it in years. The flat tombstone with its stone cross was overgrown with moss.

There was a sprig of withered leaves that someone must have left months before. Only one inscription in the stone was still legible: 'Simon Rimet, 1911–2002.' Perhaps the family had died out.

The sole sign of the man I had come for was a small gold plaque inscribed, 'Jules RIMET, 24/10/1873 – 15/10/1956.' It didn't mention anything he had done in life. Only the golden colour evoked the gold of the Jules Rimet Cup – the original World Cup trophy, which has vanished even more fully than its creator.

Rimet's name lingers in football memory, but the man himself is forgotten. Who was the white-haired Frenchman with the careful little moustache who stood at the centre of every group portrait of football officialdom? Very little has been written about him, and that almost entirely in French. But even in France, he is 'practically unknown', writes the historian Renaud Leblond.

Nonetheless, the World Cup that we know today bears the fingerprints of its maker, a man whose desire to create the tournament stemmed partly from his years fighting in the First World War. After encountering nationalism in its rawest forms, Rimet helped steer international football through a second war, during which he collaborated (uneasily) with France's pro-Nazi Vichy regime. He oversaw every World Cup between 1930 and 1950.

Who was Jules Rimet, and how did he shape this tournament?

Most of the moustachioed Europeans who created the great international sporting competitions ranged from upper class to full-blown aristocratic. Rimet was different.

He was born to a peasant family in the eastern French village of Theuley in 1873, three years after his country's catastrophic defeat in the Franco-Prussian war. The Prussians had swallowed France's Alsace and Lorraine regions to create a united Germany. The Franco-German frontier had shifted westwards to just sixty miles from Rimet's village. The French economy had been devastated and Rimet's father had sold his farm and become a grocer.

Rimets had lived in Theuley since at least the seventeenth century, but during Jules's childhood his parents migrated to Paris, leaving their eldest son and his four siblings with their grandfather, who ran a windmill. Jules became a prize-winning pupil and a choirboy, but when he was about eleven, poverty forced the family to sell the windmill. After the boy took his First Communion, he followed his parents to Paris, where they ran a grocery on the rue Cler, in what was then a lower-middle-class neighbourhood a few streets from the Eiffel Tower.

Rimet would recognise the street as it is today: a lively shopping district, dotted with a few Haussmannian buildings. The facade of a horse butcher's that probably dates from his era is still there, but it's now a fancy seafood restaurant. Groceries advertise 'bio' fruits in four languages to tourists and local bourgeois shoppers.

The most modern sport in Rimet's village had been conkers. He probably discovered football in the streets around the rue Cler. Another French biographer, Jean-Yves Guillain, has him kicking balls (as well as playing a medieval fighting sport called *barres*) on the nearby Esplanade des Invalides.

But play was never a big part of Rimet's life. He was what Parisians call, with some disdain, *un ambitieux:* a pious provincial striver. He worked in the family grocery, but also read the classics, took evening courses and studied law at university. Later he worked for a debt collection agency, which would have brought him into intimate contact with the local poor. He established himself several cuts above them: one photograph captures the young man and two friends in top hats.

By the 1890s, football clubs were sprouting in Paris. In 1897 the twenty-four-year-old Rimet and some friends met in a bistro to create their own club. They called it Red Star, a name suggested by Miss Jenny, the British governess employed by the Rimet family. As well as football, the club had sections for fencing, cycling, running and literature (Rimet was a bad poet).

Rimet served as Red Star president until 1910, and afterwards remained vice president of the Catholic-inspired football federation CFI. His speeches were heavy on abstractions ('liberty', 'youth', 'moral and physical progress') but he was also a canny diplomat and a bureaucratic tiger. In short, he was a born football official.

He doesn't seem to have fallen in love with the game itself. He only played in matches if a Red Star side was a man short. Rather, being a pious Catholic with a social conscience, he saw the game as an instrument to uplift the poor. He wanted them to rise as he had. Football would give working men dignity, and a sense of solidarity. He'd been inspired one day watching players who battled and sweated during a match, then had a drink with their opponents afterwards. In sport everyone worked together, referees were respected and cheats were punished. If only the world worked like that, he liked to say. It was his version of what Victorian Britons called 'muscular Christianity'.

The grocer's son understood that if poor men were going to play the game full-time they would need to be paid for it. His support for professional football – which was already thriving in Britain – put him firmly on one side of the great sporting argument of his age. Also in Paris in the 1890s, a slightly older Frenchman named Baron Pierre de Coubertin was reviving the ancient Olympics. Like Rimet, he thought that sport could help moralise the masses, but Coubertin's creed was amateurism and he didn't see why athletes needed to be paid. The baron's modern Olympics were strictly amateur. He was happy for football to remain a niche elite sport.

The provincial *ambitieux* Rimet took on the baron, writing: 'The Olympic ideal is of a refined essence. It's the ideal ethic to lead men to perfection, but is perfection of this world?' In an unfinished polemic that he wrote later in life, he denounced amateurism as a way to allow 'the arbitrary domination of a privileged oligarchy'. By the 1910s, Red Star was signing international footballers from the Netherlands, Belgium and Germany, and paying them semi-covertly – in so-called 'expenses', or by giving them sham jobs.

Victorian Britons invented most modern sports but couldn't see the point of playing them against foreigners. That left it to the world's rival elite, the Parisians, to create international sporting competitions, which they did in a whoosh around the turn of the twentieth century.* Coubertin staged the first modern Olympics in 1896. The newspaper *L'Auto* created the Tour de France in 1903. A year later, two international federations were founded within a few minutes' walk of each other in central Paris: the Fédération Internationale de l'Automobile began writing the rules for motor racing, and in May 1904, on a courtyard off 229 rue Saint Honoré, seven European men created the Fédération Internationale de Football Association, or FIFA.

Today, the shopfront at number 229 is a travel shop selling luxury suitcases. The historical plaque in front describes a seventeenth-century Cistercian church that stood on this spot. There's no reference anywhere to FIFA. Number 229's courtyard still houses various small businesses, as it probably did in 1904 and in the main downstairs space, where FIFA might have been founded, there's now an orthopaedist – the foot tradition lives on.

As early as 1905, FIFA's official bulletins raised the notion of holding a championship of national teams, but at this stage it was still a pipe dream. The only existing international football tournament was the Olympics. On 27 and 28 June 1914, at

---

* I told this story in my 2024 book about Paris, *Impossible City*.

a FIFA congress in Norway, a motion was passed to recognise
'the Olympic football tournament as an amateur World Cup, if
organised in conformity with FIFA's regulations'. Rimet, who was
present, grumbled quietly about the amateurism – 'We're far from
a real World Cup!' – but, knowing he was in a minority, he let it
go. Then, on the second morning of the congress, the Archduke
Franz-Ferdinand was assassinated in Sarajevo. Instead of a World
Cup, there was going to be a world war.

Rimet was already forty-one, with a wife and three young children, but he seems to have volunteered for the front. He joined the
army on 4 August 1914, the day after France entered the war, and
was still in the trenches in the autumn of 1918. It's a small miracle
that he is buried in a civilian's grave at Bagneux and not in one of
the cemetery's adjoining fields of military tombstones for French
and British soldiers killed in the Great War.

A remarkable photograph survives of Rimet's war. It is 1916,
and he is sitting in a trench, wearing his officer's kepi, surrounded
by seven black infantrymen. These must have been some of the
'tirailleurs sénégalais' – literally, 'Senegalese riflemen', though
they were in fact recruited all over French west Africa – who
fought for France in the Great War. Their presence was decried by
the Germans as a scandalous introduction of 'savagery' into 'civ-
ilised warfare'. The French themselves were embarrassed by their
reliance on black men. They rarely mentioned it afterwards, and
fobbed off the African veterans with tiny pensions. The war may
have been Rimet's only lifetime encounter with Africans – but
presumably quite an intimate one.

Even freezing in a trench on the western front, he remained at
heart a football official. His pre-war fellow official in Paris, Henri
Delaunay, a bony, bespectacled young nerd, spent much of the war
plotting to create a French version of the English FA Cup. It was
to be called the Coupe Charles-Simon, named after Delaunay's
former boss in the CFI federation, who had been killed in 1915 by
German shrapnel. On 16 April 1917, Rimet wrote from the front
to Delaunay:

My apologies, when your first letter reached me I was on the lines and very busy … I don't want to delay longer, and I send you my trusted approval. Yesterday I saw Reichel [another football official serving in the army], who took the trouble to come 15 kilometres on horseback to tell me disagreeable things about the negotiations for the competition in question …

He didn't give me good reason not to approve, and his intervention does not modify my first intention. I am shivering as I write to you, so please excuse my scribble.

Rimet was scribbling this at a fairly dramatic moment in the war: days later, French soldiers staged mutinies against their army leadership. Having lost over a million of their comrades, they were refusing orders to attack. But the French Cup was set up. (Delaunay would eventually create an even bigger football competition; he spent decades pushing for a European Championship for national teams, which finally launched in 1958, three years after his death.)

Rimet had a 'good war'. As always, he was upwardly mobile, 'promoted from private to corporal to sergeant to lieutenant and finally, in 1919, to major', write the academics Philippe Vonnard and Grégory Quin in a biographical paper on Rimet. He also invented a cheap rangefinder that, as he explained in an accompanying booklet, would allow 'everybody, the soldier like the chief, to assess a distance with the least risk of error'. A military dispatch of May 1916 singled him out: 'In a delicate position, this machine-gun officer gave proof of judicious initiative, tireless zeal and a lot of *sang-froid* during various bombardments.' Another dispatch, just before the Armistice, said:

Monsieur Rimet, lieutenant, at the front for three years now, while engaged on October 20, 1918 with determining the elements of an indirect machine-gun assault, and caught in a violent enemy bombardment, did not leave the terrain until he had accomplished his task.

He won the Croix de Guerre three times.

France lost 1.3 million soldiers in the war, including several Red Star players, while another million Frenchmen were invalided. But almost immediately after the Armistice, in the winter of 1918–19, Rimet was back in action as a football administrator. In April 1919 he became president of the new French national football federation, which united the various squabbling federations of pre-war days. Delaunay was his general secretary, and both men would remain in their posts until after the Second World War. In 1921 Rimet was also elected president of FIFA. Oddly for such a proponent of professional football, he was a strictly amateur president, only accepting travel expenses (though, given his constant motion, these would have added up).

He put his life's energy into these roles. When off duty, he lived quietly as a DIY enthusiast, a reader of Voltaire and Plato, and a gardener who liked pottering around in his clogs in his country cottage north of Paris.

He barely mentioned the Great War after 1918, but it seems to have remade his world view forever. Like many French ex-combatants, Rimet had returned from war obsessed with peace. FIFA, in his mind, was the footballing equivalent of the new League of Nations. His lifetime preoccupation became, to quote the title of a pamphlet he published aged eighty, 'Football and the reconciliation of peoples'. He would always say that FIFA sought 'international solidarity'. He thought the game could eliminate 'suspicions and rivalries that today still set peoples against each other'. Baron Coubertin believed much the same thing, but Rimet argued that Olympic amateurism was at odds with universal brotherhood, because it reserved top-flight sport for men with 'a golden paw'.

Rimet's mission in the 1920s was to realise FIFA's original dream and set up a World Cup. Finally, in May 1928, the FIFA congress in Amsterdam voted to create a competition open to all football nations. By 'all', FIFA meant Europe and the Americas; non-white peoples such as the 'Senegalese riflemen' were colonial subjects who didn't count.

Rimet's World Cup would be white, and it would be professional, unlike the Olympic football tournament, which excluded many of the world's leading players because they were paid. He was snaffling football's world championship from his posh amateur rivals at the IOC. FIFA's World Cup would never be hamstrung by the snobbish arguments about whether to admit paid players that beset the Olympics as well as rugby, tennis and American college sport. And so Rimet helped establish international football as a commercial pursuit, played and watched mostly by working-class men. There was nothing inevitable about this. When the World Cup was conceived, professional football still hadn't been legalised in France.

Once the decision had been made to create the tournament, one obstacle remained: money. 'FIFA didn't have a *sou* at the time,' recalled Yves, Rimet's beloved grandson, decades later. The federation in the 1920s was a tiny outfit, without even a bank account. Its headquarters was the Amsterdam home of its secretary-treasurer Carl Hirschmann, a stock trader who managed FIFA's money. His fellow officials seem to have thought he kept it safely in the bank. In fact, Hirschmann was investing it in the stock market. Then came the Great Crash of 1929, and he went bankrupt. He eventually admitted that he had lost almost all the 400,000 French francs that FIFA had entrusted to him. It was the first in a rich history of FIFA's financial scandals. 'Loss of money is never fatal,' shrugged Rimet. Still, Hirschmann's downfall prompted FIFA to move its headquarters from Amsterdam to Zurich, where it remains to this day.

Even with a responsible treasurer, FIFA couldn't have afforded to fund the first World Cup. The federation needed to find a host country willing to finance the whole thing. Luckily Uruguay, at the time one of the world's richest countries and planning to celebrate its centenary in 1930, volunteered. 'The host pays' has remained the tournament's organisational principle to this day.

Thirteen countries entered the first World Cup, with most of the European teams crossing the Atlantic on the same ship, the *Conte Verde*, their passages paid by Uruguay. Rimet's late-life memoir, *L'histoire merveilleuse de la Coupe de Monde* ('The Marvellous History of the World Cup'), published in 1954 and never translated into English, recounts all his World Cups. *L'histoire merveilleuse* is now so thoroughly out of print that I could only get hold of it at the Bibliothèque Nationale de France, the national library. The book's tone is light, with frequent attempts at humour. Rimet doesn't waste space on political or any other complexity, not even with the hindsight of an old man who had lived through two world wars. He seemed to have emerged from the wreckage with his optimism intact: the memoir reads like a jolly chairman's report of the lads from the first team having fun on foreign tours.

But there is some delicious detail. Rimet spends pages recalling the pleasure of that first crossing to Uruguay – sitting in a rocking chair, gazing out on the sunny Atlantic, spotting dolphins and sharks, with nobody able to phone him, and no irritating unexpected visitors. He was carrying in his baggage 'a statuette 30 centimetres high and weighing four kilogrammes' – the new World Cup trophy. He had commissioned it from a friend, the Parisian sculptor Abel Lafleur, 'of whom one cannot say that he is a sportsman, but who had acquired the sense of sport sufficiently profoundly to express it with talent'.

Sailing on the *Conte Verde* with Rimet and the footballers was the great Russian opera singer Feodor Chaliapin. The captain asked him to sing at the traditional party to celebrate the crossing of the equator. In Rimet's telling, Chaliapin refused, asking, 'If I were a cobbler, would you ask me to make you a free pair of shoes on the pretext that we were going to pass The Line?' Chaliapin was a professional, like Rimet's footballers. The ship made do with a fancy-dress ball.

Landing in Montevideo five hours late, they were 'acclaimed by a joyous crowd', writes Rimet. The president of Uruguay, Dr Juan Campisteguy, immediately invited him for a barbecue, not so much because Rimet was president of FIFA but because he was a Frenchman. Campisteguy, the proud descendant of a French émigré, regarded Rimet as 'a quasi-compatriot'. At the *asado*, he carved a choice piece from the cow's head and presented it cere-monially to his guest.

The visiting teams stayed near each other by the beach, and, writes Rimet, immediately became great friends, as if 'at a family party'. Football was creating international brotherhood. Mean-while, construction work continued day and night at the Estadio Centenario. It would only be completed days after the tourna-ment kicked off.

In the first World Cup final, Uruguay beat Argentina 4-2. Afterwards the Uruguayans ran around the pitch waving their own trophy, apparently made of silver – possibly a prize won in some other competition. Rimet, standing lost on a field packed with celebrating fans, eventually just seems to have handed La-fleur's trophy to the chubby bow-tied president of the Uruguayan FA, Raúl Jude. The first World Cup was considered a success.

Soon afterwards, Rimet's belief in human brotherhood began to collide with fascism. In March 1933, weeks after the Nazis took power in Germany, he accompanied the French team to a friendly in Munich. The German crowd listened quietly to the French anthem, and an impressed Rimet promised his hosts that on his return to France he would correct mistaken views of the new Reich.

A year later, the second World Cup was staged in Benito Mussolini's Fascist Italy. By this time, writes Rimet, the tourna-ment had grown to encompass 'the entire world' (again meaning Europe and the Americas). He did his best to get on with his Fascist hosts, though it wasn't always easy. He wrote that he often had 'the impression during the World Cup that the real president of the international football federation was Mussolini'. When the two men sat side by side during matches at Rome, the dictator watched play 'with sustained attention, without distractions', showing no interest in the Frenchman's attempts at chit-chat. Mussolini had commissioned a huge bronze winner's trophy that dwarfed the actual World Cup. Luckily, wrote Rimet, the Italians beat Czechoslovakia in the final and kept the thing, 'as we would not have known how to carry it away'.

The night after the final, the jubilant Italian dignitaries forgot about the FIFA delegation. Rimet and his colleagues felt lost until General Vaccaro, head of Italy's football federation, kindly invited them to dinner by the sea at Ostia. The general drove them there himself, a terrifying journey along a winding coastal road, but the meal was superb. Rimet, writing after the war, understood that Vaccaro might be in bad odour with some readers for his spell commanding Italian Fascist troops on the eastern front. It was not necessary to 'appreciate his political persona', grants Rimet, but Vaccaro had been a 'prestigious president' of Italian football, and a nice chap. FIFA's consistent willingness to embrace brutal regimes, from Argentina's military junta of the 1970s through Vladimir Putin and Mohammed bin Salman, was baked in from the start. It was all part of 'peace through sport'.

A photograph from the 1936 Berlin Olympics shows Rimet walking with the FIFA delegation through the swastika-bedecked streets of Hitler's capital – his French federation had opposed a press campaign to boycott the Nazi Games. In Berlin, the men of FIFA voted through another of Rimet's dreams: France was named host of the 1938 World Cup.

Rimet's six-year-old grandson Yves performed the draw for the tournament, standing on a table in shorts amid besuited officials, pulling names from a glass vase held up by his beaming grandfather. Soon after the draw was made, Hitler's Anschluss swallowed up Austria, one of the competing nations. This was a nuisance, as it left the tournament with just fifteen teams. FIFA had to cancel the match between Austria and Sweden.

The hosts France met the reigning champions in the quarter-final. Before kick-off the Italians, playing in an all-black kit for the first time, gave the Fascist salute, whereupon French fans pelted them with stones. Italy won the game. After they beat Hungary in the final at Colombes, and the Italian flag was hoisted in victory, Rimet was pleased to see the French crowd applaud, despite the 'serious political disagreements' between the two countries. He commented: 'I can see hardly anything else but sport that is capable of creating these spontaneous appeasements.'

At the FIFA congress in Paris on the eve of the tournament, Germany and Brazil had both bid to stage the 1942 World Cup. But FIFA officials, already sensing that 'politics' might intrude before 1942 rolled around, delayed choosing a host.

Rimet doesn't say a word about the Second World War in his memoir. In life, he initially tried to ignore it. Having fought one terrible war against the Germans, he entered the second dedicated to his belief that football could bring peace between nations – even if one of the nations was Nazi Germany. France declared war on Hitler on 3 September 1939. Forty-eight days later, on 21 October, Rimet travelled to an urgent FIFA meeting in Bern, Switzerland, which was attended by two prominent Germans: FIFA's secretary general Ivo Schricker, and Peco Bauwens, a senior figure in the Nazi-aligned German football federation, the DFB.

When Rimet returned to France, he found himself in trouble. Why had he been consorting with Germans? On the morning of 27 October, he was summoned for an interview at the office of Amédée Bussière, the head of the Sûreté Nationale, the French police. Later that day, one of Bussière's underlings typed up an account of Rimet's self-exculpations:

> He had thought that given the very important interests that he represents within the Fédération Internationale, in which are represented at least 50 nations, that he could go to Bern to attend the urgent committee meeting and, above all, he thought the German representatives would abstain ...
>
> M. Rimet has a son at the front, and he is profoundly saddened ... it was with tears in his eyes that he asked me to be excused.

That same day, Rimet wrote Bussière a three-page letter in purple ink, providing further explanations. He said the Prefecture of Police had granted him a visa for Switzerland. He knew he was going to meet Schricker, who admittedly was German, but the man lived in Zurich, and had assured Rimet 'that he was acquiring Swiss nationality'.

Schricker had met Rimet's train at 9.15 a.m. on 21 October. He then informed an 'astonished' Rimet that Bauwens, who headed FIFA's committee on the rules of the game, would also be attending the meeting. Bauwens had been summoned by FIFA's Italian vice president Giovanni Mauro, supposedly to discuss 'certain divergences in the translations of the rules of the game in different languages', and to opine on the regulation of Olympic football. Rimet didn't say it, but the Axis powers clearly wanted to pack FIFA's first wartime meeting with their own men.

Rimet wrote to Bussière that when he discovered that Bauwens was coming, he hotfooted it to the French consulate to ask what he should do. The consulate told him he could proceed provided that Bauwens spoke only about the rules of football, and that he and Rimet didn't talk. Rimet concluded: 'My encounter with Dr Bauwens was wholly fortuitous and involuntary.'

He told Bussière that he had led FIFA for twenty years, having repeatedly been unanimously elected. 'I have always sought to use this confidence in the service of France. Many of our diplomatic agents abroad can testify to this.' He offered to resign if that was what the French government wanted, or to hand off his presidential duties for the duration of the war to one of the vice presidents, the Italian Mauro or the Belgian Rodolphe Seeldrayers. If France let him remain FIFA's president, 'I would be very happy to receive the directives that would permit me, in this position, to serve my country as I always have.' He signed the beseeching letter 'Jules Rimet, Croix de guerre – three citations'. The Sûreté Nationale let him keep his post. After all, the FIFA presidency represented French soft power.

In June 1940 France surrendered to Hitler, and Marshall Pétain established the collaborationist Vichy regime. Rimet now saw his domestic mission, as head of the French football federation, to keep his sport going, but he soon found himself at odds with Vichy. He seemed able to live with the regime's fascism; what he couldn't accept was its support for his old enemy, amateurism in sport. The Vichyistes, like the Nazis, regarded professionalism as a profound moral evil. Also, Vichy wanted to appoint the country's football officials itself. In March 1942 Rimet stepped down as president of the French federation after twenty-three years, though he remained honorary president.

Meanwhile, the Axis powers were planning a coup at FIFA. Their opportunity came with the meeting of FIFA's executive board at the federation's headquarters in Zurich in January 1941. Football officials travelling to Switzerland from occupied Europe required German or Italian visas. The Axis powers pulled a trick: they first granted the visas, so that the meeting would go ahead, but then suddenly withdrew them.

The hope was that if officials from occupied countries couldn't travel, there would be a German-Italian majority at the board meeting, and the Fascists could capture FIFA. No doubt Schricker, the German secretary general, was in on the plot. It failed, largely, it seems, because the neutral Swiss didn't like political interference in the organisations they hosted.

As it was, Rimet and the other senior FIFA officials in their various warring countries contrived to exchange some friendly messages during the conflict. Schricker, in Zurich, helped keep letters circulating between them, and Rimet managed to visit the city twice in the war years. The footballing brotherhood treated the calamity as a mere interruption.

Almost immediately after Paris was liberated in August 1944, Rimet returned as president of the French federation. Nobody afterwards seems to have held his two-year collaboration with Vichy against him. People understood that football was much more real to him than fascism. And soon after Germany's surrender, as president of FIFA, he was once again holding meetings with FIFA's senior German, Bauwens.*

Bauwens had had a complicated journey through the Third Reich. He had applied to join the Nazi party in May 1933. A

---

* Much of my account of Bauwens and of FIFA in wartime is taken from various writings by the German political scientist Arthur Heinrich.

membership card in his name was written out. But the party never issued it, rejecting him because of his marriage to a Jewish woman, Elise Gidion.

Bauwens and Elise didn't have a perfect marriage. He would lock her in the bedroom when he received one of his mistresses. Elise became a heavy drinker, and took her own life in 1940 – or so it appears. Their son later accused Bauwens of encouraging her suicide, or possibly even adding the fatal overdose of sleeping tablets to her wine glass.

During the war, Bauwens' family construction company ran its own forced labour camp, which appeared on a post-war list of 2,500 'Slaveholders in the Nazi regime'. Yet after the German surrender, Bauwens sent Rimet a letter in which he portrayed himself as an anti-Nazi: 'Would I not be the worst person in the world, if I had performed only the smallest henchman services for the people who have my wife on their conscience?'

Other FIFA officials resented Bauwens for his 'brown' past, but Rimet didn't. Given his life experience, for him peace through sport meant above all peace between Germany and France. He and Bauwens were brothers in football.

With the war over, Rimet could focus on what mattered: the World Cup. In 1946 a FIFA congress in Luxembourg renamed the trophy the 'Coupe Jules Rimet' – 'to my great confusion', he writes modestly.

For the first post-war World Cup, in Brazil in 1950, Rimet repeated the transatlantic crossing that he had made for the inaugural tournament twenty years earlier. He aimed to restore the comity of the pre-Fascist world. The Axis powers Germany and Japan had been banned from FIFA, but Rimet was smoothing the path for their swift return. In 1950, Bauwens became president of the German football federation. A FIFA congress in Rio de Janeiro, held on the eve of the World Cup, agreed 'to not let politics introduce itself into sports'.

Travelling around Brazil during the tournament, Rimet observed that the country 'seems to live only for football and the cup'. When the Coupe Rimet itself was exhibited in a shop in

Rio, the crowds flocking to see it were so large that a security firm had to be hired. The Brazilians were certain that they would keep the cup. As Rimet noted: 'By a curious phenomenon of collective psychosis, all the city was celebrating victory before it was won.'

FIFA officials weren't invited to the opening ceremony in the new stadium, the Maracanã. Rimet explains in his memoir that for the Rio authorities, 'the World Cup is a strictly Brazilian affair'. The stadium with its 200,000-person capacity was so packed for matches that even VIPs had to fight their way to their seats. Rimet was told that the Archbishop of Rio, 'caught in a besieging crowd, could not free himself except by roughly knocking over his nearest neighbours'.

The 1950 tournament had no official final, just a second stage of group matches. But the de facto final turned out to be the Brazil-Uruguay game. A draw would be enough to make the Brazilians world champions, and a grandiose victory ceremony was planned. While their national anthem played, the Brazilian team were to walk to the centre of the pitch through a guard of honour to receive the Coupe Rimet. With the match tied at 1-1 and only a few minutes remaining, Rimet descended with the trophy through the innards of the Maracanã to the touchline, ready to make his congratulatory speech for the hosts. But by the time he emerged from the tunnel, the crowd was silent. During his descent, Uruguay had scored the winning goal.

Rimet writes: 'There was no longer a guard of honour, nor a national anthem, nor a speech in front of a microphone, nor a solemn awarding of the trophy.' Instead he found himself jammed amid a throng of pitch invaders, the cup in his hand, not knowing what to do with it. He was forced to repeat the rushed handover of 1930: 'I end up spotting the Uruguayan captain, and I give him the cup while shaking his hand, as if in secret, without being able to say a word to him.'

It was Rimet's last official act at a World Cup. Aged seventy-six, he was being phased out as president. At the FIFA congress in Bern, on the eve of the 1954 tournament, he was replaced by the Belgian Rodolphe Seeldrayers (who would die the following year).

The peasant boy from Theuley had overseen the growth of the World Cup into an event that moved the white world. During his thirty-three-year reign, the federation's membership had grown from twenty-nine countries to eighty-five. His associates at FIFA proposed him for the Nobel Peace Prize. In 1956, while they were assembling the supporting dossier, Rimet died, aged eighty-two. Though he lies forgotten in his suburban grave, his obsessions still mark the World Cup.

3

'We Are Someone Again': Germany and the 1954 'Miracle of Bern'

West Germany-Hungary, World Cup final, 4 July 1954, Wankdorf Stadium, Bern, Switzerland

Rimet's last World Cup climaxed in one of Europe's first out-breaks of football nationalism. 'The Miracle of Bern', as it came to be known, was the day West Germany advanced from being a state to becoming a nation. That day provided the first shared happy memories to stick into the new national photograph album.

The West German team that travelled to the World Cup was in many ways still the old Germany. Rimet's wartime friend Bauwens ran the country's football federation. The coach, Sepp Herberger – *Bundestrainer* of the Federal Republic of West Germany – had been *Reichstrainer* under Hitler. After the war, Herberger had passed through a denazification committee, removed the swastika from his tracksuit, and hung a portrait of the Christian Democratic finance minister Ludwig Erhard in his house.

Herberger's star player in 1954 was Fritz Walter, whom he had spotted as an eighteen-year-old in 1938. Walter had fought in the Wehrmacht during the war, and was briefly a prisoner of the Soviets. Only his footballing skills had saved him from deportation to Siberia.

The World Cup final pitted Herberger's men against the great Hungarians, who two weeks previously had hammered them 8-3 in a group game. Going into the final, a series of coincidences gave the Germans a chance. Hungary's chubby genius Ferenc Puskás picked up an injury, a Swiss marching band disturbed the

Hungarians' pre-match siesta, and a rainstorm turned the pitch into a mud bath.

The last twist of fate came with a little German help. Albert Sing, Herberger's assistant, told me in 2001: 'Before the final, the Hungarians asked the groundsman if they could use changing-room two. They had used it before the World Cup for a friendly against Switzerland, which they won. Footballers are superstitious. The groundsman told me, and I told Herberger. He said, "We're going to irritate them a little." So I asked the groundsman to hang a sign saying *Deutschland* on changing-room two.'

Long before *The Miracle of Bern* became the highest-ever grossing German film in 2003, the match itself was like a movie. The Hungarians went 2-0 up after just eight minutes, but Herberger's men fought back. Adi Dassler, founder of Adidas, had issued them with new lightweight boots, whose adjustable studs could be lengthened for better grip. The Germans flitted through the mud. Six minutes from time, their beer-loving striker Helmut Rahn scored their winning third goal. (Rahn spent much of the rest of his life having to reconstruct it for fellow drinkers in bars, using beer mats and ashtrays for players.) The final was the Hungarian team's sole defeat between 1950 and the country's uprising against communism in 1956.

The *Wunder von Bern* crystallised the German hope that hard work could raise their country from the ruins. Almost every German alive in 1954 had their own story about the match. Fifty years after the game, when I asked the West German footballer Bernd Hölzenbein whether winning the World Cup in 1974 had been the highlight of his life, he replied that it hadn't even been his favourite World Cup: 'Just like everyone, I saw the final of '54, as a small boy, on the only television set within a radius of perhaps ten kilometres. Those players were my idols. I devoured Fritz Walter's books. 1954 was a symbol of German resurrection. 1974 was less important.'

Countless Germans did gather around their neighbourhood TV sets to watch the '54 final, but far more – in both West and East Germany – followed the match on the wireless. At the final whistle, radio commentator Herbert Zimmermann whooped: '*Aus* ['over']! *Aus! Aus! Aus!* The game is over! Germany is world champion!' And then he added, as if to deflate any hubris: 'Even in this moment, we do not want to forget that it is only a game – a game, but the most popular game the world knows.'

That sequence remains one of post-war Germany's best-known passages of speech. Rainer Werner Fassbinder, left-wing film-maker and football nut, used it in the finale of his film *Marriage of Maria Braun*. Maria, a dance-hall courtesan who becomes a rich post-war businesswoman, blows herself up in her mansion by lighting a cigarette in the gas oven, while from the wireless set behind her, Zimmermann screams, '*Aus! Aus! Aus! Aus!*' To Fassbinder, a German resurrection could only be sinister.

An eleven-year-old pastor's son named Friedrich Christian Delius was listening to Zimmermann that day. Later he wrote a novel called *The Sunday I Became World Champion*. 'I still feel a personal, speechless feeling of victory,' Delius explained, 'and I am not alone. For us children the victory was a liberation, perhaps because our fathers, who had survived the war, could finally permit themselves to appear more relaxed and happy.' The day of the final, he said, was the first time he saw his father smile.

The 'Miracle of Bern' became a founding myth of the emergent Federal Republic. The train carrying the winning team home was mobbed at every station. No doubt the significance of the game grew stylised in the retelling, but something momentous did happen that day. The phrase associated with it is '*Wir sind wieder wer*': 'We are someone again.'

Post-war Germans had finally found something German that they were allowed to be proud of. They had been obliged to junk their other national symbols: the flag, militarism, the first two stanzas of their anthem and most of their past heroes. West Germany was the first nation-state without public nationalism – until that Sunday in Bern. The historian Joachim Fest, biographer of Hitler, would later say: 'The young Federal Republic had three founding fathers. Politically it's Konrad Adenauer, economically it's Ludwig Erhard, and mentally it's Fritz Walter.'

Some Germans celebrating the *Wunder von Bern* fell back on the only kind of nationalistic language they'd ever learned – the kind that had been in daily use until 1945. Spectators in Bern and people across Germany sang the taboo line of their national anthem, '*Deutschland, Deutschland über alles.*'

Two days after the final, at a celebration in the appropriate setting of a Munich beer cellar, Bauwens, no longer fully sober, told the 7,000 guests that the football victory had extinguished German guilt. He said that the players had 'shown what a healthy German, who is loyal to his country, can achieve'. He then launched into a eulogy of 'the Führer Principle', in the 'good sense of the word'. Within minutes of his taking the microphone, Bavarian radio cut off its live coverage of the celebrations.

Still, Bauwens in his own way had grasped a new truth: after 1945, football had started to replace war in Europe as a source of national pride. From 1954 on, Germans began to unite, in a mostly low-key post-war way, around their national football team. The Federal Republic built itself on the World Cup. Other countries would follow its lead.

4

The TV Years: My First World Cups, 1978–1986

When I moved from London to the Netherlands in October 1976, I was seven years old and had never heard of the country. My father had taken a job in the small university town of Leiden. Only later did I realise I had arrived in the middle of a Golden Age of football. I had barely ever kicked a ball in London, but in Holland my brother and I became regulars in the game played every evening before bedtime in the street where we lived.

We soon discovered that half the boys in the country belonged to a football club. (The Dutch FA had banned female football until 1971, in line with most other leading football countries, and during my childhood it never occurred to me that girls could play too.) In and around Leiden, which then had just over 100,000 inhabitants, there were dozens of football clubs. Some fielded as many as twenty senior teams, seven teams of under-eights, and so on. Many males derived much of their identity and social life from being the right-back or linesman of the twelfth team, for instance. Not to play football was not to exist. My brother and I joined the Ajax Sportman Combinatie, a club founded in 1892, which had once been one of the best in the Netherlands. It was no longer much good, but its ground still possessed an actual stand.

As a child, I'd get up at dawn each Saturday and race to the ground. The gates would still be locked, but my teammates and I would rattle them until, at about 8 a.m., the angry janitor arrived to unlock them. Then we'd kick around in the puddles of

ASC's gravel pitch until our match began. Afterwards we'd buy chewing gum in the canteen and hang around the ground, hoping that another team might be a player short and we'd get another game. Then we'd go to someone's house to kick balls against their garage door.

This was a fairly standard boyhood in the Netherlands. Of the fourteen million Dutch people in the 1970s, one million played football for clubs like ASC. No other country had a higher proportion of registered footballers. Franz Beckenbauer said he finally understood why Dutch players were so good when he flew over the Netherlands in a helicopter and saw that it seemed to consist chiefly of football grounds.

No wonder we all played. My parents paid ASC about £50 a year, and in return my brother and I were allowed virtually to live at the club. Twice a week we were trained by coaches who had completed long courses to get their obligatory diplomas. ASC's sole grass pitch was obsessively watered and mowed by the local council. Dutch football is a product of Dutch social democracy.

And it was world-beating. In 1974, just a couple of years before we arrived, the Dutch national team, *Oranje*, reached the final in its first World Cup appearance since 1938, displaying a style of football that tens of millions of people today still remember. In the twentieth century, each country still played its own way. A national team was the nation made flesh: those eleven men in plastic shirts embodied the country, with all its virtues and faults. You couldn't confuse the German style with the English or the Brazilian. Each international match was a miniature clash of civilisations. Nations felt that other nations' styles were immoral, or even evil.

And of all the rival footballing civilisations, in the 1970s the Dutch was the most advanced. Anglophones called the Dutch game 'total football', while Hispanic countries spoke of '*La Naranja mécanica*', or 'The Clockwork Orange', in honour of the team's amber shirts. The Dutch didn't call it anything.

It was a style that treated football as a kind of geometry. Almost every player in the country learned how to position himself, to pass into space, and to close off space after losing the ball. We didn't only learn that from our coaches. It was in the air: everyone around us understood, from the players we watched on Dutch telly on Sunday evenings to the kids kicking a ball on the street.

In the words of the man who essentially invented the Dutch style, Johan Cruyff, 'Football is a game you play with your head.' The country's sports press was full of complex and often ad hominem arguments about tactics. Cruyff turned Dutch football into a kind of intellectual debating society. He'd give endless interviews in which he showered truths about how to play. Always pass the ball a yard ahead of your teammate, he'd say, because that forces him to run, forces him to pass with his first touch, and so raises the pace of play. It sounds obvious, but when I later moved back to England, I realised that even some English professional footballers didn't know this.

In England, when two football lovers meet, the first question is, 'Who do you support?' In the Netherlands, it's 'Who do you play for?' The Dutch are footballers first, fans second.

That meant that the players at the top of the pyramid, the ones who played for *Oranje*, were recognisably members of the Dutch football family. They were like us, just better at football. Wim Rijsbergen, centre-back in 1974, had started at an amateur club in Leiden. My mother played tennis with the wife of Holland's great midfielder Wim van Hanegem, despite being approximately half her height. Some *Oranje* players of the 1970s were semi-pros, with day jobs and ordinary lives. In a favourite Dutch word of the era, they were not demigods but '*normaal*'.

This was the football I was raised in, and it's still my football. I'm not Dutch, and I left the country aged sixteen in 1986, but my team at World Cups is *Oranje*.

Argentina-Netherlands, World Cup
final, Leiden, 25 June 1978

This is my first World Cup memory. I am eight years old, and I'm sitting in my pyjamas in our living room watching the final with my parents and grandparents. The latter are visiting from apartheid South Africa, where my parents were born and raised. My family are immigrants in the Netherlands. I am often ashamed of my parents – outsiders who dress wrong, don't look like Dutch people and speak Dutch with funny accents.

Sitting in the grandstand in the Buenos Aires stadium is the moustachioed leader of the military junta, General Videla. For him, this World Cup is a celebration of Argentinian greatness. Argentina's striker Mario Kempes scores the opening goal, but after seventy-eight minutes Dick Nanninga, the big Dutch centre-forward who runs a flower kiosk in a small town near the German border, heads the ball into the confetti-strewn net. The French windows to our garden are open on the warm evening. In my memory, a communal cheer rises from the neighbouring houses.

In the ninetieth minute, with the score 1-1, the Dutch sweeper Ruud Krol strikes a long free kick forward. It bounces through to striker Rob Rensenbrink, 'The Snake Man', and he hits the post. That's how close I came to winning the World Cup at my first attempt. Decades later, a Dutch TV advert would doctor the original footage to show Rensenbrink's shot going in, under the slogan, 'Imagine if things had gone differently ...'

Argentina won 3-1 in extra time. Few Dutch people minded all that much. Even Rensenbrink said in old age that what kept him awake at night was not his shot against the post, but the theft of his beloved fishing boat. The Dutch in 1978 were proud to finish second in the world once again.

My grandparents and mother are long dead, but I can still see us all sitting around the TV that evening. I recall that night as vividly as almost anything else in my childhood. A World Cup is like Proust's madeleine. Each new World Cup reminds you of past World Cups, and the people you watched them with.

I suspect that World Cups were even more memorable when

I was a child. I grew up with almost no other live football on TV, and no second screen to mess around on during the game. Back then, we watched with a focus that no longer exists. Aged eight, I couldn't imagine anything higher than being a footballer at a World Cup. But even for a kid today, the tournament can be their first glimpse of beauty and greatness.

France-Netherlands, World Cup qualifier, Paris, 18 November 1981

On the Dutch goal line, their captain Ruud Krol and keeper Hans van Breukelen stared at each other accusingly after Michel Platini's free kick for France sailed between them into the net. France won the qualifier 2-0, and *Oranje* didn't make it to the 1982 World Cup. Four years later, a header by Belgian defender Georges Grün kept us out of the 1986 World Cup. So I watched the 1980s' tournaments the way the vast majority of the world watches every World Cup: without my own team there, looking for another country to support.

France-West Germany, World Cup semi-final, Seville, 8 July 1982

This was one of the formative matches of my childhood, even more so than the Italy-Brazil game three days earlier. I can still see myself aged twelve, sitting up late, my feet on our living-room table. I watched the German keeper Toni Schumacher fly into the ribs of the French defender Patrick Battiston, and after Battiston had been stretchered off to hospital, I watched Schumacher take the ensuing goal kick (the Dutch ref Charles Corver hadn't even given a foul). More than thirty years later, Battiston would say: 'To this day, I have a cracked vertebra and broken teeth.'

After Battiston's exit, the beautiful French players with their socks around their ankles went 3-1 up in extra time. But that night in Seville, two German footballing myths were launched: their improbable comebacks, and their invincibility in penalty shoot-outs. Klaus Fischer made it 3-3 with an overhead volley, and the Germans won the first-ever shoot-out at a World Cup. After Maxime Bossis missed the deciding French penalty, he said: 'Football is important, but life is important too.'

What are the ingredients of a classic World Cup match? Two world-class teams meeting in a knockout game and each playing their best, with a frisson of violence, a referee's blunder, an agonisingly close result, and the losers in tears at the end. Ideally, the two countries will have a rivalry that transcends football. If you narrow it down like that, there have been only a handful of classic matches in the tournament's history.

The extra ingredient that made Seville a game for the ages was the Second World War. Any European aged over about forty-five in 1982 remembered the war. Many French people still used the wartime pejorative '*Boches*' for Germans.

By 1982, Europeans increasingly felt able to talk about the war. They even felt able to desacralise it by associating it with football. The French TV presenter Georges de Caunes said that for French people of his generation, Schumacher's assault brought up feelings from wartime.

For decades from 1954 onwards, the Second World War added meaning to World Cups. It was a one-way emotional process, only felt by teams playing against West Germany: the Germans themselves could hardly experience every game against France, the Netherlands, Poland, Serbia, the USSR, Russia, Ukraine, the US, Canada, Belgium, England, Scotland, Wales, Northern Ireland, Greece, Norway, Denmark, the Czech Republic et cetera as a grudge match.

Usually, the Germans won. The football writer David Winner says that in the story of twentieth-century World Cups, Germany played the role of the villain: the bad guy who kills the beautiful teams, like Hungary in 1954, Holland in 1974 and France in 1982. In Winner's phrase: 'A World Cup without Germany would be like *Star Wars* without Darth Vader.'

France's great playmaker in Seville was Michel Platini. Decades later, when he was president of UEFA, I asked him about the match, and he told me that the French players that night hadn't been thinking about the war. 'The older people, yes,' he conceded. 'But players don't feel involved with history. We cried not because we were reminded of history. We cried because we didn't go to the final, because we lived through very, very strong moments, and we were at the end of our tethers.'

And yet, Platini said, for him Seville was a happy memory. 'It was a great joy to have lived all that: the emotions with your mates, a moment that was magnificent, difficult, catastrophic. You experience something for an hour and a half, and people are still talking about it thirty years later. That's a true joy.' I think he meant it.

Belgium-USSR, second-round match, Léon, Mexico,15 June 1986

In the 1980s, when the Netherlands didn't qualify, the country was represented at World Cups by their neighbours, Belgium. That means that despite Diego Maradona's two goals against England in the Aztéca Stadium, the team from 1986 that sticks in my mind are the Red Devils.

The Dutch in 1986 had mixed feelings about the Belgians. People supported them until they progressed too far in the tournament, and then got anxious: surely they weren't going to win the thing before we did?

I watched the Belgium-USSR game at a friend's house. It was one of the rare fantastic matches at a World Cup. The Belgians won 4-3, despite a hat-trick by the fragile little 'Soviet' Igor Belanov. (Only much later would we realise that he and most of his teammates were Ukrainian. As the Soviet joke went, the USSR team in the 1970s and 1980s was Dynamo Kyiv 'weakened by a few players from other clubs'.)

My friend and I were captivated by the drama in the way only children can be. We felt directly connected to the centre of the world. That evening, we swore that we'd go to the next World Cup. He didn't.

5

Early Forays, 1988–1996

These were the years when I finished school, went to university, began going to football tournaments, and started working life with the *Financial Times* in London.

My university degree was in history and German, which turned out to be fortuitous. When I started it, in 1988, there were still two Germanies, West and East. The Berlin Wall fell during my second year. I spent my third year studying in Berlin, and was there for the night of German reunification in 1990. Since West Germany also won the World Cup that year, it was a good time to observe the nexus of German football, German nationalism and German fear of German nationalism.

During these years I had illuminating encounters with Diego Maradona (not necessarily to his advantage), FIFA's president João Havelange, and with a footballer who told me that the highlight of his career had been training sessions at the 1978 World Cup. I also witnessed the unscheduled premiere of the song 'Three Lions', better known as 'Football's Coming Home'.

Netherlands-USSR, European Championship final, Munich, 25 June 1988

I finished my A-level exams in London the day before the final, then stayed up all night celebrating with school friends.

Early the next morning, I flew to Munich to watch the Netherlands against the Soviet Union – the first tournament game I'd ever attended. My parents bought my plane ticket as an exam present;

the editor of *World Soccer* magazine had promised to arrange a ticket to the final for his Holland correspondent, unaware that his Holland correspondent was eighteen years old and wrote his articles in his bedroom, cribbing the content from Dutch magazines.

When the plane took off, I fell into the comatose sleep of an eighteen-year-old. I woke up once, stretched my arms, and knocked a glass of orange juice over the dazzling white shirt of the press photographer next to me. He was livid. I immediately fell back to sleep.

My match ticket was waiting for me at reception in an expensive Munich hotel. From there, I got straight on the bus to the stadium. I was going to worry later about where to sleep. I had enough money to pay for two nights in the youth hostel, and even to eat something. Football journalism paid well in those days, especially if you were a teenager living at home.

Then two ticket inspectors got on the bus.

'Ticket,' one of them said.

I showed him my ticket.

'Forty Deutschmarks,' he said.

I hadn't stamped my ticket.

'Otherwise, you'll come with us to the police station, and we'll sort this out at our leisure,' he said.

After a lengthy discussion, I handed them forty marks and tried not to cry too obviously. Now I was almost penniless.

The final itself was the best thing that happened to me in Munich. First Ruud Gullit scored, and in the second half Marco van Basten hit his famous volley high into the goal behind which I was sitting. As I recall it, there was a second or two of silence before we all grasped that the ball had gone in. Then the German chancellor Helmut Kohl handed Gullit what is still the only football trophy that the Netherlands has ever won.

I didn't know anyone in Munich, but I'd hoped to be dragged along in a collective Dutch party. I wasn't. Nobody even gave me a glance. I eventually drifted towards the train station. There I got talking to a homeless Italian man, who had been living in West Germany since childhood but spoke only a few German words.

He sometimes baked pizzas, but usually he was unemployed. He had become an expert in the art of sleeping in train stations. The secret, he explained, was to lie down behind the baggage lockers. A few times that night, the police came and kicked us awake, but now and then we managed to grab a few minutes' sleep.

I spent the next day by myself in Munich's English Garden. That evening, I reported back to the station. This time I got talking to a middle-aged local man. 'You can sleep at my flat,' he offered.

Of course I didn't trust him, but the alternative was another night behind the baggage lockers. He gave me a mattress, I slept as if I'd been anaesthetised, and I was allowed to leave for the airport the next morning.

I've been back to Munich several times since. I've stayed in the Marriott hotel, and have eaten in Italian restaurants that would probably never have employed the homeless man I met. On these visits, the city somehow looked different – nicer.

The England team's hotel, Turin, 3 July 1990

The night before the England-West Germany semi-final at Italia '90, the English players sat in a team meeting waiting for their manager, Bobby Robson, to walk in and deliver his motivational speech. Robson's beloved white-paper flip chart stood at the front of the room. Gary Lineker, the striker who doubled as the squad's bookmaker, turned over the top sheet and wrote on the second page: 'Even money he mentions the war.' Then he covered it again with the top sheet.

When Robson walked in and opened with, 'We beat them in the war,' the players collapsed laughing. The football-and-war hysteria that my generation had grown up with was starting to fade into camp.

Bösekendorf, East Germany, July–August 1990

I had travelled to Italy at the start of the World Cup. Weeks later, the tournament ended with West Germany beating Maradona's Argentina 1-0 in a very boring final. Maradona explained afterwards that Argentina had lost because of a complicated FIFA-orchestrated conspiracy against the Argentinian people.

The final was West Germany's last ever match at a World Cup. The two Germanies were scheduled to reunify three months later. Franz Beckenbauer, the West German coach, said: 'We're number one in the world. Now the players from East Germany are going to be added on. I'm sorry for the rest of the world, but for the next few years we're going to be unbeatable.'

A week or so after the final, I arrived in an East German village named Bösekendorf as part of a team of students doing anthropological research. Bösekendorf lay smack in the middle of soon-to-be-reunited Germany, only about 300 metres from the freshly redundant East–West German border.

The Iron Curtain here consisted of what looked like a white ribbon a few metres wide, winding through the countryside along the east–west border. This was the 'Death Strip': land that the East German regime had kept bare with poisons, so that guards could see and shoot any escapees trying to cross the border. That summer, we wandered around the abandoned Death Strip.

Bösekendorf had been so near the border that during the Cold War the inhabitants could hear the church clocks in West Germany, see people walking there, even wave to them. Because of that proximity, the communist regime treated everybody in the '500-metre zone' as a flight risk, and sealed the area off even from the rest of East Germany. People needed a pass to enter or exit the village.

Suddenly, with reunification, the villagers were upgraded into 'Germans'. During the World Cup, they had cheered on their new national team. I became friendly with a young man of about my age, Gerhard, who had been particularly low-status because East Germany had classified him as 'disabled', though it wasn't clear what his disability was. In the month I spent in the village, he seemed to wear his West German football shirt every day. He had risen from East German to world champion.

Berlin, 3 October 1990

That September, I moved to East Berlin as a student. On 3 October 1990, I walked down the pompous Unter den Linden boulevard watching Germans celebrate reunification. The avenue was packed, but apart from a few East Germans scarfing champagne, most people were wandering around quietly, not celebrating. I was starting to realise that many Germans were worried that their mighty new country might backslide towards Nazism.

In 1990, German dominance in football felt like an omen. The triumphant national team seemed to stand for a triumphant Germany. I was awestruck by the country I encountered. Its economy couldn't stop growing. A West German bus driver I met had invited me for beers at his house – a villa with a veranda in a spotless village.

But German dominance scared many people. Would the mighty new country start wars again? Fear prompted the British prime minister Margaret Thatcher and the French president François Mitterrand to try to block reunification.

The people most afraid of German dominance were probably Germans themselves. Many of my fellow history students at Berlin's Technical University felt almost guilty for being German. They didn't believe that the old demons had gone away. In fact, some of the demons still walked among us. In one of our classes on the Third Reich, there was a mature student, a woman of about seventy, who had lived through Nazism and seemed to approve of it. She saw it as her job to correct my generation's trendy anti-Nazi biases. She'd make articulate interventions in defence of Hitler, and point out Soviet and American atrocities. Her message was: why pick on the Nazis?

You could see why Germans, especially in lefty, countercultural Berlin, might dread an ascendant new Germany. Amid the anxiety of the time, the country's triumph at the World Cup could seem almost an embarrassment. The only public reference to it that I saw in Berlin was a poster on subway walls quoting Beckenbauer ('We're going to be unbeatable'). I assumed at first that the posters were celebratory. In fact, they were using his words to warn against incipient Nazi-style triumphalism in the new Germany.

It was as Henry Kissinger, who had grown up a football fan in pre-war Germany, wrote in 1986: 'The Germans' often outstanding national soccer team has not brought a proportionate amount of joy to a people that may not in its heart of hearts believe that joy is its ultimate national destiny.'

Foxborough Stadium, Boston, June–July 1994

In 1994, the year that the World Cup was hosted by the US, I happened to be living in Boston, doing my last stint at university. I wrote letters to newspapers and TV stations across America, begging for a job covering the tournament. One evening, the phone rang in our shared student house. It was a senior guy from ABC Television, offering me a gig as the network's lowliest production assistant, based in Boston.

Then, shortly before the tournament, the *Financial Times* hired me as a graduate trainee, to start work that autumn. (Thirty years on, I'm still there, no longer a trainee.) I wrote my first articles for the paper during the World Cup. I used to read them down the phone line to a copytaker, as if it were the 1950s.

I visited the team camps in the Boston region. The Greek squad, under their Greek-American manager, spent many evenings trekking to receptions hosted by Greek-Americans. Meanwhile, the Nigerians loafed in the lounge of their Holiday Inn, watching TV with journalists and other hotel guests. I had one long conversation with the team's goalkeeper about the wisdom or otherwise of turning in a crooked member of the Nigerian camp. This culminated in the keeper and I standing in the hotel lobby holding hands – a Nigerian custom, I think – for a couple of awkward minutes.

I spent most of my days hanging around Foxborough Stadium's broadcast compound. One morning, a white-haired old gentleman limped by, surrounded by hordes of curiosity-seekers. Somebody said he was the Uruguayan journalist Diego Lucero (real name Luis Alfredo Sciuotto), born in 1901, at that point the only person on earth to have attended all fifteen World Cup tournaments. He had seen his home country win the very first title against Argentina in Montevideo in 1930.

A year after the World Cup in the US, Lucero, aged ninety-three, was shown the red card by God. But that morning in Boston, as a naive twenty-four-year-old, I had decided: one day I'm going to be the next Diego Lucero.

I was starting at the bottom. During matches at Foxborough I worked as a 'spotter'. I'd sit in the commentary box behind the commentators, and whenever a player did anything noteworthy, I had to identify him instantly, so that the producers could put his name on screen.

I was terrible at the job. Some people are 'super-recognisers', who can memorise and remember thousands of faces from the briefest glimpse; I am the opposite. Early in my first match, Argentina-Greece, an Argentinian player fell over. Having no idea who he was, I guessed. 'Balbo, number 15!' I called out. The moment the producer put Balbo's name on screen, the player stood up and looked into the camera. It was Chamot. The producer was not happy.

I think the one time I successfully managed to identify a player was when Maradona (helpfully a head shorter than anyone else) smashed a shot into the top of the Greek net. Aged thirty-three, he had somehow managed to get off cocaine and slim down for his final World Cup. In triumph, he raced to our touchline, stuck his face into one of our cameras, and roared with bulging eyes. Argentina won 4-0.

My facial recognition skills didn't improve. South Korea-Bolivia (0-0) was particularly challenging. Eventually, when the producers asked me to identify a player, I'd stay silent until the point when everyone in the stadium had seen his shirt number.

ABC ditched me after the last game at Foxborough. Maradona had just been banned for taking five different variants of the banned stimulant ephedrine, so he and I exited the tournament simultaneously.

Oxford, autumn 1995

Oxford isn't the place where you'd expect to run into Maradona, but that is where I met him the next year. He'd been invited there by a rabbi called Shmuley Boteach, a tiny charismatic self-promoter who later became Michael Jackson's spiritual adviser and then a cheerleader for Israeli war crimes during the invasion of Gaza from 2023.

Rabbi Shmuley ran a fringe religious cult movement at Oxford. One of its members, an Argentinian student, had previously worked as a bellboy in a Buenos Aires hotel, where he got to know Maradona by running certain errands for him.

I gather that Shmuley's cult managed to lure Maradona to Oxford with the suggestion that he was going to receive an honorary degree, something that Shmuley had no power to confer. And so Maradona flew to the country where he was supposedly still public enemy number one after his 'Hand of God' goal of 1986. I got myself invited along as a journalist.

The evening started with a dinner. Shmuley had drawn up a rota of a few favoured people – including me, the only journalist – who would each get to spend five minutes in the seat next to Maradona. Of course, we all used every second of our time to talk to him. I had rehearsed some questions in careful Spanish, and when it was my turn in the chair, I beamed into his face, pointed to his young daughters who were sitting at the back of the room, and said, 'Your children are very beautiful, Mr Maradona.' 'Thank you,' he said, before gazing forlornly across the room at the only person there he wanted to speak to, his old mate Ossie Ardiles, who had driven up from London to see him.

I continued doggedly. How did he feel about coming to England, after the 'Hand of God' goal? 'Time heals all wounds,' he said, and smiled at Ardiles. When my five minutes were up, I realised that I had done what almost everybody in Maradona's life did: I had tried to take a piece of him.

Next, the Oxford Union debating society took its piece. Shmuley dressed Maradona up in a university mortar board and gown, and presented him with a scroll that said, 'Inspirer of Dreams', though Maradona may have thought that it was an honorary degree. The audience asked questions, and Maradona wheeled out the line he had honed for the English: 'Time heals all wounds.'

Then a student in the audience shouted, 'Mr Maradona, I've heard that you can juggle a golf ball. Is it true?' Well, said Maradona apologetically, he was wearing brogues, and so …

'Just try!' shouted the student, and he lobbed the golf ball onto stage. Maradona juggled it with his feet for about a minute. The Union went wild.

The moment the event ended, Shmuley and his entourage chucked Maradona into a van and raced him down the motorway to Heathrow. If all went well, he'd just about make his flight back to Buenos Aires. I'm guessing that they must have hit traffic, because eventually Maradona found himself on a Piccadilly Line Tube train trundling to Heathrow. Wearing a hat and a long coat with an upturned collar, he managed to travel a few stops unnoticed, until a passenger recognised him and exclaimed, 'Maradona!' Then a carriage full of English people swarmed the national enemy, lavishing praise on him and begging for autographs.

Wembley Stadium, London, 18 June 1996

The England-Holland game at Euro 96 felt literally incredible, in the sense of being impossible to believe. Somehow England broke out into brilliant Dutch total football and won 4-1. During the tournament, a new song called 'Three Lions (Football's Coming Home)' had been playing on British radio stations. Late in the game, the ecstatic crowd spontaneously began to sing it.

I was sitting in the press stand, a few seats from the song's co-writers, the comedians David Baddiel and Frank Skinner. While the crowd sang, the duo stood up, open-mouthed, gazing around the stadium entranced. They realised they had written a folk anthem.

The song's genius is that it combines the two contradictory beliefs held by England fans: that England always loses, and that it has a manifest destiny to triumph. The lyrics express a post-imperial jokey kind of nationalism. Elgar's 'Land of Hope and Glory' this isn't. 'Three Lions' is such a perfect football song that the German players (who, inevitably, won Euro 96) used to sing it in their team bus. Today it remains the unofficial English football anthem, much better than 'God Save the King'.

Finland-Hungary, World Cup qualifier, Helsinki, 11 October 1997

Finland were on the verge of qualifying for their first-ever World Cup, but two minutes into extra time, Hungary snatched a draw. A Finn told me years later that he'd seen old men in tears as they left the Olympic Stadium. They knew then that they would never see their country play in a World Cup.

Downing Street, London, 11 March 1998

England were bidding to host the 2006 World Cup, and FIFA's president, João Havelange, had come to London to meet Prime Minister Tony Blair. We journalists were invited into Downing Street for the occasion. We waited in a gaggle outside the black door until Havelange came out.

'I have just met the prime minister, Mr Tony –,' began the

eighty-one-year-old Brazilian, and then paused while he tried to remember Mr Tony's surname. He tried again: 'I have just met Mr Tony –' No luck.

Finally, he gave up. He had met Mr Tony, and was giving England 'his personal support'. After all, explained Havelange, 'World football was born in England. The rules of the game were created in England.' In 2006 it would be forty years since England hosted a World Cup. And, he added, in 2010 it would be sixty years since Brazil hosted. The implication was clear: Havelange was backing England, and as a quid pro quo, the English and their friends would vote for Brazil for 2010. FIFA's long-time autocratic leader was stepping down that June, but he could surely arrange one last deal. My front-page article in the *Financial Times* began: 'England's bid to host the 2006 football World Cup was significantly boosted ...'

Looking back, I realise that Havelange used to pledge his support to every bidding country he visited.

The Amsterdam Arena, May 1998

The Ajax stadium was hosting a new kind of event: a football business conference. Dutch clubs had gathered to talk about previously unimagined phenomena, such as floating on the stock market and pay-per-view TV.

At the drinks reception on the field afterwards, I got chatting to the former Dutch midfielder Willy van der Kerkhof. With another World Cup about to start, he reminisced about playing for *Oranje* in Argentina in 1978 alongside his twin brother Rene. He told the stories that veterans of that team always do: the wintry cold of their training camp up in Cordoba, the Argentinian fans banging on the doors of their bus as it arrived at the Monumental Stadium for the final, and the armed soldiers lining the touchline. The Dutch players usually say they were relieved to lose against the hosts, because if they hadn't the Argentinians might really have got angry.

'It doesn't sound fun,' I said.

But Van der Kerkhof's middle-aged eyes lit up. He said, 'You know, those were the best five weeks of my career.' It wasn't just reaching the World Cup final, he explained. It wasn't even particularly the matches. What he loved best were the training sessions. Every day in Cordoba, he had trained with the best teammates and the best manager (the Austrian Ernst Happel) he would ever have. What the World Cup had meant to him was the experience of excellence.

6

World Cup 1998: France Discovers Football, and I Discover France

I took the Eurostar from London to Paris in June 1998 without any sense that this World Cup would change my life path, but I did feel that my life needed changing. The *Financial Times* at the time inhabited a sick building on Southwark Bridge in London, where the windows didn't open. On winter days, the only time I felt daylight on my face was on my two-minute walk from home to the Tube station each morning. I was one of the worst-paid journalists on the paper, stuck writing a daily report on the currencies market. Leafing through my cuttings book from the era, I see that my last effort before the World Cup is headlined, 'Yen rallies on prospect of G7 cavalry.'

I was really looking forward to the World Cup, even if the host country wasn't. The French, famously, didn't have a football culture. I watched their first game, a 3-0 win over South Africa, in a café on the Left Bank where the other customers ignored the TV set in the corner.

Lyon, June 1998

Early in the tournament, I spent a fortnight in this delightful provincial city. I'd wake up in late morning, then have a long lunch on a *terrasse* reading the French sports newspaper *L'Equipe*. The low point of the day was, generally, covering a group game. In one spell, I travelled to five matches in six days and saw a total of four goals. A game like Austria-Chile (1-1) was not meant to be enjoyed, and the stadiums were usually dominated by a French silent majority.

'I wish I was home,' a Dutch colleague at the tournament lamented one day. 'My whole street in Rotterdam is getting together to watch the matches on TV: chips, beer, kids – it's fantastic. And they tell me, "You're so lucky to be in France!"'

But every evening after I'd filed my match report, I was free. That's because in 1998 the internet still barely existed. The *FT*'s website was a neglected appendage, so I only wrote for the newspaper. When it went to press at around 7 p.m. French time, there was nothing more I could do. Nor did I have to worry about emails. I had a Hotmail address, but I didn't check it all tournament.

So almost every night, a few colleagues and I would go out for dinner on some outdoor terrace in Lyon, the capital of French gastronomy. Our newspapers weren't yet competing with free online content, so they were still selling lots of copies, and paying us generous expenses. That was journalism before the internet.

Travelling around France, June 1998

The big story in the first weeks of the tournament was hooligan-ism. In Marseille, English fans and locals skirmished on and off for days. In Lens on 21 June, German hooligans beat the French policeman Daniel Nivel into a coma. He would spend the rest of his life half-paralysed and wheelchair-bound, with limited speech, no sense of smell or taste, and blind in one eye.

Non-violent fans typically travelled to the World Cup for a single game, expecting to find the 'all-out hooligan war' that they'd been hearing so much about in the media. They were deter-mined to show that some fans were different, which explained the scene that I witnessed day after day: a supporter clad in national regalia would walk into a café or train station, and be greeted with a cheer by supporters of the opposing team. Then everyone would embrace as if they'd just met their future spouses.

In fact, it was the yobs who were the exceptions – and apart from the thugs who attacked Nivel, almost all of them were English. One country had a near monopoly on hooliganism at tournaments that decade, from Sardinia in 1990 through Malmö and Trafalgar Square to Marseilles in 1998. Everyone still remem-bered the Heysel disaster of 1985, which had prompted a five-year ban on English club teams playing in Europe. A debate restarted about whether England should be banned from international tournaments.

When England played Romania in Toulouse, the city practi-cally went into lockdown. I only popped in and out to see England lose. A colleague who had been deputed to 'hooliewatch' – a major occupation of English journalists in the 1980s and 1990s – grew so angry with the thugs he was watching that he began policing them himself. It helped that he was six foot four. He marched up to a small English hooligan who was kicking a parked car and asked, 'What do you think you're doing?'

'They're French, innit,' explained the hooligan.

'You are in France!' shouted my colleague.

The overriding sentiment at the World Cup towards English thugs wasn't fear, or loathing. It was bafflement. Here we all were (the reasoning went) in midsummer in a beautiful country with pretty decent food and wine, somehow having got our hands on World Cup tickets for what might prove the only time in our lives. Yesterday we'd seen Jairzinho on the train. Everyone was acting as if the French government had put LSD in the water supply (and maybe it had). So why were the English yobs so upset? Why did they wear a look of grim intent as if they had come to gorgeous French town centres for an unpleasant job that had to be done?

It wasn't that English people were morally inferior to foreigners. It wasn't even that English fans were morally inferior to foreign fans: club games in Italy, Poland, Scotland or the Netherlands were uglier affairs than in England. And English hooligans were vastly outnumbered by the harmless football geeks that the UK produces in unique quantities; earnest men in shorts and grey socks racking up their 457th ground, and comparing the architecture of Nantes' Stade de la Beaujoire with a Finnish stadium witnessed in 1976.

But it was only the English whose nastiest fans followed the national team. Foreigners increasingly associated England's hooligans with other modern expressions of English nationalism: drunken monolingual tourists on the Costa del Sol; Margaret Thatcher belittling other countries; and the endless glorification of the Second World War. For many people around the world in summer 1998, that fat skinhead chucking stones in Marseille *was* England.

Iran-USA, group match, Lyon, 21 June 1998

The encounter between the Islamic theocracy and the Great Satan was being billed as 'the mother of all games', the geopolitical grudge match. I took a fantastically expensive taxi from Lyon to the American camp deep in the French countryside. The players were sitting around on deckchairs in the grounds of a mansion, quietly going mad. The most thrilling activity on offer to them was feeding the ducks. The keeper, Kasey Keller, reflected later,

'After five minutes, everybody was ready to kill themselves. And each other.' (And especially their coach, Steve Sampson.)

There was a lot for us to ask them about. A French TV channel had just screened *Not Without My Daughter*, a movie about an American woman's attempt to reclaim her daughter from her cruel Iranian husband. That had prompted Iran's ambassador to France to threaten that his country's team would walk out of the World Cup.

The American players weren't getting drawn into geopolitics. From his deckchair, the defender Alexi Lalas said, 'It's valid to be upset about any movie that Sally Field is in. But none of the players are viewing this as anything other than an incredible opportunity to get three points against a team we should beat.'

Conversely, the Iranian mullahs weren't too bothered about the Americans either. The conflict that really worried the regime was Iranians versus Iranians. Exiled opposition groups were planning a protest at the match. Iranian secret policemen and officers of the Revolutionary Guard had flown to France with orders to stop them.

That evening, when spectators arrived at Lyon's stadium for the game, security officials checked their clothes for political slogans. But the precautions failed. Minutes before kick-off, thousands of Iranian spectators stood up from their seats to unveil T-shirts bearing the image of a woman named Maryam Rajavi. In the press box, rapid collective upskilling in Iranian politics revealed that Rajavi was the leader of the anti-regime Mujahedin-e-Khalq (MEK) movement. At the time MEK was headquartered in Iraq, and funded by Iran's enemy Saddam Hussein. Several western countries classified it as a terrorist organisation.

Collectively, we journalists managed to piece together what had happened. MEK's supporters living all over Europe had bought tickets to the game. They had hidden bits of banners from the security checks, and now, in their seats, were sticking them back together with Velcro. One sign attacked the country's Supreme Leader: 'Down with Khamenei.'

The Iranians jeered their own national team while it warmed

up. When the anthems were played, a balloon bearing Rajavi's portrait floated past the line of Iranian players, who studiously ignored it. Eventually the referee picked up the subversive object and carried it fastidiously to the touchline.

For the whole match, every time the ball went into the stands, Rajavi's followers jumped from their seats and jabbed their fingers at her picture on their shirts. The mass protest made for a more compelling spectacle than the two mediocre teams labouring on the field. The MEK imagined that they were delivering their message to a worldwide TV audience. However, the TV screens by our seats in the press box (a thrilling innovation) revealed that the cameras didn't ever film the crowd, not even when the ball went into the stands. FIFA's media officer for the game, Iranian-born Mehrdad Masoudi, explained later that cameramen had been pre-issued with photographs of people and objects that couldn't be shown. Nobody who wasn't in the ground that night ever saw the protest.

Iran won 2-1, in what was the football-mad country's first-ever victory at a World Cup. Afterwards their players wept on the field. 'I know I shouldn't say this,' the American striker Eric Wynalda remarked much later, 'but there was something beautiful about it.' Wynalda was seething because the coach, Sampson, had left him on the bench.

Several American players bashed Sampson – 'If this was the master plan, good God, it was pretty masterful,' said Lalas – and the eliminated US team clinched the inaugural *Financial Times* award for worst side of the tournament.

Night train from St Etienne to Lyon, 23 June 1998

Tired Scottish fans sat slouched in the packed train corridor, behind the driver's compartment. Their team had just been knocked out of the tournament after losing 3-0 to Morocco. It was a bit of a low.

That was when the French train driver emerged into the

corridor and began handing out cans of Kanterbräu beer. He didn't speak any English, but an interpreter was found who introduced the driver as Eric Foucault. Instantly, the Scots broke into a chant:

There's only one Eric Foucault
One Eric Foucault
Gave us a beer
So give him a cheer
Walking in a Foucault wonderland.

Maybe, Foucault asked through the interpreter, the Scots were better at rugby? 'No!' the fans chorused. But nobody on the train will have got a bad impression of *l'Ecosse*. At one stop, a Moroccan fan carrying his national flag got on. He looked startled to find himself surrounded by enemy supporters, and even more startled when they all gave him a cheer. He went around the corridor shaking hands with every Scot.

The Scottish fans began to debate their team's penchant for failure. Scotland had played in six of the last seven World Cups but always failed (sometimes with high drama) to reach the second round. The fans agreed it was time to break the tradition of romanticising defeat. After all, Scotland was about to get its own parliament; on the field, too, its destiny ought to be in its own hands.

Foucault reappeared and led the Scots in a French singalong. Then he gave them a microphone to broadcast over his PA system. They sang 'Flower of Scotland' for the whole train.

Update: As of 2025, Scotland-Morocco remains the last match the Scots have played at a World Cup.

England-Argentina, second-round match, St Etienne, 30 June 1998

The passage of play from the sixth minute to the forty-seventh in this game is one of the most gripping I've seen at a World Cup. It started when Argentina's Diego Simeone seemed to have pushed the ball too far in front of him, only for England's keeper David Seaman to catch his legs. Gabriel Batistuta netted the resulting penalty.

Three minutes later, eighteen-year-old Michael Owen, who had started the World Cup on England's bench, hared into the Argentinian box at an inhuman pace, and, like Simeone, found an opponent to bump into. Alan Shearer hit the perfect spot kick.

For Owen's next solo from the centre circle, the English journalists around me rose from their seats, pounding their desks and screaming, 'Go on, my son!', until he put the ball into Carlos Roa's top corner.

Years later, I asked Owen whether he hadn't wondered, as a teenager playing against Argentina at a World Cup, 'My God, what am I doing here?' 'No,' he replied. 'That was probably why you could succeed, and why a lot of youngsters burst onto the scene in any sport.'

I wrote in my match report, 'Owen revealed himself as the best forward in the world,' and asked, 'How good is he going to get?' It would turn out that he'd never be any better than during those seven minutes in St Etienne.

In the dying seconds of the first half, Argentina made it 2-2. Only when the half-time whistle went did I realise that my hand was jammed halfway down my mouth from excitement. I caught the eye of my colleague Paddy Barclay, a Scot. His hand was jammed down his mouth, too. We raised our eyebrows at each other – neither of us even supported England. For almost the first time that tournament, I remembered why people love football.

Two minutes after half-time, David Beckham, after being floored by Simeone, stupidly flicked up his leg and nudged him. Simeone collapsed and Beckham was sent off. England held on for a penalty shoot-out, which Argentina won when Roa saved David Batty's kick.*

---

* Roa would retire from football a year later. He had decided that the Apocalypse would come in the year 2000, and had holed up in an Argentinian

The height of media technology in 1998 was attaching a mobile phone to a laptop and sending an article from St Etienne to London. It took me about twenty-five minutes, but I finally succeeded – though perhaps only after the last edition of the paper had gone to press. Our sports editor didn't speak to me for days afterwards.

Then I got into a car with two German journalists and dozed on the back seat as we drove south through the night to a village on the Riviera. At about 5.30 a.m. I woke to find us turning into the drive of a villa that looked like something out of a TV ad. It had a sprawling garden, and a pool in which my six German journalist housemates and I played water polo every night. If the FIFA president Sepp Blatter had suddenly announced that he'd decided to extend the World Cup by a year, I'd have been delighted. I was dragged out of the villa kicking and screaming a week later.

England, night of 30 June 1998

But what happened in England after the team went out? The 1998 elimination is the platonic ideal of English eliminations from World Cups: defeat by a former military enemy, on penalties, with a designated national scapegoat, this time Beckham. Each elimination is typically the most watched British TV programme of the year (in the case of 1998, there were twenty-four million viewers) and therefore the nation's biggest communal experience. How does it impact the English?

Firstly, the TV broadcast kills some viewers. 'Risk of admission for acute myocardial infarction [a heart attack, in layperson's terms] increased by 25 per cent on 30 June 1998 [the day of England-Argentina] and the following two days', found a study led by Douglas Carroll of the University of Birmingham. In all, there were about fifty-five more heart attacks than usual in such

---

mountain village 'to prepare for the end of the world'. Though he later returned to football, his career never quite recovered.

a period. The risk is probably higher for people actually in the stadium. Paul Weiland, who wrote and directed the film *Sixty Six* about the 1966 World Cup final, told me that he'd met a man whose father died in the stands at Wembley when Geoff Hurst scored England's fourth and final goal.

By now there is a lot of academic research into heart attacks during football matches. A meta-analysis in 2020 led by the Chinese scholar Huajan Wang found that mortality rises 19 per cent in a country that loses a match at a major international tournament. Conversely, winning a game reduced national mortality by 12 per cent. If you extrapolate the damage across all the participating countries, it seems likely that the average World Cup causes more deaths than goals.

The next thing that happens in England on the night of a typical elimination is a slight increase in street violence – albeit less than you'd expect from millions of disappointed, drunk people leaving pubs simultaneously. To indicate the modesty of the mayhem: during the World Cup in Qatar in 2022, police in England and Wales made 115 football-related arrests up to the point when both nations had been knocked out.

Then, when drunk men get home after the game, there is a spike in domestic violence. The awful 'holy trinity' of sport, alcohol and 'hegemonic masculinity' encourages some men to hit their partners, write Damien Williams and Fergus Neville of the University of St Andrews.

English police forces only began seriously recording domestic violence in the twenty-first century, so we don't have figures for the 1998 elimination. But a study led by Allan Brimicombe of the University of East London found 'a significant increase in the rate of reported domestic violence' on nights that England either won or lost a game at the 2010 World Cup. (Draws didn't seem to increase violence.)

By the morning after the elimination, all is usually peaceful again – or as peaceful as England gets. Almost everyone in the country understands that elimination is nothing more serious than the end of a party.

Suicides don't spike after the elimination. (To the contrary: as Stefan Szymanski and I showed in our book *Soccernomics*, suicides decline slightly in European countries participating in major tournaments, probably because lonely people briefly feel more part of the national community.) Almost everyone in England goes to work as usual the next day, grumbles for a few minutes about the useless manager, and then gets on with life, fortified by the communal experience. Except for a few damaged fanatics, fans lose and move on.

La Colombe d'Or restaurant, St-Paul-de-Vence, 3 July 1998

The heyday of journalism. Author on the far right.

I still have the photograph. It shows four young journalists having lunch in a sunlit flower garden. Inside hung the restaurant's famous art collection: paintings by Picasso, Matisse and Chagall, supposedly left behind as payments for lunch. My friends and I were experiencing the life that Germans describe with the phrase, 'Living like God in France'.

Of course, like many spots in *la France profonde*, the Colombe d'Or had become a facsimile of the rural French idyll, so perfectly designed that it was accessible chiefly to rich foreigners. In 1998, journalism was still a moneyed profession.

For us, a World Cup was a chance to spend a month being paid to discover a new country. During that tournament, I learned to live like God in France – to eat bouillabaisse beside a swimming pool in Marseille, or andouillette on a little *place* in Lyon. These were clichés, but they were seductive ones. I glimpsed a better life in France than I was living in London. The consequences would be fateful.

Brazil-Netherlands, semi-final, Marseille, 7 July 1998

With the score at 1-1 in extra time, and *Oranje* within sight of another World Cup final, I had to stop watching. It was too stressful. Instead I scanned the stands, picking out famous ex-players. The moment the game went to a penalty shoot-out, every Dutch fan knew that Brazil was going to win, and I felt strangely relieved. This was an excellent Dutch team, but it wasn't quite the perfect *Oranje* of my dreams. If this lot won the World Cup with me there when I was only twenty-eight, what would I have left to look forward to for the rest of my life as a fan?

The Dutch winger Boudewijn Zenden later recounted to me the conversation he had with his friend Ronaldo outside the changing rooms after the match. The two had met as seventeen-year-olds at PSV Eindhoven, Ronaldo's first European club. Everyone at PSV realised at once that Ronaldo was special. One day after training, a few players were practising *levandos*: a blasted, rising shot that suddenly dips under the crossbar. A good footballer might manage one *levando* in ten attempts. Ronaldo had a try. He hit seven *levandos* out of nine. Then he chuckled, 'You guys keep practising, I'm going in.'

Zenden, a keen linguist, was learning Portuguese, and he and Ronaldo made friends the way footballers do. One day in their first preseason, they were in a hotel in Mexico City when

Ronaldo burst into Zenden's room and tried to playfight him. He didn't know that Zenden had been a junior judo champion. Within seconds Zenden had pinned his arm behind his back. 'Ow! Ow! Stop!' cried Ronaldo. Then he ran off, and returned with his fellow Brazilian, Vampeta, yelling, '*Dois Brasileiros*!', 'Two Brazilians!' Seconds later, Zenden had both their arms behind their backs. 'Let go!' they pleaded.

After Ronaldo joined Barcelona and then Inter Milan, he and Zenden would exchange the odd phone call over crackling lines from Moscow, Lisbon or wherever else they happened to be playing. Like many top-class footballers of the era, they were becoming citizens of the world.

So they were delighted to run into each other after the Brazil-Holland match. The two probably had more in common with each other than with the average Brazilian or Dutch fan back home. They chatted for an hour. When they parted, Ronaldo clasped Zenden's shoulder and said, in his broken Dutch: 'Doesn't matter. Third place for Holland is good too.'

When Zenden repeated this to me, I realised that Ronaldo had been quite right. Third place for Holland was fine. This small, successful, self-satisfied country didn't need to win a World Cup to feel superior. It was competing to be moral world champion, the tournament's Beautiful Loser: the one pure, attacking team.

It's a foreign misconception that *Oranje*'s World Cup history (three defeats in three finals by 2010) is a tragedy. The Dutch are proud of their record. No other small country has done as well in recent decades. After losing the final of 1974, the team were welcomed home by cheering crowds. Johan Cruyff always argued that *Oranje* had 'really' won that World Cup. How so? Well, he said, people still talked about the Good Football they had played, and that represented victory.

The mission of later Dutch sides seemed to be to repeat that moral victory. Only bigger, unfulfilled countries – countries like Brazil – need to win World Cups.

*

After Brazil-Holland, my German friend the writer Christoph Biermann argued that it was the best football match ever played. His reasoning went like this. Football improved every year, so the most recent great match was by definition the best ever. At any World Cup, there were only a handful of games between two top-class teams playing well. At this tournament, Brazil-Holland was the best of those games. Ergo, said Christoph, it was the best ever.

I think he was right in 1998. At that time, the leading national teams were probably the best teams in football. Clubs had only recently acquired the freedom to sign almost any player of any nationality, so Manchester United was mostly still a collection of top-class British and Scandinavian players, Bayern Munich of German ones, and so on.

But in the twenty-first century, the best football is no longer played at World Cups. Now, a dozen or so rich club teams monopolise the best global talent. That talent trains together daily, honing collective mechanisms that barely exist in international football. Club teams deploy sophisticated zonal defences, whereas many national teams still use old-fashioned man-marking. Today, Real Madrid or Liverpool could beat any country. The World Cup has become an inferior product.

France-Croatia, semi-final, Stade de France, Paris, 8 July 1998

A minute into the second half, newly independent little Croatia, still emerging from the Yugoslav war and playing in its first-ever World Cup, took a 0-1 lead against the French hosts. In that moment, the men in red-and-white tablecloth shirts were less than forty-five minutes from a World Cup final.

But almost immediately from the restart, their playmaker Zvonimir Boban allowed himself to be pushed off the ball just outside his own penalty area, and the French right-back Lilian Thuram equalised. Thuram sometimes went years without being seen up front – he didn't always even know during a game how many goals his team had scored – but in the seventieth minute, miraculously, he scored a second. These were his only two goals in 142 internationals. France reached the final. Boban had blown his generation's chance.

In 2021, during a pandemic-era Zoom interview, he recalled for me what he called 'the biggest error of my life':

Boban: I was a very serious player, I was captain of the team, and we scored. I was screaming and yelling to everyone to be serious now, because this is – in Italian, they say 'Zona Cesarini'. That's five minutes before the end of the first half, the second half for [the first] five minutes, the last five minutes of the game. And also Zona Cesarini, it means these five minutes when you score or when you [concede] a goal.

So I was screaming: 'We can't relax. Now it's concentration. Now we have to be—' Then one minute later, I lost the ball in the red zone, 20 metres from our goal, and France equalised. This I will never forgive myself.

Me: You don't think, 'Look, we're a small country, it was our first World Cup, we finished third, that's incredible'?

Boban: Yes it is incredible, but without my error we would be in the final. Until the match for third place against Holland, I lost two kilos. I didn't sleep. I just can't overcome it. My spirit is not strong enough! When we speak about it, it's very difficult. Still now.

Me: Did you feel that people blamed you?

Boban: They blamed me a lot, and they had a reason to blame me. Later, they understood that I gave a lot of this team and I played really – I have to say, without false modesty – excellent football for my national team.

Me: Did your teammates blame you too?

Boban: No, zero. They have been my teammates from the childhood. They respected me a lot, they respect me till now. So they just try to make it easy for me. They have been very close to me in those days.

Netherlands-Croatia, third-place match,
Parc des Princes, Paris, 11 July 1998

The only time the hierarchical relationship between me and a great footballer broke down a little was with Jorge Valdano. The Argentinian had won the 1986 World Cup, alongside Maradona. He's also a world-class dresser and, unfairly, a gifted columnist and short-story writer who feels at home among journalists. When an interviewer once laid out two tape recorders in front of him, he remarked: 'Ah! One to record my words, the other to record my thoughts.' When we met at a dinner in London a few days before the 1998 World Cup, he formed the incorrect impression that I was involved with the beautiful woman sitting opposite me. I won his respect.

A few days later, I was loafing around the media centre in Paris when there was a stampede right behind me and somebody began hugging my back. I turned around to find that it was Valdano, pursued by a horde of Latin American journalists.

He and I, and a few other like-minded souls, spent much of that tournament travelling around France together, unhindered by my basic Spanish. He shared my love of Dutch football, and he took to referring to *Oranje* as '*los Kupers*'.

Just before the Holland-Croatia third-place game in Paris, we had dinner on the terrace of the stadium's media centre. I commiserated with him on Argentina's elimination, but he said, 'The elimination of *los Kupers* was much worse.'

A heavy-set man lumbered past our table, and waved. 'He was a good footballer,' Valdano told me in an aside, and waved back at the legendary German Günter Netzer.

'That was a fun evening in London,' Valdano said.

'You should come over more often,' I said.

'I'd like to live there,' he continued. 'Do you think I could manage an English club without speaking a word of English?'

'No,' I said. 'You should come to London, meet a beautiful Englishwoman, and move in with her. Then you'll learn English and you can work at any club.'

We shared his dessert. He said, 'The beautiful woman – that's realistic. But learning English is not.'

Boban's Croatia beat Holland 2-1.

France-Brazil, World Cup final, Stade de France, Paris, 12 July 1998

Michel Platini, organiser of the 1998 World Cup, casually admitted many years later that FIFA had manipulated the draw to maximise the chances of a France-Brazil final. It was one of those rare plans that worked.

To my amazement, I was granted a press ticket for my first-ever World Cup final. We younger journalists got to the press stand hours early, and whiled away the time taking photos of each other. When volunteers arrived with the team sheets, there was a collective exclamation of shock: Ronaldo wasn't playing! Minutes later, the volunteers returned, confiscated the original team sheets, and replaced them with new ones: now he was playing!

As the match unfolded, it became clear that the original team sheet had been correct: Ronaldo was there but not there, wandering the field like a zombie, barely touching the ball. The most plausible supposition is that a pre-game panic attack had left him exhausted. He knew that Brazil needed to win the tournament – no team in the modern World Cup has played under such unbending expectations as the Seleção in 1998. As the best player, he felt that he personally had to win it for his country.

Instead, Zinedine Zidane headed in two first-half corner kicks. (The French coach Aimé Jacquet, spotting gaps in Brazil's marking during set pieces, had suggested that Zidane 'take a stroll to the near post' on corners.) France won 3-0.

Twenty-three million French people watched the final – the country's record TV audience up to that point. For many, it was possibly the first football game they'd ever seen. That World Cup was when France began developing a serious football culture. The

1998 final kicked off a twenty-four-year period in which France reached four out of seven World Cup finals, but I later met two Frenchmen who had been tortured by the question of whether, or how, to watch the game.

The first was a Parisian who spent the tournament working for a TV station. He had accreditation for the final, but decided after some soul-searching not to go. He sensed that he would always remember that night and he wanted to spend it with friends, watching the match on TV. Looking back, he felt he had made the right call.

The other Frenchman was a footballer who had been left out of the national squad in the final cut before the tournament. He knew in his heart that he wasn't quite good enough for *les Bleus*. In the French changing room, he'd sometimes watch Zidane before a game. Zidane would sit there silently, pulling on his socks, getting ready to go out, dominate, and win the match for France. Zidane felt detached from the pressure. No match awed him.

The player told me, 'I knew what he was feeling, because I sometimes felt the same before a game in the French league.' If this man was in the changing room getting ready to play Nice, say, he'd feel invincible too, the hero of the story. But, he marvelled, Zidane felt this when he was playing with and against some of the world's best players.

Around the start of the World Cup, this player left France for a foreign city, where he had signed for a new club. There he watched the tournament on TV. In the early matches, he more or less supported France. But when his old teammates reached the final, it was too much for him. He said, 'I had the feeling of missing something unimaginable – winning a World Cup in my own country.' Had the cards fallen slightly differently, or had one or two guys been injured, he might have been there himself, about to become an immortal. He couldn't watch France win the final.

A note on hosts

A victory for the host country felt normal back in 1998. Five of the first eleven World Cups, between 1930 and 1978, were won by the hosts. Stretching the concept of home advantage more broadly, every winning team in twentieth-century World Cups except Brazil in 1958 was playing in its own continent.

But home domination ended with the millennium. As I write in 2025, no host has won since 1998. The only subsequent host even to reach the semi-finals was Brazil in 2014, and we all remember how that one ended.

Home rule at World Cups faded partly because countries without a strong footballing tradition like Japan and South Africa began hosting tournaments. But something else changed too: travel and venues became homogenised. Long-ago teams used to arrive overfed and undertrained after transoceanic boat journeys. Their next challenge was exotic food: England's hopes in Mexico in 1970 exploded with the stomach of their goalkeeper Gordon Banks, who was stricken by diarrhoea on the eve of the quarter-final against West Germany. Then there were Latin American political shenanigans. Argentina's victory in 1978 probably owed something to the ruling General Videla's awe-inducing visit to the Peruvian changing room before their match against Argentina.

Today's visiting teams feel practically at home – or as home as they are anywhere. The modern footballer spends half his life in five-star hotels, where he plays on his Xbox, idly wondering whether he is in Azerbaijan. Players hardly notice the difference any more between a World Cup match in Paris, Johannesburg or Doha.

Postscript

Many people in 1998 thought that the World Cup would have a lasting impact on France. They were proved wrong. Instead, the tournament turned out to have bigger consequences for me.

The winning, united, multiracial French team briefly became

a symbol of a winning, united, multiracial France. The football victory was going to melt away racial divides.

It didn't. After 1998, France went through a quarter century of economic stagnation, fading global power, terrorism, ethnic riots, the uprising of the 'yellow vests', and recurring fear that the anti-immigrant far right would win the French presidency. A World Cup can't heal a country.

But it can divert an individual's life path. Three days after the tournament ended, I was back in the *FT* building writing the currency report: 'Money traders see higher UK rates.' I soon realised that I couldn't take it any more. Within a month, I resigned. 'I shall be sorry to see you go,' said the editor politely, then added hurriedly, 'But I shall do nothing to stop you.'

I went off to be a freelance football writer. Later I drifted back to the *FT* as a columnist, but I've never again worked in a corporate office. In 2001 I bought a little flat in Paris. In 2002 I tried living there. I'm still here. That flat is now my office. It's where I wrote this book. I've become a French citizen, and I'll probably die in Paris. The World Cup changed my life.

7

1998–2001: Champions and Adulterers

Dortmund, November 1998

It was a routine training session on a freezing Tuesday afternoon, and the Borussia Dortmund squad was doing a peculiar exercise. Two players stood in a little goal, one of them threw a ball into the air, and a third came diving in and tried to head it in. It was good practice for diving headers.

For two German world champions of 1990 it was approximately the 3,000th training session of their careers, yet they were still giving it their all. Centre-half Jürgen Kohler, broad as a boxer, back home after years with Juventus, netted a header and screamed in delight. After practice, the little playmaker Thomas Hässler ran a few laps, giggling to himself. Each time he passed the collected balls at the end of a lap, he picked one up for a short dribble.

Then, long after their teammates had gone back to the changing rooms, the two champions juggled a ball together. Kohler whistled each time he managed a back-heel, though Hässler probably wasn't impressed. When Kohler missed a ball, he rolled around laughing on the grass. Finally, he went for a shower while Hässler bashed some last shots at goal.

Afterwards, I waited for Kohler in a hut with a couple of chairs and a pot of coffee. With me were two adolescent girls who were going to interview him for their school newspaper. The smaller girl was nervous, because she needed to pee. Should she wait till after the interview, or go quickly before Kohler arrived?

She finally chose the latter option. She had hardly locked the toilet door when Kohler walked into the hut. In the tiny space, the noise of her peeing was deafening. After a noisy flush, she emerged, blushing, to do the interview. Luckily, it consisted of only one question: 'What are the differences between German and Italian fans?'

Kohler laughed: 'If I'm very honest, Italian fans look better.'

Then he described to me the standard of excellence in the German national team. Aged twenty-two, he had played in the West German side that reached the semi-final of the European Championships against Holland in 1988. There he encountered Marco van Basten, at the time the world's best centre-forward. In the eighty-seventh minute, Van Basten scored the winning goal.

I had brought along a photo of the two men sliding to the fateful ball together. Kohler examined it. 'He was that toe-end, those two centimetres quicker to the ball than me,' he sighed. 'In that tenth of a second, he was the better one.'

In almost any country, Kohler would have been praised – a promising youngster who had got so close to an international final, bested only by a genius. But in Germany, a semi-final was nothing. Kohler was savaged. He felt he deserved it.

Like everyone invested in the German national team – the manager, the media, his teammates – Kohler set the highest standards. That had been the culture of the *DFB-Mannschaft* since 1954. True, there was some booze, poker and illicit sex (in 1980 a Montevideo prostitute was asked at gunpoint to hand back $100, the amount by which she was judged to have overcharged a player), and players were always squabbling. But that was the consequence of throwing together driven personalities.

I asked Kohler if the humiliation of 1988 had traumatised him.

'Yes,' he said. 'But I told myself, "OK, you have to work on yourself even more." Over the years, I learned a lot from that match. I think Van Basten was a very, very important player for my career.'

So Kohler wouldn't have got so good without Van Basten?

'You could say that. Precisely. That's exactly right. I must say that very clearly.'

Two years of obsessive self-improvement later, Kohler won the 1990 World Cup. Listening to him, I realised that the German habits of playing worse but winning, winning in the last minute, and winning on penalties didn't have much to do with luck. Striving to meet the standard of excellence, nobodies won World Cup medals.

There's little demand for excellence in non-sporting life, but you can glimpse unusually high standards in a few companies, ministries or university departments. You almost smell it when you walk through the door: people are fulfilling themselves through their work, fascinated by its detail, benchmarking themselves against the best in the world. But any institutional tradition of quality is fragile – and by the time I interviewed Kohler, that German tradition was dying.

A playground in Rio de Janeiro, 21 August 1999

It was a beautiful Rio morning, and Carlos Alberto Parreira, strolling through the neighbourhood, stopped to pat a child on the head. The boy didn't even look up. Parreira was getting used to being snubbed. He had coached Brazil to victory at the 1994 World Cup, but the entire nation – including, literally, his mother – had complained about his team's boring, defensive, un-Brazilian *futebol-força* ('football of force'). 'We never taught defensive ways!' he protested, tapping me repeatedly on the shoulder. 'We taught balance.'

Next door to the playground, his current club, Fluminense, once a Brazilian powerhouse, had sunk to the third division. Parreira's career since 1994 (as well as most of it before, to be fair) had been a disaster.

'Winning the World Cup changed my life,' he told me. 'After being a world champion, a coach should change jobs. I should have become a football director. I didn't know that then. I told myself, "This is not going to change my way of living, my behaviour." Afterwards I still found excitement in the daily workings of a club. But at the end of the day, if you win or lose, the emotions are not the same as if you win with Brazil in the World Cup.'

Salpêtrière hospital, Paris, December 1999

In the city where he had experienced his footballing nadir, Ronaldo underwent a knee operation that he hoped would save his career. Recovering in bed, he received a visitor he barely knew: Zinedine Zidane had dropped in to wish him well. 'And without cameras,' Ronaldo would add, in a story he often told. There's a solidarity between greats.

Christie's auction house, South Kensington, London, 27 September 2000

Geoff Hurst, the scorer of England's hat-trick in the 1966 World Cup final, was auctioning off his memorabilia. The highlight of the 129 lots was the red shirt he'd worn in the final. I had come to interview him, with a Dutch TV crew that had agreed to pay his fee of several hundred pounds.

When we asked how we should address him, he joked, 'Only my children call me Sir Geoff.' He explained that when he'd asked them what they wanted to inherit from him, they'd said the settee, some money and a painting. That's when he'd decided to sell his memorabilia.

Winning the World Cup was like landing on the moon: it overshadowed the rest of your life. People only asked Hurst about that day, just as nobody ever asked Neil Armstrong about anything he did on Earth. At the end of the interview, I thanked him for his courteous answers. He replied that he was a professional. We had paid his fee, and so he put in a serious performance.

The next day, the sale of his stuff netted about £150,000, including what was then a world record of £91,250 for a football shirt. It now hangs in the National Football Museum in Manchester. Hurst later sold his World Cup winner's medal to his old club, West Ham. Seven of his England teammates sold theirs too.

I only realised much later that monetising his World Cup final had become Hurst's job. Like most of his teammates, he had been pushed out of football without much money. He then sold insurance for years, before the 'boys of '66' got together and built a business on the one day in their lives that other people still cared about.

For decades, the players travelled England in small groups, staging joint events about the final. Hurst recalls in his autobiography: 'Once, in Newcastle, only 13 people turned up, so the performers and the audience reconvened to the bar and did the show there instead.' They held events at the NEC in Birmingham ('like *Star Trek* conventions', writes Hurst) where paying punters queued for autographs. Hurst says England's full-back Ray Wilson 'calculated that he made more money from these events than he did in the entirety of his playing career'.

Studying the photographs of his teammates lifting the Rimet Cup at Wembley, Hurst reflects: 'One day in that future, though we don't know it yet, we will sell the medals in our hands and the shirts on our backs while holding on to our memories of today until half a dozen of us will lose those too.'

The boys of '66 succumbed to an epidemic of dementia, probably brought on by heading the heavy leather balls of their playing days. By 2025, Hurst, aged eighty-three, was the last of the team still alive, still touring England to talk about 1966.

Le Parisien newspaper, November 2000

The French world champion Emmanuel Petit was complaining to the newspaper about the increasingly overloaded football calendar. He said, 'Considering the number of games we have to play,

I wouldn't be surprised if we were soon forced to take drugs. And more and more footballers' wives will cheat on their husbands because they are never at home!'

He was right on the latter count. I knew of a journalist who, shortly before a World Cup, went to interview an international goalkeeper at his house. The journalist met the keeper's wife, and they clicked. Once the tournament began, he returned to the house, this time to see her. He felt safe from discovery; he only had to turn on the TV to watch her husband making heroic saves in another country. The keeper ended up winning the World Cup, so perhaps everyone was happy.

Brazilian Congress, Brasilia, 10 January 2001

A Brazilian parliamentary commission of inquiry was investigating the national team. It was a bit like the US Senate's Watergate hearings or the UK's Covid inquiry, except that a lot of the inquiry was focused on trying to explain a defeat in a football match – the 1998 World Cup final.

This particular day, Ronaldo himself had come to testify. One deputy asked him, ludicrously, who should have been marking Zidane. Ronaldo grinned: 'I don't remember. I also think that whoever should have marked him didn't mark him very well, right?' When another deputy asked him why Brazil didn't beat France, Ronaldo finally lost his patience:

Why didn't we win? Because we let in three goals, because we lost, because – I don't know … How many times has Brazil won? And no one asked why, or a few people asked why we win. But you win and you lose. We lost. Be patient. Just because we lost are we going to invent a bunch of mysteries?

He had got over it.

8

World Cup 2002: Lost in Japan

This was the most exotic World Cup to date – the first time the tournament had ventured beyond western Europe and the Americas. Japan and South Korea were co-hosting, and the *Financial Times* was sending me to Japan.

I had some sense of Japanese obsessions going into the tournament, because in 2002 there was still such a thing as well-paying freelance journalism, and Japanese magazines kept commissioning me to write articles about hooligans.

Fan violence gets exaggerated before every World Cup, mostly because it looks good on TV, but I'd never seen exaggeration on this scale. Since few Japanese people cared much about actual football, the World Cup was being discussed chiefly in terms of the impending destruction of their cities. Hooligans (or, as the Japanese had rechristened them, given their language's historic lack of an 'H' sound, 'fuligans') grew into foreign ogres of Japanese fantasy, successors to the giant American GIs who arrived in 1945.

The hysteria reached a crescendo in the days before the tournament. One of my editors had attended a funeral where hooliganism was the only topic of conversation. The England-Argentina group game in Sapporo was to be the bloody climax. Some Japanese wanted to know whether it would be safe to play golf 100 miles from the stadium that day. There was frenzied speculation over the identity of the 600 people said to have booked seats at a Sapporo barbecue restaurant on the night of the game, even though they were almost certainly business types on a sponsor's jolly.

I wrote for one Japanese magazine:

Going to the average European football match is approximately as dangerous as going to Buckingham Palace. The greatest risk spectators run is probably from eating the burgers. Indeed, the startling fact is how little football violence there is, given that football represents a large chunk of European male leisure time, that men commit almost all violent crime, that they do so mainly in their leisure time, and that a football match can assemble 70,000 men.

I don't think I changed Japanese perceptions.

What explained this obsession? I wasn't in a position to say, given that I couldn't read a single character of the three Japanese alphabets. That left me reliant on the Japan-explainers I knew: a few Japanese people who spoke English, and an English friend who had moved to Tokyo and learned fluent Japanese, an accomplishment on a par with sprouting wings and learning to fly.

Above all, there was my university friend Henry, with whom I'd travelled to my first World Cup in Italy in 1990. By 2002 he was teaching English at a university in rural Japan. Henry was a connoisseur of English culture in all its forms, and he helped me understand what hooliganism meant to the Japanese.

He told me that when they found out that there were football fans who had fights at matches, they initially struggled to believe it. They regarded it as an inexplicable foreign custom, like eating grasshoppers. The Japanese had almost no recent experience of public violence. Their police habitually punished any stray miscreants by making them write 'apology letters', a trick that seemed unlikely to work with English hooligans. So vast was Japanese incomprehension that when their police held anti-hooligan training exercises before the World Cup, the policemen acting the parts of hooligans wore Nike shoes and face paint, like the football fans in commercials on Japanese TV.

Henry sensed that the hooligan question went to the core of both English and Japanese culture. How this worked dawned on him one day while reading the Japanese English-language newspaper *Daily Yomiuri*. In the paper's 'View from Europe' supplement, Henry saw a photograph of Lee Owens.

Owens looked much like any other English hooligan being led away by police: belly, tattoos and a scowl of defiant pride, but no face paint (we should be so lucky). It turned out that although he had officially been banned from all English grounds in 1994, he still got in to watch Middlesbrough weekly and followed England abroad. No doubt he was planning to attend the World Cup too.

Henry cut out the photograph and showed it to his students. 'This is England,' he told them. Owens, he explained, stood for a significant chunk of the culture they were studying: the pissing in public fountains abroad, and the fighting amid piles of vomit in English towns on Saturday nights.

The students were embarrassed for Henry, but they were also mystified. They had always thought of England as a country of gentlemen. In the 1970s, when English hooligans made their first incursions on the continent, Europeans had experienced the same bewilderment.

Trying to explain what made a man look and behave like Owens, Henry breached a rule of Japanese etiquette and talked about the Second World War. He told the students that hooligans saw themselves as representatives of England's warrior tradition. When they broke shop windows or threw plastic chairs (because contrary to Japanese fears, their violence was usually minor and symbolic), they were doing it for England. They were fighting for the Queen, and for granddad who'd been in the war. Like British soldiers in Normandy or the Falklands, the hooligans were conquering foreign lands.

Their behaviour diverged from the English norm, but their perception of history didn't much. The British, more than any other European people, took pride in their military tradition. Whenever Britain went to war, as it did in Afghanistan just before the 2002 World Cup, there was strong public support.

Japan's self-image was the opposite. Since 1945 most Japanese had come to regard themselves as a 'peaceful people', whose mission was to end war on earth. Henry showed the students an

essay from that same issue of the *Daily Yomiuri*. It was written
by a senior diplomat named Hisahiko Okasaki, whose picture
marked him out as the anti-Owens: a neat and prissy Japanese
mandarin type.

Okasaki's essay, a typical sally from the Japanese right, tried
to minimise the 'Rape of Nanjing': the rape and murder of tens
or perhaps hundreds of thousands of Chinese by Japanese soldiers over about six weeks from December 1937. Questioning
the Chinese account, Okasaki was tasteless in all the familiar
ways. He turned 'rape' into 'massacre' and then 'incident', and
explained that the Japanese soldiers had in fact been civilising the
Chinese. 'By and large,' he wrote, 'Japanese people may be proud
that their wartime army was one of the most disciplined armies
in the world.'

Okasaki was making a common Japanese argument. The
nation hadn't done much honest accounting of the atrocities it had
committed in the war. Most Japanese regarded the atomic bombs
on Hiroshima and Nagasaki as acts of unprovoked aggression.
There were 'Peace Parks' and 'Peace Centres' across the country.
Even kamikaze pilots were honoured in a 'Peace Museum'.

Henry said he read Okasaki's article 'with that smug feeling
you get when somebody else is making a fool of themselves in
print'. But then, at the end of the piece, Okasaki caught him out.
The article concluded: 'It may antagonise some people to say that
Japan excels over other nations when it comes to discipline and
civility. But let me state a fact that nobody can dispute. Are there
any large cities in major nations other than Japan where women
can safely walk around at night?'

Here Henry had to admit that Okasaki had a point. True,
Europe was safer than most Japanese thought (one of Henry's
students told him that Finland was 'very dangerous', and that she
would probably be killed in Prague) but it wasn't half as civil as
Japan. On the downside, Japanese civility came at the cost of
glossing over the country's past atrocities. Few of Henry's students knew much about the Second World War. Commentators
such as Okasaki who did mention the war tended to lie about it.

Japanese behaved peacefully because they had deluded themselves that they were a 'peace nation'.

That self-image was false, but it was also a bit of a blessing. It encouraged Japanese people to be civil, so much so that their fans tidied their stands after matches at the World Cup in France. Hence their obsession with foreign hooligans. Sociologists like to say that groups of people define themselves in opposition to an imaginary Other. The Japanese had found their perfect Other in English 'warrior people' like Lee Owens – and in 2002, those Others were about to land in Japan.

Roppongi Prince Hotel, Tokyo, May–June 2002

My headquarters for most of the tournament, the Roppongi Prince, was a favourite hotel among foreign pop stars. Anyone feeling overwhelmed by cultural alienation could chuck their TV set straight out of the window of their room into the kidney-shaped swimming pool in the courtyard.

The Roppongi neighbourhood was the traditional base of Tokyo's westerners. On my first few mornings I'd wake up jet-lagged at 4 a.m. and go out looking for breakfast, but Roppongi at night seemed to be mostly a red-light district. 'Massage?' the women hanging out by the traffic lights would ask me. 'Coffee?' I'd reply hopefully.

Once the tournament kicked off, I started taking Shinkansen bullet trains to matches around the country. On the first day I ran into my colleague Michael Walker from the *Guardian*. We'd become friends in a restaurant in Lyon at the previous World Cup, after Mike tried to recruit me to a newspaper that turned out not to exist. He had been in Japan for days already, and it showed. When I pointed through the train window at a Buddhist temple, Mike told me it was actually a Shinto shrine. 'I didn't know you were an expert in Japanese religions,' I said. 'Oh,' replied Mike modestly, 'in the part of Belfast where I grew up, the Shintos and the Buddhists would be ambushing each other every day.'

I had hoped to discover Japan, but for me, the World Cup mostly meant the Shinkansen. Sometimes we'd travel 500 miles for a match, then move on at six the next morning. We'd whizz past traditional Japanese landscapes of rice fields and shopping malls while salarymen in the carriage flicked through their morning porn mags and I surfed the internet, using a miraculous new invention called Wi-Fi. The *Financial Times* had attached a thingy to my laptop that allowed me to send emails without a phone line. It didn't surprise me that the contraption existed; the astonishing thing was that it worked. Emails poured in from home, annoyingly saying things like, 'I am sooooooooo jealous of you.'

By this World Cup, my fourth, I'd grasped that journalists always whine about being at World Cups. I know this might sound incomprehensibly churlish to normal people, but then journalists don't watch World Cups like normal people. We go to a game a day, working and travelling nonstop, and mostly watching teams we don't care about. Our days are spent in a sea of testosterone. Male journalists (almost the only variety at the World Cup back in 2002) are always pushing or squabbling with each other over scarce match tickets, or to get near a player spouting inaudible clichés in a language they don't understand. I've never appreciated women as much as I do during World Cups.

A World Cup in Japan posed a whole additional set of problems. At night, after a game, I'd often go out with a colleague to hunt for a restaurant. The problem was that from the outside most Japanese restaurants didn't look like restaurants. Somebody explained to me that a restaurant here was meant to be an escape from the urban frenzy, so it wasn't so much a window onto the street, like in Europe, as a private club behind a closed door. One night in Osaka, a *Financial Times* colleague and I scrutinised several facades trying to work out whether they were restaurants. But in Japan, we were like four-year-olds: we couldn't read a word of the signs. Eventually we gave up and went to bed hungry – together in the same room, given the *FT*'s legendary stinginess. I think peak occupation that World Cup was four *FT* journalists sharing one small room.

I'd typically sit up till 2 a.m. writing a column while simultaneously watching the day's goals on Japanese TV – a dizzying
spectacle. The Japanese producers cut out the passes leading up
to the goals as irrelevant, so you'd see an endless succession of
balls flying into the net without any context. It was much more
fun than football.

Japan-Belgium, Saitama Stadium, 4 June 2002

Several days into the tournament, none of us foreigners had yet
managed to spot a single hooligan, but some Japanese had. One
of my Japan-interpreters explained to me that to an old-fashioned
Japanese person, the drumming Latin Americans and cheery
Irishmen drinking on the streets (and possibly even littering!) *were*
hooligans. A policeman broke up a Latin American kickabout in
a park in the city of Niigata, saying it was 'dangerous and against
the rules'. A railway worker grumbled about Mexican noise.

The young Japanese fans who filled Saitama Stadium for their
match against Belgium felt differently. They loved foreign football
culture, and had advanced it a stage by converting it into camp.
Mixing European face paint with Latin American drums, they
celebrated their team's throw-ins as if they were goals, but they
also applauded the Belgian national anthem.

In the country with the oldest average age in human history, the
atmosphere felt like a youth festival: several Japanese players with
hair dyed blond were being cheered on by fellow twenty-some-
things dressed up for a night at the football. So many of the fans
were women that it was the first football crowd I'd ever heard
that had a soprano voice. They created such a brilliant atmosphere that when Takayuki Suzuki scored Japan's first goal of the
tournament, half the foreign journalists (including me) jumped
up cheering.

Sixty thousand spectators were waving Rising Sun flags, and
grinning as they showed the referee their middle fingers. There
were none of the faces contorted in rage that you saw at games in

Europe. At one point the whole crowd was jumping, clapping and singing in unison to the opening bars of *Aïda*.

In the 'mixed zone' in the stadium's catacombs after the 2-2 draw, Peter van der Heyden, the Belgian left-back who had spent most of his career traversing the small towns and villages of his country's league, marvelled: 'It will probably stay with me forever. This is the most beautiful stadium I've ever played in, better than the Camp Nou.'

The morning after, I had breakfast with Yoichi Funabashi, an august Japanese commentator on international relations (and football nut), and his eyes were still shining. He and his wife had delighted in the very un-Japanese activity of booing the referee with the crowd. 'Japanese sport used to be joyless, about dedication to the nation and to the state,' Funabashi explained. 'Sport had been part of the martial tradition – "Samurai culture".' A Japanese marathon runner at the Tokyo Olympics of 1964 had killed himself after failing to win the gold medal. Now you saw Japanese footballers with dyed platinum hair smiling during a World Cup match!

Argentina-England, Sapporo, 7 June 2002

That afternoon, I headed for the urban park in central Sapporo, where the tournament's 'all-out hooligan war' was supposed to kick off. But all was quiet, except for a dozen singing Argentinians. Fat English fans sat around on the lawns drinking beer in tranquillity. They were being accosted as celebrities by young Japanese fans, many of them elaborately made up in England decorations. One woman had a skull painted on one cheek and a St George's Cross on the other. A group of teenage girls had brought England flags, and literally squealed when the 'fuligans' signed them. I guessed that when young Japanese saw unkempt Englishmen slouching around in public, it was like when English people saw scantily clad Brazilians dancing in public: they wished they could do it themselves.

Elderly Japanese watched the tableau from their benches. Further along in the park, a Japanese man was contemplatively walking on his hands. I suspect that some Japanese were secretly disappointed that the fuligans hadn't shown up. Instead, football had become love.

A confession: in nine World Cups, I still haven't seen a single act of fan violence. The 1998 tournament was the last to feature any hooliganism of significance. As far as I can tell, the death toll from violence at all World Cups since 1930 is still zero.

Everything in football is repetition. That night, in a rerun of the 1998 England-Argentina game, Michael Owen won another penalty (brought down by right-back Mauricio Pochettino, the future coach, who according to my match report had been 'widely identified as a weak link'). David Beckham achieved redemption for his sending off in 1998 by netting the spot kick, and England won 1-0.

Ueno Station, Tokyo, 12 June 2002

Argentina were knocked out after drawing their group game with Sweden in Miyagi. After the game, a colleague of mine took a slow (for Japan) train back to Tokyo. Travelling in second class, he spotted a familiar bald head across the compartment. He wandered over to take a look, and yes: it was Juan Sebastian Verón. The Argentinian captain was sitting crammed around a little fold-out table with his teammates Hernán Crespo, Claudio Lopez, Juan Pablo 'Juampi' Sorín and all their luggage. By the looks of it, the Argentinian federation had left them to find their own way back to Buenos Aires.

The four men were hunched over their DVD players. Sorín's eyes were red from crying. In Tokyo they staggered out of the train, weighed down by their bags, and started pushing their way through the hordes of commuters. (Inevitably, it was rush hour.) Nobody seemed to notice them. Amid a barrage of *ojes* and *ches* they went hunting for a taxi to the airport. Because those lucky bastards were going home already.

Japan-Turkey, round of sixteen match, Miyagi, 18 June 2002

Turkey won 1-0 in the rain, Japan were out of the World Cup, and the Japanese spectators in plastic ponchos, who had been singing for the whole match, fell silent for a few seconds. Then they burst into applause. They clapped the Turks, who bowed to each stand in turn, and when Japan's players ran a lap of the field, the fans gave them an ovation too. The Japanese had never thought their team was very good, and they didn't particularly mind that they had been eliminated.

Many of Japan's players were crying, and I cried a bit too. This embarrassed me until I ran into a British colleague who told me that he had also cried.

Turkey's coach, Şenol Güneş, observed, 'Look at the Japanese, they are applauding their team even when they lose.' Güneş had just taken his team to the quarter-final, in Turkey's first World Cup since 1954, but Turkish newspapers had been calling him 'a disgrace to football' and 'a coward full of complexes'.

The Kakegawa Grand Hotel, June 2002

On nights when there were no games, the people I knew in Tokyo would take me to eat some of the best food of my life, in streets I'd never be able to find again. On those occasions, the football faded away. Most Japanese people knew that the 'Warudo Capp' was happening, like Britons might know that the World Chess Championship was being held in Brighton, but they were busy living their lives. While the world obsessed over France-Senegal or Brazil-Turkey, baseball fans from the Japanese provinces were busy cheering on the Yomiuri Giants in the Tokyo Dome.

I loved my brief visits to Japan. Mostly, though, I lived in the parallel country that is the World Cup – living off plastic-wrapped rice balls in over-lit media centres, watching teams play out 0-0 draws.

There was little atmosphere in the stadiums. Japan in 2002 was still an expensive country, and few foreigners had come (except for hordes of Irishmen who seemed to be everywhere), so at some matches there were just a few hundred foreign fans, watched respectfully by Japanese people. At times you could hear individual voices sing. The silence at the Argentina-Nigeria match was particularly poignant. The collapse of the Argentinian peso had kept almost all the country's fans at home. Watching a game alone with my thoughts was often the one meditative moment of my day.

During the group stage, when a World Cup is at its most relentless for journalists, I saw sixteen forgettable games in twenty-one days and Lord knows how many cities. I'd get off the train thinking, 'It's Saturday, so perhaps this is Niigata, though who really knows.' One friend in Tokyo told me that I visited more of Japan in a month than many Japanese do in a lifetime. I was soon so visibly shattered that when one colleague saw me in a media centre, he came up and took my pulse.

I think it was in Sapporo that a colleague with whom I was sharing a room told me a story about a rock star on tour. Every day, the rock star checked into a new hotel room in a new city. Eventually he began to suspect it was always the same room.

One day he broke the mirror in his hotel room. 'Why did you do that?' asked a fellow band member. (Why not just chuck your TV into the swimming pool?) The rock star explained, 'When we get to the next hotel, I'll know it's a new room because the mirror won't be broken.'

The moment they arrived at the next hotel, the fellow band member dashed ahead to his friend's new room and smashed the mirror. When the rock star opened the door and saw the same broken glass as the night before, he had a breakdown and was taken to hospital. (Coincidentally, the man who told me the story in Sapporo was taken to hospital that same night.)

A few days later, in the Kakegawa Grand Hotel, I felt like that rock star. Alone in my ninth-floor room on four hours' sleep, in a town I couldn't find on a map, I wanted to go home. I just couldn't remember where that was.

A week later, I had another night in the Kakegawa Grand, and by then it felt like home – I could tell by the broken mirror – or as much as anywhere else did. This time I was sharing a room with Matt, an *FT* colleague who had flown in after covering the first round in South Korea. Matt was impressed by the Kakegawa Grand, especially after his Korean hotel room where there had been two handprints on the wall three metres above the bed. He was still ruminating on what might have happened there. A mafia execution? Very experimental sex? Or both?

Team camps, Japan and South Korea, May–June 2002

I suspect many of the players at the 2002 World Cup experienced a version of what I went through in the Kakegawa Grand. In fact, it was probably worse for them: at least I could occasionally leave the tournament.

A test for any team aspiring to win the competition is: can you survive weeks in camp together? This had been an issue since the first World Cup in 1930, when, as Jules Rimet recounts, the Uruguayan host team were practically held captive in their gorgeous hotel. One of their goalkeepers, unable to bear the 'monastic' regime, jumped over the wall one night and went out on the town. Returning home 'on the sly', writes Rimet, 'his shoes in his hand', the keeper was caught by his coach and expelled from the competition.

Footballers have been known to admit years after a World Cup that it was the unhappiest time of their careers. A training camp is a bit like being in the army: a couple of dozen men with all the usual social tensions cooped up in an upscale version of barracks. Some players miss their young families back home. Some are bullied by teammates. And they all know that if they get knocked out, two days later they'll be holidaying on some exotic beach with their loved ones.

Then there's another issue: many footballers don't like football. They enjoy the money and the lifestyle, but not the training sessions, the stress, tactical talks and changing-room life. During the club season, this isn't a huge problem. Players typically train in the morning and have the rest of the day to themselves. But at a World Cup, there is only football.

By 2002, the camp test was tougher than ever. As Emmanuel Petit had bemoaned, the football calendar had grown so packed that by the time the club season ended, leading players were desperate for a holiday. The journalistic cliché went that the World Cup was 'every footballer's dream'. It was for some. If you were an Ecuadorean or Irish or Japanese international, you would tell your grandchildren about your World Cup. But for the most successful footballers it was just another work trip, to be survived on painkillers.

Their exhaustion was also mental. They lacked time to look forward to the tournament, to fantasise about it, to remind themselves that it was supposed to be special.

A few weeks before the 2002 World Cup, I'd flown to a European city to watch an England international play in the Champions League. After the game, I sat up with him in a hotel bar till after midnight, talking over beers. The England team had recently sparked national overexcitement by beating Germany 1-5 in Munich, but the player was downbeat, possibly jealous. He hadn't played in the game, and said the result was ridiculous. Germany should have scored when it was still 1-1, and afterwards things had got silly. I asked whether 'God Save the Queen' stirred him. 'To be very honest, no,' he said.

In two hours of conversation, he did not mention the coming World Cup once. He talked about horse racing, his family and his club. I left with the impression that if he weren't picked for the tournament, he wouldn't mind.

Around the same time, the US captain, Earnie Stewart, told me that after the horrors of the team's chateau in France in 1998 ('we were literally in a monastery'), he had come close to skipping 2002. In the event, the only major player who chose to sit out the World Cup was Germany's Stefan Effenberg, unless you took the view that the entire Dutch team had voluntarily skipped the tournament by failing to qualify. Everyone else went, presumably driven by irrational hope ('Maybe I'll score the winner in the final') and rational fear. In many nations, the patriotic press was tough on 'traitors'. If the Englishman I spoke to had pulled out of the World Cup, the tabloids would have run pictures of him sunning himself on holiday while his erstwhile teammates 'fought for England'.

But 2002 was a particularly hard tournament to play in. Fear of terrorism (a more serious risk than hooliganism) turned the team hotels in Japan and Korea into sealed camps. When a team won a match, the nation back home may have caroused in the streets, but the players got straight on a plane, couldn't even get a beer from the trolley, then checked into their new hotel at 4 a.m.

Italy's Paolo Maldini missed his family so much he'd sit in his hotel room watching them on a webcam. Zinedine Zidane flew to South Korea a couple of days after his wife gave birth. He cannot have been in the mood for a World Cup; France went out in the group stage without scoring a goal.

Ireland did get to the second round, earning themselves a flight from Japan to Korea. That night, their winger Jason McAteer gave a bittersweet paean to his room-mate Steve Staunton. 'It's another week with Steve. Half of me is hoping we'll get separate rooms in Seoul. No, he's great: another week listening to his conversations with his dad.'

Sometimes, once a group of players has done enough to return home to applause, they semi-consciously long to get knocked out. Everyone at home is telling them that they can't wait to welcome them with open arms, their agents have a stack of offers to show them, and they're done with the fatigue and cabin fever.

I think that partly explains how the last stages of the 2002 tournament unfolded. The quarter-finals featured two teams whose nations expected success (Brazil and Germany), two countries that had learned to expect failure (England and Spain) and four teams whose nations were astounded – and delighted – that they had got this far: Turkey, Senegal, the US, South Korea. The Germans reached the final against Brazil in part because they had to. They weren't better than the Cinderella nations, but they forced themselves to climb two more mountains because their fans demanded it.

The media centre in Nagai Stadium, Osaka, 22 June 2002

Then there were factors outside the players' control – such as the refereeing.

The day of the Senegal-Turkey quarter-final, the media centre in Osaka was packed with sweaty, sleep-deprived men eating packaged rice balls. Before going into the stadium to see the game, we watched South Korea-Spain on TV.

There were already suspicions about the refereeing of Korea's matches. Portugal had two players sent off when they played the hosts in the group stage. At South Korea-Italy in the round of sixteen, the frog-like Ecuadorean referee Byron Moreno awarded the Koreans a dubious penalty almost from kick-off, showed Italy's Francesco Totti a second yellow card for diving when Italy arguably should have had a penalty, and disallowed an apparently good Italian goal in extra time that would probably have won the game.

Afterwards the Italian minister for public offences, Franco Frattini, called Moreno 'a disgrace'. The *Gazzetta dello Sport* newspaper said he was 'the worst referee, ever'. A new set of public toilets in Sicily was named after him. The Italian theory was that FIFA needed Korea to reach at least the semis, or else the tournament in Korea would fizzle out. Moreover, this was part of the well-known long-running global conspiracy against the Italian people. I thought the Italians were exaggerating. Moreno struck me as just your common-or-garden incompetent home ref.

In extra time of the South Korea-Spain quarter-final, the Spanish forward Fernando Morientes headed home what would have been the winning goal, only to have it flagged off by a lines-man who indicated that the ball had gone behind the goal line before Joaquin crossed it. When the replay revealed his call to be ludicrous, the Osaka media centre erupted in a howl of rage.

'We have become just one more victim,' Spain's manager José Camacho said afterwards. 'I thought that as we were playing in a quarter-final the officials were going to be more fair.'

At the time, I dismissed this as whining.

Japanese parliament, Tokyo, 25 June 2002

Seishiro Eto, an MP for the ruling Liberal Democratic Party and director general of the Japanese Parliamentarians' League for promoting the World Cup, worked from a 1960s' room with cheap furniture and a grey carpet that looked straight out of the Bulgarian Communist Party's Central Committee building. The atmosphere was more like the Mad Hatter's Tea Party. Nothing Eto said quite made sense. When I asked how he had experienced the World Cup, he replied, 'Japanese people have seen shadow hooligans this time. I would have liked to see real hooligans and hooligan acts.' He laughed, so this may have been a bit of a joke, but then he went on: 'I don't want people to think that the moderate version of hooligans we have seen out here are the real hooligans.'

The only hooligan incident at the World Cup had been some Slovenian fans fighting among themselves during their defeat to Paraguay. Surely, I asked, Eto didn't still think hooligans were a big problem in Europe? 'I believe hooligans only exist within sports at the moment, but in Europe especially, because of the immigration problems, which lead to unemployment, poverty and uncertainty, if hooliganism occurs at the time of an election, it can be a big political problem. And it could become linked with terrorism.'

Was this crazy thinking or not? Eto said he wanted to take a football team of Japanese parliamentarians to the Middle East to try to bring peace there. I told him it was a brilliant idea.

Brazil-Germany, World Cup final, Yokohama, June 30, 2002

Germany had only just qualified for the World Cup. Their 5-1 defeat to England in September 2001 was the national team's lowest point since the 1920s. Yet now they had reached the final with a team built around a goalkeeper, the impregnable Oliver Kahn.

'So much of getting to a World Cup final is luck,' their midfielder Marco Bode told me over Zoom in 2024. By this time, Bode looked like a north German doctor on his day off: a well-preserved fifty-five-year-old with grey hair and glasses seated in front of a bookcase. A bright man, he had enough distance from the 2002 final to reflect on what it had meant in his life.

He had spent his whole club career at modest Werder Bremen. He said, 'I think that Werder, all told, was more important for me than the national team, also because I was usually more important for Werder than for the national team.' And football hadn't been his only life: during his playing career, he had studied maths and philosophy at university.

He was already twenty-six when he made his debut for Germany, against South Africa in Johannesburg in 1995. The South African president, Nelson Mandela, had come out to greet the players before kick-off. When he got to Bode, he remarked, 'You look exactly like Steffi Graf!' Bode told me: 'Mandela was right. We do look alike, in our eyes, and at the time also in our haircuts.'

The German squad in Bode's day was drawn mostly from Bayern Munich and Borussia Dortmund. The role of the small Werder contingent, said Bode, was 'like Switzerland': to keep the peace between the great powers. He wasn't usually a regular starter, but he played forty internationals and was in the side that won Euro 96. Over time he grew into that classic German phenomenon: the *Turnierspieler*, or 'tournament player'.

Bode started the World Cup 2002 on the bench, but came on as sub in the do-or-die group match against Cameroon, and scored the opening goal. That remained the high point of his international career: for once, he had been decisive for his country. Decades later, some Germans still came up and talked to him about that goal, though they usually couldn't remember which African team he'd scored it against. 'A game at a World Cup makes you better known than a hundred games at Werder,' he said.

After Cameroon, Bode played every match in the tournament. Germany made hard work of an easy run to the final. Thanks largely to Kahn in goal, they beat Paraguay, the US and South Korea by 1-0 each. Bode said that the 2002 side was the last German team to rely chiefly on 'order, passion, discipline' – the so-called 'German virtues'.

The night before the final, he stood by the window of his hotel room, watching the usual Saturday-night party crowds swarm in and out of Yokohama station. Behind the soundproof glass, he couldn't hear a thing. That's how he had lived the whole tournament, in isolation. It had felt like 'an unreal World Cup', he said. Many Japanese people in the stadiums had never watched football before. Even when they cheered, it was usually for the wrong thing: a hopeless cross hoofed high into the box, say. It had taken him time to get used to that.

In the final Germany were facing the Brazilians, the tournament's best team with their 'Three R' forward line of Rivaldo, Ronaldo and Ronaldinho. But Germany had so often slain better opponents at World Cups. They could do this.

I was dreading the journey from the Roppongi Prince hotel to Yokohama for the final, until a British colleague told me that he was going to rent a limo to the stadium and put it on his expenses. He said I was welcome to join him, and who cared what his editor said. It was the last hurrah of sports journalism. Our industry was about to be decimated by free online websites that meant nobody had to pay for news ever again. Soon after that World Cup, my friend lost his job.

As our limo neared the stadium, we passed Ronaldo – or at least a professional Ronaldo lookalike, bucktoothed, round-faced, wearing the Brazilian No. 9 shirt, and like the great man himself, sporting the world's worst hairstyle, with something resembling a moustache sprouting from the front of an otherwise shaven head. He was making money posing for photographs with passers-by.

The real Ronaldo had barely played club football in the four years since his panic attack on the day of the World Cup final in Paris. Injuries had wrecked his body. Now he had returned to football on his own terms – and going into the final, he had already scored six goals at the World Cup. An intimate of his, who visited him twice at his club Inter Milan before the World Cup, emailed me during the tournament:

> Ronaldo didn't say it explicitly, but I always felt he was fooling everyone. For him only one thing was important: the World Cup. He had to be present there, to shine, make Brazil world champion, equal Romario, take revenge for 1998, etc. etc. I think that the last two years he consciously hid himself (with Inter's approval, I think; I can't judge how that game works. I do know that Nike and his agents are directing it, as ever.) All his so-called 'returns to football' had no meaning.

Going into the match, Marco Bode was thirty-two years old, and had already decided to retire immediately after the tournament. The World Cup final was going to be the last game of his career. That knowledge relaxed him, he said. 'I noticed during the anthems that I was less tense than usual. I felt happy. I enjoyed it.'

At half-time the score was 0-0. I wrote in my notebook: 'Bode's control is not up to this level.' Even so, he might have scored the opening goal. He pulled a sprint from deep, alone into the box, just as he had against Cameroon, but this time the pass didn't come.

With sixty-seven minutes gone, Ronaldo bundled Didi Hamann off the ball and fed Rivaldo, a brilliant egomaniac who always shot, even from the halfway line. This time, the instant that Rivaldo shot, Ronaldo was twenty yards from goal. Yet when Kahn spilled the ball, practically his first mistake of the tournament, Ronaldo was there to tap it in, having made up the distance in a second or two. For his second goal, he found the inside of Kahn's side netting, the only vacant corner of the net. He was too good for this level: a double against these Germans was routine for him. Brazil in 2002 were the only side that I've seen win a World Cup without ever being truly tested.

Bode was substituted after eighty-four minutes. By the time the final whistle went, his adrenalin had already dropped, and he felt able to accept defeat. 'Maybe that's my own particular mentality,' he told me. He walked up to Kahn, who was sitting immobile against his goalpost, destroyed by his error, and told him: 'Without you, we wouldn't even have been here.' Over two decades later, Germans still sometimes mentioned that moment to Bode. But Kahn was inconsolable.

Meanwhile, Brazilian players were cavorting around the ground wrapped in national flags, some of them wearing Jesus T-shirts. The one point of stillness amid the euphoria was Ronaldo. He wandered alone around the pitch, speaking consoling words to prostrate Germans, accepting the congratulations of their coach Rudi Völler in Italian, thanking the referee, Pierluigi Collina. Having achieved his life's goal, he wanted to experience it with a clear head.

The Germans stayed on the pitch a long time, partly, I suspect, to soak up the emotional peak of their careers. They collected their medals for second place, able to handle defeat. 'I don't think it was such a challenge for most of us,' said Bode. He wasn't the sort to tear a 'loser's medal' angrily off his neck. He would have found that 'disrespectful'.

At the post-match press conference, Ronaldo told us, 'Slowly, slowly, I'm starting to understand what's happening. I think it will take some time for me to figure it out.' And then: 'I would be telling a lie if I didn't say that every time I step on the pitch it's a victory for me. So I think that even if I weren't a world champion, I'd definitely be happy now.'

A Brazilian journalist grabbed a microphone and started lecturing him. 'We are not interested in the past,' he said, meaning the World Cup that had just been won, 'only in the future.' Didn't Ronaldo want to win an Olympic gold? And what about the next World Cup, in four years' time?

Ronaldo answered, quietly: 'I don't want to feel any pressure now about the future. I don't want to think. I don't want anything except to celebrate. Thank you very much.' He had learned to fend off the vultures.

Frankfurt, 1 July 2002

The next day, the returning German team were welcomed home by a huge crowd. 'So we were not seen as losers,' said Bode. At this point, he could have signed one last fat contract. An English Premier League team was interested. But he was keen to retire on a high. He did, and it ended up helping him in his transition out of football. He hadn't tarnished his name by sitting on a bench somewhere for two years, or getting injured, or fighting with a club manager. In most Germans' eyes, he remained a *Vizewelt-meister,* a 'vice-world champion'.

I asked how he now placed that final in his life. He said, 'A positive ending – as stupid as that might sound. I know I'm not a Maradona or a Cruyff or a Lothar Matthäus, but I am proud of my career – also because of this final.'

Then he quoted the line from the end of the movie *The Commitments,* when the band falls apart: 'Sure we could have been famous and made albums and stuff, but that would have been predictable. This way it's poetry.'

In the film, the response is, 'It's a pisser is what it is, Joey,' but Bode didn't quote that bit.

Paris, July 2002

Returning from a month in Japan, I suddenly realised how rude and noisy Europeans were.

Postscript

I later had to revise my theory that the defeated Italians and Spaniards were indulging in self-exculpatory whining at referees. Three months after the World Cup, the Ecuadorean FA gave Byron Moreno, the ref of South Korea-Italy, a twenty-match ban. In a game between Liga de Quito and Barcelona Guayaqil, he had signalled six minutes of extra time but then allowed thirteen. In those thirteen minutes, Quito scored twice, to win 4-3. The match also featured two controversial penalties and two sendings off. At the time, Moreno happened to be running for a spot on Quito's city council.

Freshly returned from his ban in 2003, he was suspended again after sending off three Deportivo Quito players in a match. He then retired from refereeing, saying, 'I'm leaving through the front door with my head held high. I prefer to die standing up than to live kneeling down.'

Moreno's downfall came in 2010. After landing at JFK airport in New York, he was arrested when a customs official found 'hard objects on the defendant's stomach, back and both of his legs'. Moreno was carrying ten plastic bags of heroin. He was sentenced to thirty months in a New York jail. Few media reported the news. Nor did many fans show interest in what seemed like an important story about the World Cup.

Moreno served twenty-six months before being granted an early release for good behaviour. He went on to present a programme on Ecuadorean TV in which he analysed refereeing errors. He described South Korea-Italy as 'one of my top three career refereeing performances. I'd give myself an 8.5 out of 10.'

His corruption wasn't necessarily an isolated case. In 2012 the Chinese referee Lu Jun was sentenced to five and a half years in jail for taking nearly $130,000 to fix seven league matches. Hardly anyone outside China noticed. But Lu Jun had refereed two games at the 2002 World Cup.

Most football fans took it for granted that FIFA was corrupt. They'd heard the stories of officials stashing bribes in secret bank accounts. However, fans care more about what happens on the field. Once we start to doubt that the matches we are seeing are real, the emotion we invest in World Cups becomes pointless.

9

World Cup 2006: How We All Learned to Stop Worrying and Love the Germans

The usual speculation before a World Cup – almost the only interesting thing that journalists *can* write – is whether the stadiums will be ready on time, the hooligans will come, and the host country can handle the organisation. Going into 2006, nobody was asking these questions. Everyone knew that Germany could organise a World Cup.

Germans were respected. Their goal for the World Cup was to become loved. The tournament's slogan was 'A Time to Make Friends', accompanied by a logo of smileys. Germany's manager, Jürgen Klinsmann, had been tasked not with winning the tournament but with playing attractive football. Germans were sick of being the Darth Vader of World Cups.

Sixty years after the end of the Second World War, official Germany aspired to become 'a normal country' – one that wasn't forever apologising for its past and anxiously keeping watch for old demons that might resurface. This aspiration went far beyond football, but the World Cup was the moment when a 'normal' Germany hoped to present itself to the world. I was curious to see how that went.

The other big story ahead of the tournament was the return of the best European player of his generation, Zinedine Zidane. He had retired from the French team after Euro 2004, but in August 2005 he announced that 'a voice' had persuaded him to return.

Which voice? By this time, after a few years in Paris, I had begun watching French TV. *Les guignols de l'info*, the country's equivalent of *Spitting Image*, ran a sketch in which a mystery voice addresses 'Zizou' while he sleeps at night, clad head to toe in sponsors' gears. The voice turns out to belong to France's president Jacques Chirac, who is hoping to distract the population from his own travails. At first, Zidane rebuffs him. Muttering the names of certain new *Bleus* in his sleep, he comments, 'They're rubbish.' 'Exactly,' replies Chirac, and tells Zidane he needs him.

Zidane later revealed that the actual 'voice' had been his brother's. No matter: he came back, along with fellow oldies Claude Makélélé and Lilian Thuram. A repeat of the French triumph of 1998 hung in the air.

Before Germany, I had always been delighted to go to a World Cup. But I had become a father in February 2006. I left my wife and baby daughter at home, seeing them only once during the tournament on a brief dash back to Paris. At every World Cup from 2006 on, I wrestled with the sense of being in the wrong place. I'd sometimes literally count the hours till it was over.

Trains around Germany, June–July 2006

This was the best organised World Cup, down to the perfect summer weather. About the only blemish on the tournament was the chorus of frogs who disturbed the sleep of the Ukrainian squad at their Potsdam hotel.

Accredited journalists got free first-class train travel. This was confusing, because German second-class was so palatial that I initially took it for first. First class was like renting your own small apartment. And if you missed the 1.30 a.m. train after the game, you could catch the 2.30 a.m. one. Thank you, German taxpayers.

The new stadiums were beautiful, packed for every game, and not fated to become white elephants. When the World Cup ended, they would be handed over to clubs that could fill them for decades to come.

But what made this tournament special was the nationwide party. After three World Cups in the US, France and Japan, it was a joy to experience one in a country that cared about football. There has probably never been a World Cup so widely followed in the host country. Stepping into cafés decked out with mock green turf floors, it felt as if the private perversions of your childhood had gone universal. Fans from everywhere dressed up in national colours (sometimes of their own country) and celebrated together in a beer-fuelled international love-in.

A new German nationalism had emerged from the first day of the World Cup, taking everyone by surprise. German flags sold out almost at once, because nobody had anticipated much demand in a country where flag-waving had been taboo since 1945. I read that a child might come home from school and say, 'Mummy, Daddy, let's put up a German flag outside our house like everyone else!'

The parents, raised on the old taboos, would reply brightly, 'Well, how about a German *and* a Brazilian flag?'

And the child would ask, puzzled: 'But why a Brazilian flag?'

A friend in Berlin told me that her mother, who had never paid the slightest bit of attention to football, was flying a German flag from the handlebars of her bike. Post-war Germans were finally claiming the same right as every other nationality: to love their country and its football team.

The team was possibly their weakest in decades, and it was

easier that way: the new Germany wasn't '*über alles*', but just another country. It was also multicultural: there were players of Polish or African origin, and the Swiss-raised Francophone Oliver Neuville. Germans cheered them on in a merry self-deprecating way that foreigners found unthreatening. Fans painted the flag on their faces and belted out the anthem, but they wouldn't dream of dying for Germany. It felt like a new kind of nationalism – a great big party.

Argentina-Ivory Coast, Hamburg, 10 June 2006

I travelled to the game with a British friend who goes to every World Cup. He always registers as a supporter of a team that won't bring many supporters, because it's the easiest way to get tickets. In 2006 he was an official Ivory Coast supporter. Arriving at the stadium, we noticed large numbers of white Ivory Coast fans.

Watching Italy-Ghana in the ZDF 'Arena', 12 June 2006

Ulrich was a Berlin friend from my student days. Back then, we had mostly talked about Nazism and German reunification, but during this World Cup we just imbibed football together. His girl-friend, Margarete, said she saw more matches that month than in the rest of her life put together.

For Italy-Ghana, Ulrich had scored seats in the studio audience of the ZDF TV studio. We watched the game on a giant screen, and then watched ZDF's experts discuss it. One pundit – a lanky blond thirty-something, with teeth so white they must have been visible from outer space – entranced the studio. Apparently he was the coach of a small German club. He explained the teams' tactics with such wit and charisma that he was more compelling than the game itself. His name was Jürgen Klopp.

Brazil-Croatia, Berlin, 12 June 2006

The moments before kick-off were the last peak of the modern veneration of *jogo bonito*, the Brazilian 'beautiful game'.

Going into the tournament, Brazil seemed to be football's lone superpower. About half their starting line-up had won the previous World Cup. Ronaldo was back, albeit looking like an XL blow-up doll version of himself. Even Brazil's president Lula said that he looked fat. But their other striker, Adriano, was arguably fatter.

Most of the 72,000 people flocking into Hitler's Olympic Stadium for the Croatia game seemed to be Brazilians in yellow shirts. Only when I got nearer did I realise that they were speaking all kinds of languages. There were Germans, Japanese, Brits, all self-identifying as Brazil supporters – a new post-nationalistic fandom. Fairly typical was a Finnish friend of mine who had flown in from Beijing and paid a tout €300 for a match ticket. When the Brazilian anthem was played, hardly anyone in the banks of yellow shirts sang along, because they didn't know the words.

Brazil had become an experience, a tribute act more than a football team. They couldn't possibly meet expectations, which were essentially to reincarnate Pele's Brazil of 1970. Even given that, their performance was a let-down. Hardly any of their players moved off the ball. Roberto Carlos insisted on taking free kicks, which he blasted high into the stands, his faith in his own accuracy undimmed either by experience or by the presence of decent alternative kickers such as Ronaldinho and Ronaldo. Brazil won 1-0 through a stroke of genius from Kaká.

This was the tournament when when the notion of *jogo bonito* began fading into history. The languid style with its dribbles and tricks against unfit, semi-competent defenders was the product of a particular era. To expect its return was like hoping for the revival of Byzantine art, yet Brazilians continued to hope.

Public Viewing of Germany-Poland, Leipzig, 14 June 2006

Germans had discovered something that they called, in their impenetrable language, 'das Public Viewing'. Huge screens were set up in city centres around the country. The avenue in front of my old university was turned into a 'Fanmeile' centred around the Brandenburg Gate. The screening of Germany-Sweden there reportedly drew a million people – possibly the largest gathering for a football match in history. After games, some spectators would wander over to check out the nearby Holocaust memorial.

I watched Germany-Poland (played in Dortmund) sitting on a balcony overlooking the main square in Leipzig. Below me, thousands of white-shirted Germans massed around big screens, waving flags and chanting, 'Deutschland!'

I'm Jewish. I studied German history. I grew up despising the German football team. But sitting on that balcony, drinking German beer, when Oliver Neuville scored their last-minute winner, I almost cheered.

Portugal-Netherlands ('The Battle of Nuremberg'), round of sixteen match, Nuremberg, 25 June 2006

Before the game I met a Dutch colleague in the media centre, who delivered the ritual lament of a journalist in the middle of a World Cup. 'I'm shattered, man. I'm so happy I'll be going home tomorrow.'

'Hang on,' I said, 'you'll stay here if Holland win tonight.'

He looked at me as if I were five years old. 'We're playing Portugal.'

I saw his point. Holland always lost to Portugal. For the Dutch, the Portuguese are what Germans call an Angstgegner, the opponent of fear. I think it's because the Portuguese control the ball – and with it the tempo of the game – which in those days Dutch teams were used to doing. We'd have had a better chance against Brazil or Germany.

Portugal won 1-0, but the game is remembered chiefly for

the four red cards and sixteen yellows handed out by the Russian referee Valentin Ivanov – at the time, a record number for any FIFA tournament. Three of the sent-off players, Holland's Giovanni van Bronckhorst and Khalid Boulahrouz and Portugal's Deco, ended the game chatting amicably on a bench together. Van Bronckhorst and Deco were teammates at Barcelona. Footballers were becoming global citizens.

There was no historical rivalry between Portugal and Holland, but there was between Germany and Holland. I was watching the match just behind Willem van Hanegem, the best Dutch player in the World Cup final of 1974, who as a baby in 1944 had lost his father and seven other relatives when a bomb – dropped by an Allied plane – fell on their village. Van Hanegem had always frankly disliked Germans. When the ones in the stadium sang that they were going to Berlin without Holland, he raised his shoulders like a human hedgehog. He was one of the only people at the 2006 World Cup who still mentally inhabited the Second World War.

Loetje Café, Laren, Netherlands, 28 January 2025

Nearly twenty years later, I was granted a troubling insight into how refereeing had worked at the 2006 World Cup.

I had a coffee date in a small town near Amsterdam with Mario van der Ende, a former Dutch referee who had sat on the FIFA Referees Committee from 2003 to 2007. Van der Ende had taken the role soon after Byron Moreno, the discredited referee of South Korea-Italy, was banned by the Ecuadorean FA. Van der Ende told me that he didn't remember the committee ever discussing the Moreno affair. 'Maybe that sort of thing was consciously avoided,' he said.

He explained how referees for the 2006 tournament had been chosen. The chairman of the Referees Committee at the time was Ángel María Villar, who also wore another hat: he was president of the Spanish federation. Villar's number two on the committee was Ricardo Teixeira, president of the Brazilian federation. Both men sat on FIFA's mighty executive committee too. Van der Ende said, 'I always found it surprising that someone who was head of a big federation also ran the Referees Committee. It is different today.'

The conflict of interest didn't seem to bother FIFA, but it did bother people in the refereeing world. Van der Ende said that in the run-up to a big tournament, some referees would ask not to be assigned to a Spain match in case they made a decision that upset Villar and so weren't picked for the tournament. During the World Cup itself, Villar and two Spanish associates within FIFA chose the referee for each match.

It's impossible to say whether Villar's influence in this era helped the Spanish team. True, they lost to France in the round of sixteen in 2006, but they won the World Cup in 2010. Villar remained president of the Referees Committee until 2013, and returned to the job from 2015 to 2017. Was he a man who could always be trusted to do the right thing? After meeting Van der Ende, I checked up on Villar's recent doings. He had had to give up his posts in football in 2017 after he, his son Gorka and two associates were arrested in Spain on suspicion of financial wrong-doing. In March 2025, Spain's public prosecutor's office demanded a fifteen-and-a-half-year sentence for Villar for alleged corruption and embezzlement.

Let's move from the probity of refereeing to its quality. You might think that FIFA would pick the best refs on earth for the World Cup. Van der Ende believed that if, say, Luxembourg had three excellent referees, all three of them should be chosen. But FIFA didn't work that way. Van der Ende said, 'It surprised me that there had to be one [referee] from each country, so they weren't choosing on quality.' Influential countries were able to get their referees placed on the list. That's how Ivanov, the Russian who lost control of Portugal-Netherlands, had made it to the tournament at the last minute, instead of the German Herbert Fandel.

FIFA aimed to choose referees and linesmen from as many countries as possible so as to maximise the number of happy federation presidents. As a referee at the 1994 and 1998 World Cups, Van der Ende had been assigned linesmen from countries like Paraguay and Vanuatu. They met for the first time at the tournament, so they never had the chance to practise together.

When he raised selection issues with FIFA's president Sepp Blatter, Blatter would reply, 'You're completely right, my son, but don't forget: football is all politics.' Blatter was in the business of pleasing FIFA's member countries. Van der Ende had retorted that in that case, the elevator music at FIFA ought to be Simon & Garfunkel's 'Keep the Customer Satisfied'.

The problem, he told me, was that most Asian or African referees weren't as good as their European peers. They had no way of gaining regular experience of high-intensity top-paced football. Some were also overawed by star players like Zidane or Roberto Carlos. Van der Ende said, 'I've seen referees pose for a picture with players before a game.' He thought the quality of refereeing at World Cups was worse than in the knockout stages of the Champions League.

Postscript

FIFA still spreads the refereeing around. The thirty-six refs for the 2022 World Cup came from thirty-one different countries, including seven Asians, six Africans and a Guatemalan.

Switzerland-Ukraine, round of sixteen match, Cologne, 26 June

This was possibly the most boring game I've ever seen, the nadir of 10,000 years of human civilisation. Neither team even pretended to attack. It was worse than watching Sven-Göran Eriksson's England. Here's the measure of the impossibility of a goal: no journalist ever goes to the toilet during a World Cup game because someone would inevitably score in their absence.

During the second half of Switzerland-Ukraine, the journalist next to me went to the toilet.

The game was goalless after extra time, and Switzerland couldn't even score on penalties. They went home despite having not conceded a goal in their four matches. Ukraine progressed to the quarter-finals, where they were hammered by Italy.

The problem was that Switzerland-Ukraine was only a slightly worse version of many matches in 2006. Approximately twenty-seven of the thirty-two teams had come not to win the World Cup, but to avoid a humiliating thrashing.

Underdogs at earlier World Cups had been spectacularly terrible, like Zaire in 1974, or weird, like the Australian amateurs in 1974 with their skintight Aussie Rules shorts, or brilliant, like the Cameroonians in 1990 who beat Argentina. By 2006, all that was over. Some football teams are born to mediocrity, some teams have mediocrity thrust upon them, and some teams achieve mediocrity through their deeds. With apologies to Shakespeare and Joseph Heller, for a team like Switzerland it was all three.

Swiss mediocrity had been hard-won. This had long been a country of downhill skiing, with a few semi-professional footballers who were ignored by the wider population. In only one decade before the 1980s did the *Nati* (as the national team was fondly nicknamed) win even 40 per cent of their matches: the 1940s, when most of their opponents had certain well-publicised problems.

But from the 1980s, Switzerland globalised, and immigrants arrived from football countries. Their children, known in Switzerland as 'Secondos', preferred football to skiing. Like the rest of the world, the Swiss also began watching the leading European leagues on TV. The better Swiss players joined a global middle class of footballers who earned a decent living at respectable European clubs, where they absorbed the basics of defensive organisation even if they mostly sat on the bench.*

---

* The pinnacle of this middle-class-isation would be attained at Serbia-Ghana at the 2010 World Cup, when both teams' goalkeepers were reserves at Wigan Athletic.

To achieve mediocrity, a team had to follow just a few simple tenets. Become top-fit. Take the field intending to bore the pants off tens of millions of blameless TV viewers. Set up a ten-man moving screen behind the ball. Defend thirty yards from goal, to avoid accidents in the penalty area. Ration fouls, so as not to draw red cards or dangerous free kicks; instead, 'spend' your fouls on the opposition's best attacking player. Never attempt an unexpected pass or dribble. Don't even aspire to the high-paced attacking pressing game played by the best club teams. Dismiss the thought that the World Cup would be a better place without your team.

Smaller nations ascended from cluelessness to hyper-organisation. Trinidad and Tobago, for instance, conceded only four goals in three group matches in Germany, but I suspect that a well-drilled select eleven of accredited journalists could have done just as well.

Not only did almost every team at the tournament have the same style, but the fans did too. A universal uniform had emerged, copied from football supporters in TV ads, of team shirt, face paint and cheese-eating grin. The Swiss fans sang a song ripped off from the Germans: 'Stand up if you are Swiss [or Nigerian, or Inuit – fill in desired nationality].'

Part of the problem for spectators was that by 2006 we were being spoiled by the rising quality of the best leagues. The average team at this tournament was worse than, say, Everton, especially in the summer heat after a ten-month season. (The World Cup has a 'June problem'.) I sat in the Cologne stadium thinking what I often thought at World Cups: why are so many people watching this?

Brazil-Ghana, round of sixteen match, Dortmund, 27 June 2006

On the face of it, this was an unremarkable game. Brazil still weren't playing like a team, but they had wonderful individuals and won 3-0, their record eleventh straight victory at a World Cup. Afterwards Ghana's coach whined a bit about the refereeing, but admitted, 'If you give them just deciles of seconds, they will finish with you as they finished with us.' There was no shame in Ghana losing to Brazil. They could fly home with honour.

I left the stadium not suspecting that I had witnessed a rigged game. But two years later, the Canadian journalist Declan Hill published *The Fix*, a book about football and organised crime, which provides evidence to suggest that Asian gamblers bribed the Ghanaians to lose by more than two goals.

A match fixer in Thailand, whom Hill calls 'Chin', let him sit in on a pre-tournament meeting. 'They fixed the World Cup at an anonymous KFC in northern Bangkok,' writes Hill. 'There were four men. They sat at a little table hunched over so they could hear one another while they spoke.' Hill was sitting at the next table, trying to eavesdrop. One of the quartet was an African, said to be Ghana's under-seventeen coach. Hill took a grainy photo of him with a hidden camera.

During the World Cup, when Hill and Chin spoke on the phone, the fixer predicted the outcome of four matches, three of them correctly: victories by a margin of at least two goals for Italy against Ghana, Italy against Ukraine, and Brazil against Ghana. The only result Chin got wrong was England-Ecuador: the English were supposed to win by at least two goals, but managed just one, by Chin's account because they were useless.

All this was intriguing but hardly proof. After all, none of these results was unexpected. (Match fixers often arrange for favourites to beat underdogs by a certain margin, partly because that allows them to bet the same way as most ordinary punters. This arouses less suspicion than if they staked fortunes on improbable outcomes.)

Hill needed more evidence. Nearly penniless, he flew to Ghana to look for the Ghanaian he'd seen in the KFC. Improbably, he found him. The man turned out to be a youth coach named Abou Damba. He admitted to Hill that he had often introduced an Asian named 'Alan' to Ghana's internationals. Damba said that anything that Alan and the players agreed after that was not his business. Ghana's captain Stephen Appiah gave Hill an interview in his car in Accra. He confirmed that he often spoke to match fixers, but denied ever arranging for Ghana to lose.

If the match I saw in Dortmund was fixed, the Brazilians would never have known it. Even some Ghanaian players might not have known. There was enough evidence for FIFA to investigate these matches. It didn't.

Argentina-Germany, quarter-final, Berlin, 30 June 2006

There was a tiny kid on the Argentinian bench who had just turned nineteen but looked fourteen. Argentina's coach José Pekerman had known him a long time. In fact, when the adolescent Leo Messi was playing in Barcelona's youth teams, it was Pekerman who had advised Argentina's federation to claim him before Spain did.

Given some playing time in early matches at his first World Cup, Messi shone. His performance in the dead-rubber game against Holland (both teams had already qualified for the knock-out stages) prompted his Dutch teammate at Barça, Giovanni van Bronckhorst, to reminisce: 'Two years ago we played with part of the first team against the youth team. He played for them. Sixteen years old. Man, I didn't know what I was seeing. There are players who can't be marked.'

With eleven minutes to go against Germany, and Argentina 0-1 up, Pekerman decided to replace Hernán Crespo with another forward. The coach must have glanced at the kid further down the bench and thought, 'Not today, not against the big boys.' Instead he sent on a respectably sized adult named Julio Ricardo Cruz. A minute later, Germany equalised. Messi never came on, and Argentina lost on penalties.

France-Brazil, quarter-final, Frankfurt, 1 July 2006

France had barely played a good game in two years, but tonight they knocked out Brazil, with thirty-four-year-old Zidane setting up Thierry Henry for the only goal. The average age of the French team was thirty.

What struck me about the match was that everybody, especially in France, understood it as a repetition. Zidane and several other world champions of 1998 had slain Ronaldo's Brazil again. The crowds celebrating on French streets sang the team's song of 1998, 'I Will Survive'. They were 're-enacting 1998, a time of happiness', explained Albrecht Sonntag, a German sociologist who worked in France. As in 1998, a grinning President Chirac was omnipresent, again implying that football could heal the country. Again, the 'president of hearts' was Zidane, or 'Zizou', as in '*Zizou Président!*' World Cups allow you to travel back in time.

So much of a modern World Cup is repetition, especially as you grow older. After decades of tournaments shown live on TV, each new France-Brazil or England-Argentina or Holland-Germany is just a repeat of earlier versions. Each victory or red card or controversy is a quotation of past ones.

A match can never mean as much as it did the first time around. Win or lose this one, you know it isn't the end of the story: at some point in the next few decades, there'll be a replay. Repetition turns down the emotional dial of World Cups.

Italy-Germany, semi-final, Dortmund, 4 July 2006

After the giant Italian central defender Marco Materazzi permitted a harmless German shot, his captain Fabio Cannavaro stalked up to him, gave him a lecture, then reached up and slapped him in the face. Cannavaro believed that a defender didn't permit shots, or corners, free kicks or even throw-ins.

To appreciate this World Cup, such a party off the field but so dull on it, you had to appreciate defending. I've never seen a team with higher defensive standards than Italy in 2006. They conceded only once on the way to the final, and that was an unstoppable own goal.

They beat Germany 2-0, and the Germans were lucky to get nil. The German public seemed happy to lose. That night, police in Berlin had to stop people throwing themselves into the Spree river. The fans weren't trying to drown themselves – they were just partying.

Oliver Bierhoff, the German team's general manager, remarked with surprise that fans seemed to have become less interested in results. And you could take that insight a step further: as the football got duller and the party got better, fans were replacing players as the World Cup's main characters. Even when their team was losing or the match was bad, they generally sang rather than booed. The 'main-character effect' was enhanced by the new digital cameras on mobile phones. You'd see supporters filming themselves while jumping for joy.

Wannsee, early July 2006

I was sitting in the garden of a grey villa in Wannsee, on the south-western edge of Berlin. It was another glorious summer's day at the German World Cup, and in front of me was Lake Wannsee, packed with thousands of noisy, bathing Berliners.

Behind me was the villa where fifteen senior Nazis had gathered around the dining-room table on 20 January 1942 to plan the Holocaust. The participants on one side of the table would have had a view through the windows of the cascading garden leading down to the lake. After the meeting, the bureaucrat Adolf Eichmann wrote in the protocol that the 'Final Solution' should 'concern approximately 11 million Jews'.

I was in the Wannsee villa for a conference on the two eternal German themes: football and Nazism. Several German attendees expressed fear of the nationalism that had emerged during the tournament. An older woman said: 'When I see those big squares full of young football fans, in their white shirts, chanting,

'*Deutschland!*', I think: that's a Goebbels scene.' Another attendee worked for a German charity that ran projects like maintaining Jewish cemeteries and rebuilding destroyed synagogues. He had been to the Germany-Ecuador game, in a VIP box full of German intellectuals. He said that watching the other people in the box chant '*Deutschland!*', he felt they were shouting the word at themselves, at their own past. It had sounded to him like an exorcism.

For most Europeans in 2006, though, the war was finally over. In Wannsee I went for a walk in the woods with an official from the DFB, the German football federation, whose job was to handle historical questions. Any journalist who asked anything about the DFB and the war would be passed on to him. I asked him if many journalists had called about war-related issues during the tournament. 'Nobody,' he said.

This World Cup was a pan-European celebration of reconciliation for the Second World War. That's why, logically, it had to end in Berlin.

Unter den Linden avenue, Berlin, 9 July 2006

Early on the last day of the tournament, a strange legion formed on the Unter den Linden, the avenue where I had witnessed the muted celebrations of German reunification in 1990. Sixteen years on, celebrations were a lot more raucous for a side that had lost in the semi-final. Half a million white-shirted young people, many of whom had waited hours in the heat, had come to thank their team. Practically in the shadow of the *Siegessäule*, the victory column that is a monument to nineteenth-century militarism, this was a losers' parade.

German football's era of ugly winning had spanned the history of West Germany: from 1954, just as the post-war 'economic miracle' was beginning, to 1990, three months before German reunification. In football, West Germany had been the villain who killed the beautiful teams. The highbrow weekly *Die Zeit* called the feeling *Siegesscham*: shame in victory. The ugly teams of 1982,

1986 and 2002 that reached World Cup finals had been embarrassing to many Germans. And once your country has won the World
Cup once or twice, it's generally enough. The more you win, the
less it matters.

In fact, it was often the losers of World Cups who lived in
memory: Puskas in Bern in 1954, Cruyff in Munich in 1974, Platini
in Seville in 1982. At last, in 2006, the Germans got to be lovable
losers – the ideal incarnation for a country that no longer scared
anybody, not even Germans themselves.

The World Cup had lost its Darth Vader. We had all learned to
love the Germans. There might never again be a European football
match as loaded as France-Germany in Seville in 1982. Football
had stopped being war. All that was sweet, but it took some of the
spice out of World Cups.

France-Italy, World Cup final, Olympic Stadium, Berlin, 9 July 2006

The moment of the match was Zinedine Zidane's headbutt of
Marco Materazzi, but most of us only saw it in the replay. Our
eyes had been elsewhere, following the ball, when, twenty minutes
into extra time, it happened: Materazzi said something to Zidane,
who was jogging away but then stopped, turned, and nutted the
Italian in the chest. The Argentinian referee Horacio Elizondo
missed the headbutt along with everyone else, but the fourth official spotted it, and Zidane was sent off for the fourteenth time in
his career – this time effectively forever, as he was retiring after the
tournament. It was an epic exit for an epic figure.

For years, people speculated about what Materazzi might have
said to provoke him. Finally, in an Instagram Live appearance in
2020, the Italian told his story. He explained that the altercation
had begun soon after Zidane, on his own in front of the Italian
goal, had struck a bullet header that was improbably stopped by
goalkeeper Gianluigi Buffon. Had that ball gone in, with the score
tied at 1-1 in extra time, France would surely have won.

The Italians were stunned by their uncharacteristic lapse in marking. Materazzi was ordered to stick even closer to Zidane. He did, to such effect that they collided more than once. Materazzi said he apologised to Zidane, who retorted, 'If you want my shirt, you can have it after the game.' As Materazzi tells it: 'I replied that I'd rather have his sister.' The clichéd macho jest cut through to Zidane. His sister, Lila, was looking after their unwell mother, and had phoned him several times in the hours before the final. Zidane later confirmed to the French newspaper *L'Equipe*: 'He triggered something talking about my sister.'

No doubt Zidane had felt triggered, but it was surely his frustration at the game that made him snap. He wouldn't have nutted Materazzi if his header had gone in, but he must have felt France's strength seeping away. His two great lieutenants Patrick Vieira and Thierry Henry had gone off, and the thirty-four-year-old's bent back was sagging beneath the weight of a nation.

After his exit, the final went to a penalty shoot-out – which, despite everything, is the best drama that a World Cup can produce. To see a player walking from the halfway line to take his kick is to watch a man face to face with fate. France lost because David Trezeguet's penalty bounced out off the underside of the bar when it could just as easily have bounced in.

Leaving the stadium, I ran into a French colleague and commiserated with him. He said, 'I don't mind losing. I just feel bad that it ended like this for Zidane.'

In the French changing room after the game, the coach Raymond Domenech made a speech praising Zidane, and asked the players to applaud their captain. 'There was only the grinding of teeth, and my applause was not spontaneously followed,' Domenech recalls in his memoir, 'Certain players really hated their captain.' They could not forgive Zidane for sabotaging victory, he writes. Nor, it seems, could Domenech.

Perhaps some French players did hate Zidane (Domenech is an unreliable narrator), but the French public didn't hate him. The French slang for headbutt is a *coup de boule*. That summer holiday, the hit song in the dance clubs of French beach resorts was 'Coup de boule', in which the whole dance floor would do the headbutt.

The French philosopher Jean Baudrillard died in 2007. In his posthumous essay *Carnaval et cannibale*, he eulogised Zidane for 'refusing to be the idol and the mirror of globalisation at such an emblematic event'. Baudrillard explained that Zidane, by sabotaging his own success on the field, had rejected the modern notion of performance. He called the headbutt 'the most glorious' scandal in ages. He said Zidane was expressing 'derision for the entire system', for 'the Nothingness at the heart of globalisation'.

Well, perhaps. What's certain is that Zidane's spontaneous, authentic and perversely elegant farewell to football made him more beloved than if he had jogged away from Materazzi and won another World Cup.

Postscript: The Left Bank of Paris, 7 March 2007

The 2006 World Cup was when spectators became participants. One participant at the tournament did the reverse, and became a spectator: the French benchwarmer Vikash Dhorasoo. I knew him from the French league as a lovely waiflike number ten, a player who would have been chief creator in most national teams. Dhorasoo's bad luck was that he was a French number ten in the era of Zidane. It meant that he played just eight minutes at the World Cup. Instead, unbeknown to his teammates, he spent the month making a documentary about his situation with the magnificently named French director Fred Poulet. The film was released seven months after the World Cup, under the English title *Substitute*.

Most of *Substitute* consists of Dhorasoo filming himself with a handheld camera as he mooches around the French camp alone, forgotten by his coach Domenech. We watch Dhorasoo reading in bed, not knowing what to do with himself. He reflects, 'I played one World Cup, it's the only one.' After France beat Brazil, he tells the camera: 'They've beaten Brazil.'

Before the final, Dhorasoo films his own arrival in the French dressing room. On the day of the biggest game of his life, he is just a film-maker. He tries to cheer himself up by telling himself that once every four years, only forty or fifty footballers get to a World Cup final, and he's one of them. He tells himself that if France win, he will deserve his medal; at least he helped the team qualify. After the defeat, he films the changing room again – the starters getting dressed in silence, Trezeguet, the man who missed, blankly straightening his shirt.

The film premiered in a small arthouse cinema on the Left Bank of Paris. After the screening, Dhorasoo came out to meet the audience. He told us that in the last few months, he had gone from international footballer to unemployed film-maker – which, with his long hair, beard and beanie hat, was exactly what he looked like. He said, 'The film succeeded because my World Cup failed.'

He explained that the film reflected certain realities of football: the countless hours spent alone in hotel rooms, and the second-class status of substitutes. 'When we went to the Elysée, with President Chirac, there was a table of first-teamers and a table of reserves. That's football.'

Someone asked if any of his teammates had seen the film. 'No,' said Dhorasoo, 'unless they are here in disguise. Cinema doesn't interest them.'

The discussion of his film continued until the Parisian audience got sidetracked into an argument about Jean-Luc Godard, sparked by a middle-aged man in a white silk scarf.

Marriott Grand Hotel, Moscow, May 2008

I flew to the Chelsea-Manchester United Champions League final in Moscow as a guest of UEFA, the European football authority. I had a fabulous room in the five-star Marriott Grand Hotel. (Did UEFA corrupt me? I don't think so.)

One day, I left my room at the same moment as the chap staying in the room opposite mine: Sepp Blatter. We nodded to each other. That afternoon in the corridor, I met two women holding a massage table waiting outside his door. They asked me if I knew where Mr Blatter was. He hadn't shown up for his (undoubtedly non-sexual) massage. I apologised on his behalf. It was a glimpse into the everyday life of FIFA's president.

PART TWO
NEW WORLDS

10

May 2004 – May 2010: South Africa, The Chosen Country

'Sport is a major value of South African life.'

Leo Kuper, sociologist, 1965

'When I left the plane this morning and I arrived on the African soil, I started to make a little – dancing. Dancing, dancing, dancing.'

Sepp Blatter, FIFA president, September 2008

The World Cup that has meant most to me was the one played in South Africa, in my parents' back garden, in 2010. It's the only World Cup that I'm writing about with a run-up of decades, trying to show how the tournament impacted the country.

I had been visiting South Africa since I was baby. But anyone using the words 'South Africa' about this fantastically divided and diverse country needs to answer the question, 'Which South Africa do you mean?' The first South Africa I knew consisted of the white northern suburbs of Johannesburg, where my relatives lived, but I gradually realised that there were many other South Africas. For instance, the white-flight business district of Sandton was separated only by a highway from the black township Alexandra, as if the City of London sat next to a Brazilian favela. When I became a journalist, around the time that apartheid fell, I went looking for the South Africas I didn't know. Most of them played football, and following the game helped me understand the country.

Then, in the late 1990s, South Africa began bidding to host
the World Cup. The impetus was largely emotional. South Africa
(like Argentina) suffers from a sense of *terra finis*, of being 'at the
end of the earth'. It yearns to be part of the world, of which most
South Africans know little.

After South Africa was chosen as host, I tried writing a book
about it all, though for reasons I'll explain I found that I couldn't.
I watched the 2010 World Cup in fascination, and returned in 2024
to see what the tournament had left behind. I hope the thirty-year
journey adds up to an X-ray of the country.

My family's connection with South Africa was an accident. Like
so many South Africans, both white and black, the Kupers came
from elsewhere. I think the first Kuper arrived from Lithuania in
the 1880s. It was a case of both push-and-pull migration: in an
era when there were pogroms against Jews in the Russian empire,
diamonds were found in Kimberley, South Africa, and, in 1886,
gold was discovered in Johannesburg. The new city was rough
even then, and growing so fast that already no one remembered
who Johannes had been.

The original Kupers could have landed up in the US, or Argentina, but it happened to be Johannesburg. They didn't find gold.
Like many Johannesburgers of the time, they ran a pub, a few
minutes' walk from the future World Cup stadium Ellis Park. And
they prospered in South Africa. For most of the country's history,
all the wealth was channelled to its small white population.

By the time my parents were born during the Second World
War, Johannesburg's white northern suburbs housed the only
African-born bourgeoisie south of the Sahara. The streets were
tree-lined, the gardens vast, and in the 1940s my father's family
had two cars, a swimming pool, a tennis court and servants.
Johannesburg's climate was unbeatable. Perhaps no cohort of
people ever lived as well as their generation of white South Africans underneath the purple jacaranda trees.

Though the climate didn't kill you, the people sometimes did.
There was always a whiff of the Wild West about Johannesburg.

On the evening of 8 March 1963 my father's father, another Simon Kuper, a judge, was sitting at home with his daughter, when an intruder hiding in the garden shot him in the head through the window. In the ambulance my grandfather scribbled illegible words on a scrap of paper. He died after twelve speechless days, without revealing more. The police think they know who killed him, but it remains yet another unsolved Johannesburg murder.

My parents left South Africa in the early 1960s, fleeing unhappy families, a country that still felt like a distant province of Britain, and apartheid. Even in Europe they remained South Africans. One rush hour in the London Underground, my mother spotted a familiar face. She tapped the man on the shoulder, and said, 'The day you escaped from jail was the most exciting day of my life.' 'It was quite exciting for me too,' replied the ageing anti-apartheid fighter.

My parents didn't boycott apartheid. When they could afford it, they took their children back for Christmas holidays. We would leave dark Europe and land the next morning in South African midsummer. Still today, when I close my eyes and think back to apartheid, it's a blazing December morning in Johannesburg in 1984 and I'm sitting on my grandparents' veranda by their rose garden. I've just had a swim in their pool. My grandfather is listening to the cricket on the radio. Nester Dlamini, the black maid, is cutting a chocolate cake. She lives behind the kitchen in the dank servants' quarters, where on Sundays she hosts services for her church. In the garden below, tended by a gardener who lives in a shed 300 miles from his children, Nester's grandchildren are playing in our old underpants from Europe. My encounters with apartheid were so startling, so different from anything I experienced growing up in Europe, that these are my sharpest childhood memories.

By the 1980s an inner voice had got into almost every white South African's head, whispering that the whole edifice rested on racism. But most of the time, most white people I knew were able to turn off the voice. My mother's parents managed their cognitive dissonance by inveighing against apartheid (I think sincerely) while enjoying its fruits.

White South Africa was sports-mad. My mother's mother had been a provincial-level tennis player, as well as a hockey goal-keeper. Aged ten, I'd walk down the road alone with my scorebook and a couple of rand for an ice cream to watch the cricket at The Wanderers. But one sport barely existed in white South Africa. Football was for black people.

Black townships, 1930s–1940

In black South Africa you only existed once you had a nickname. Members of the Zulu and Sotho ethnic groups were traditionally given praise names, *izibongo*. And so South African footballers were re-baptised 'Scotch Whisky' (because he 'drives the sorrows away and brings happiness'), 'Once a Year', and 'Kalamazoo'.

Nicknames coloured the British sport black. The footballer John Makuronts was known as 'Herr Hitler' – not because he was a mass murderer, but because black South Africans, cut off from the world, yearned for the exotic. Players were dubbed 'Buick' (after the American car), Russia 'The Horse' Jacobs (a double nickname!) or 'British Empire'.

South Africa's oldest great club, the Orlando Pirates, who play in black and white, were named for the Hollywood pirate movie *Sea Hawk* (1940). A group of lads from the Orlando neighbourhood had been to see Errol Flynn's film at the bioscope. 'Pirates' was a touch of America for black South Africans who would never get there.

South Africa-Australia cricket Test match, Durban, January 1950

Every player and almost all the spectators were white. One small decrepit stand, known as 'The Cage', was reserved for non-whites. Like almost everyone else in The Cage, the young lawyer Nelson Mandela supported Australia. At the time, he couldn't have imagined supporting a South African sports team. A team representing the South African nation was an impossibility under apartheid. You could have a team representing South Africa's whites, or a black team, wrote my great-uncle Leo Kuper, a sociologist and the brother of the murdered judge, but you couldn't have a team of the whole nation, because under apartheid 'South Africa is not a nation'. To the country's white rulers, the future President Mandela wasn't a South African.

Durban, 1950s

Leo was a gentle, liberal sociology professor. He opposed apartheid but didn't have the stomach for dangerous activism, so in 1961 he and my aunt Hilda, an anthropologist, emigrated to the US, where they spent their final decades in a sun-filled bungalow in Westwood, Los Angeles, near the UCLA campus.

Mandela only heard they had left much later, when as a prisoner he tried to order Leo's banned 1965 book, *An African Bourgeoisie*. 'I met the Kupers only once,' he wrote to Alan Paton from jail in 1979, 'in their house in Durban. Although I am confident that they will never cease burrowing wherever they may be, I was sorry to hear they had emigrated. Their exit must have weakened their school of thought in several directions.'

When I went looking for serious studies of South African football, I found almost nothing. Then I happened on *An African Bourgeoisie*, the book denied to Mandela. In an era when scholars ignored football, Leo, a keen tennis player, had devoted a chapter to the black South African game. Through football, he showed what power meant to black men under apartheid.

Any non-white South African aspiring to power before about 1990 couldn't find it in politics. So non-white power-seekers (almost all of them men) often became either clergymen or football officials. Mahatma Gandhi, who lived mostly in Durban from 1893 to 1914, tried in vain to become a football official of a local federation. Chief Albert Luthuli (president of the African

National Congress, and in 1960 the first African to win a Nobel prize, for peace) was active in the Durban and District African Football Association. Leo explains: 'Political energy, denied any other expression, is projected onto the Football Association.'

The association's meetings could last all night. Officials sometimes debated procedural rules for hours, in English – generally their second or third language. During one constitutional argument in 1932, Mr Kuluse, of the Mountain Blues club, made a long intervention about the exact meaning of the word 'shall'. You could laugh at these men. But what Leo called the 'emphasis on ritual' mattered to them. They wanted to prove (including to themselves) 'that Africans can successfully manage their own affairs'.

South African black football became – and remains, in the twenty-first century – a facsimile of politics. At big games, a proud club official would lead his team onto the field. Everyone wanted to be that official, and so there were often quarrels and schisms; fifteen new clubs split off from Durban's Wanderers FC alone. The Durban FA's election in the late 1950s became a battle between two factions, 'Russians' and 'Japanese'. Leo recounts: 'The rebellious groups met in secret, at night, and in the most obscure places.' The emotional investment was tremendous. Where else could a black South African vote at the time?

For those football officials, this was their world, the only one they had. They couldn't have imagined that one day non-white South African football officials would organise a World Cup. For Mr Kuluse, connoisseur of the word 'shall', the 2010 tournament was a posthumous triumph. I wish he could have sat on the Local Organising Committee.

Atlanta, US, 1968: Kaizer Motaung's electric typewriter

In 1968, Phil Woosnam, British coach of the Atlanta Chiefs in the North American Soccer League, sent an SOS to South Africa: he needed good footballers. A man called Ali Twala recommended a young striker: Kaizer 'Chincha Guluva' Motaung of the mighty Orlando Pirates.

Motaung crossed the Atlantic and debuted as a sub for Atlanta in a friendly against Manchester City, scoring twice. In his first season, 1968, his goals won Atlanta the NASL's first championship, and he was named rookie of the year. But he was more than a footballer. Returning to Soweto around 1970, he found Pirates in the usual administrative chaos. Four of his friends had been thrown out of the club. Kaizer's faction wanted Pirates to be run professionally, like the Atlanta Chiefs. Nobody in the club listened.

In the sort of schism my uncle Leo had described, Kaizer and friends left Pirates to found a new club, the Kaizer Chiefs. They borrowed the Atlanta Chiefs' logo without paying for it. The American club folded in 1981, but the native American head that adorned its shirts remains iconic throughout southern Africa.

Under apartheid, joy for black South Africans came from music, God, love, beer, the remains of family separated by migration, and the Chiefs and Pirates – practically the only two clubs most fans cared about. The Chiefs-Pirates Soweto derby became South African football's 'Clásico', overshadowing the national team. To quote Cape historian Leslie Witz: 'You could say that the Kaizer Chiefs *are* the national team.'

Motaung's story illustrated Leo's point: the only realm where an ambitious black man could accumulate power in apartheid South Africa was football. Motaung, along with his frenemy Irvin 'Iron Duke' Khoza of the Pirates, would bestride the South African game into the 2020s. He and his children ran Chiefs as a family company. They set up fan clubs all over the country, selling the members Chiefs-branded products, from toiletries to funeral plans.

But Motaung never forgot the man who launched his career. In the 1980s he presented Ali Twala with an electric typewriter.

Kaizer Chiefs-Orlando Pirates, Orlando
Stadium, Soweto, around 1976

The golden age of black South African football, from about 1975 to 1985, was played out on Saturday afternoons in Orlando Stadium, a tiny ground with multicoloured walls and roofless stands in the Orlando neighbourhood of Soweto.

Almost nothing of those Saturdays has been preserved. Barely any of it was shown on TV and the few newspapers that covered the matches don't tell the story either – the results and scorers can differ depending on which edition of the same day's paper you read. South Africa's white rulers didn't care about Soweto; the place didn't even appear on maps of the country. And as for the people at those matches, many died young. You really had to be there. Sanza Tshabalala, a South African radio DJ, spent dozens of Saturdays of his childhood at Orlando Stadium. He told me what it had been like.

Kick-off was at 4 p.m., but Sanza would get to the stadium just after 7 a.m. to start selling his apples. By 9.30 they would all be gone. By the time Brenda Fassie sang at 11 a,m. the stadium was already packed, and smelling of cannabis, which was as integral to South African football as pies and beer were to the English game. Drunks would be crying outside the gate because the 'Congo' end was sold out.

After Fassie sang, there were competitions in which you could win a car. The stadium would be packed, 'too full', says Sanza. 'And all the gangsters were there, and even thieves, because all the money is there. It was dangerous. If Pirates lose, it's hard to get out of the stadium. It's a dull game without the violence, somehow. All those nicknames: "Welcome to the Slaughterhouse", "Welcome to the House of Pain". As kids we fought other kids even to sell apples.'

Meanwhile the Pirates' playmaker Jomo Sono (who had once sold apples at matches himself) might be in the Indian market watching pirated videos of old FA Cup finals. An hour before kick-off he would park his car at the stadium, change out of his snakeskin shoes, and get in the mood by kicking some balls through tyres. Jomo moved to the US in 1977 to become Pele's understudy at the New York Cosmos, but black South Africans know which of them was the better player. Not that it mattered: football outside South Africa was a mere notion to most Sowetans, like life on Mars. At most, you might see a foreign game in the 'bioscope' on 16mm film years after it had been played. Danny Jordaan, chief organiser of the 2010 World Cup, was thirty-eight when he first saw a World Cup game on TV, in 1990. On Saturdays, Orlando Stadium was Wembley and the Maracanã rolled into one. Being the best here was all that existed.

The hour before kick-off could be a scary time. The Pirates specialised in schisms. One day in 1985 two teams, both calling themselves 'Pirates', appeared simultaneously at kick-off at Ellis Park, each claiming to be the real thing. That evening, Pirates official Bra China 'Dibaba' Hlongwane was stabbed by rivals a reported twenty-seven times in front of 30,000 spectators and the TV cameras. He survived, possibly protected by his layers of fat. He would later survive a shooting, only to die, anticlimactically, of a heart attack.

On this Saturday in Orlando, only one Pirates team shows up. The teams' witch doctors take their seats in the stand, having washed their players in oxen blood, and cast spells on the opposition's penalty area. Witch doctors are so important that they are sometimes lured from rival clubs with fat contracts. If they fail, they are sacked like managers are.

Before kick-off, the Orlando crowd sings – in flawless harmony, but just raw enough – the call-and-response miners' anthem 'Shosholoza', in a mix of Zulu and Ndebele. Every spectator knows every word:

Shosholoza
Ku lezontaba
Stimela siphum' eSouth Africa

It's the best communal song on earth, and Sowetan fans – schooled from childhood in church choirs – are the best communal singers.

Then, finally, Jomo plays. In an era when apartheid tried to turn all black people into unskilled labourers, here was a master. Sanza, who was born to be a DJ even if he first spent years selling cannabis, says, 'When Jomo touches the ball, the entire stadium, including the opposition fans, goes "Haaaaa!" He would stand on the ball with his hands raised. When the black man had nothing!'

Standing on the ball with hands raised might draw bigger cheers than a boring goal. Just as isolated Australia has animals and plants that don't exist anywhere else, isolated black South Africa evolved its own indigenous style of football. Fans still call it 'ticky-ticky', a football of pointless tricks with names like 'tsimayas' and 'shibobos'.

After Jomo returned from New York, he founded Soweto's first Kentucky Fried Chicken and his own club, the Jomo Cosmos (another American name). Some mornings, Sanza would ring his 'bedroom number', wake him up, and make him tell stories on the radio from those lost Orlando Saturdays. Like the time Jomo got married on the day of a Pirates game. At half-time Pirates were losing 2-0. Sanza recites the myth: 'They came to get him at his wedding, mafia-style. He scored two, created the third. Pirates won 3-2. Then the entire stadium came back to celebrate his wedding.'

In 2010, black South African fans yearned to show the world their game in all its ticky-ticky glory.

Soweto, 16 June 1976: We didn't bury him because he was ash

Soon after that Soweto derby, the slow-motion fall of apartheid began. Thousands of young Sowetans gathered at Orlando Stadium to protest against the white regime's law that all teaching in black schools had to be in Afrikaans, the dialect of Dutch spoken by the white settlers. The police fired at the peaceful crowd. That sparked the Soweto Uprising.

It's commemorated in the Hector Pieterson Museum. I was given a tour by a Sowetan woman named Fuzi, a friend of my grandmother's. Fuzi said that when the uprising began, my grand-mother had phoned and said, 'Bring the children to us, because otherwise they will be wounded.' That didn't happen.

Fuzi's brother ended up fleeing into a beer shop, which was set on fire. Fuzi, who by the time I met her had cancer, which in Africa was usually a death sentence, said, 'We didn't bury him because he was ash. We didn't even find him.' In the Hector Pieterson Museum, it's hard not to feel ashamed of being white.

Orlando Stadium was more than a football stadium. But by the twenty-first century, Chiefs and Pirates played most of their matches in white Johannesburg. In 2006 the little ground was torn down and later rebuilt as a training venue for the World Cup. The tournament would mostly be played in white South Africa.

FIFA Congress, Zurich, June 1992

Sixteen countries joined FIFA at this congress, but only one received an ovation from the hall. The new South Africa was the chosen country, with a universal mission. Its struggle to reconcile the different colours resounded worldwide. South Africans in workplaces and schools began scribbling their fantasy line-ups for the new national team that was going to win the World Cup.

Pretoria and Ellis Park, 10 May 1994

A fortnight after Mandela won the first-ever non-racial elections, he was inaugurated as president – an event that my parents had only imagined possible after a bloody civil war. He gave a speech promising to build a 'rainbow nation'. Then he was driven straight to Ellis Park to watch South Africa's football team, recently christened the 'Bafana Bafana' (literally, 'Boys boys') beat Zambia.

Los Angeles, summer 1994

A month after Mandela's inauguration, South African football's power brokers flew to the World Cup in the US. For most, it was their first World Cup. Danny Jordaan was there, Kaizer Motaung, and Solomon 'Stix' Morewa, the corrupt, lazy boss of the South African Football Association (SAFA, nicknamed 'Suffer'). In Los Angeles, they began talking about bringing the World Cup to South Africa. They said to each other, 'I'm sure we can do this.' Imagine the chutzpah of a new FIFA member that had never hosted an international anything before. The chosen country lived by its own rules.

South Africa-New Zealand, rugby World Cup final, Ellis Park, Johannesburg, 24 June 1995

It's best known as the scene from Clint Eastwood's movie *Invictus*, but it happened in real life. The rugby World Cup of 1995 was the first big international sports tournament played in South Africa. The final, South Africa-New Zealand, was tied 12-12 in extra time when the little South African fly half Joel Stransky kicked the winning drop goal.

Mandela, wearing a Springbok jersey, handed the cup to the giant white Afrikaner captain Francois Pienaar, and said, 'Francois, thank you very much for what you have done for the country.' Pienaar spoke into a microphone to a watching nation, 'No, Mr President. Thank *you* for what you have done for the country.' They had performed an allegory of white-black reconciliation.

Other fathers of fatherlands such as Washington or Garibaldi built their nations on armed uprisings. Mandela was building the new South Africa (born 1994) largely on sport. In other countries, sport strengthened national feeling, but South African sports teams had to *create* national feeling. For all the country's dysfunction, this sometimes worked. You could almost see the rainbow in the sky when Stransky kicked his drop goal, but also in the countless moments of casual consideration when whites and blacks interacted. When South Africans weren't murdering each other, they mostly treated each other as South Africans. The new South Africa's greatest achievement is the South African nation itself.

South Africa-Tunisia, African Nations Cup final, Soccer City, Johannesburg, 3 February 1996

A year after the rugby final, it was the Bafana's turn. Hosting football's African Nations Cup, they reached the final against Tunisia. About 130,000 people crammed into FNB Stadium, 'Soccer City', which had been built for 85,000. They waved fish and yelled 'Feeeesh!' for white defender Mark Fish (who didn't need a nickname) and 'Shoes!' for tricky midfielder 'Shoes' Moshoeu. Some fans honoured both players at once, by waving shoes attached to fishing rods.

If I were a black South African who had lived through apartheid, I think I'd have been too bitter to wave a fish for a white footballer. I might have voted for the Pan Africanist Congress, with its slogan, 'One settler one bullet'. Yet most black South Africans voted for the incompetent but non-racial ANC, and cheered on their white footballers even more vociferously than black ones. Black South African acceptance of whites has always baffled me.

South Africa won the final 2-0, with both goals scored by substitute Mark Williams, who earned the nickname 'Nation Builder'. It remains the Bafana's only trophy to date.

Then 130,000 people tried to leave the FNB simultaneously. It took my uncle Donald three hours to drive out of the stadium. He didn't mind. He had hung one of his shoes out of the car window, and was shouting 'Shoooooeeeees!' until the shoe was stolen. The traffic police weren't much help. The young poet Sandile Dikeni remembered one policeman in particular. 'This big Afrikaner guy, huge, huge guy, for all purposes he is a rugby fan,' Dikeni later told me, sitting on the stoep of his house. 'But he is standing on his car and shouting "Bafana Bafana!". I haven't seen the traffic cop again, but I'm sure he goes now every time to FNB Stadium to watch some African soccer.' Years later Dikeni was in a terrible car accident while returning home from a funeral, and he never quite recovered. He died of tuberculosis in 2019, aged fifty-three – an ordinary black South African fate.

Mandela's house, Houghton, Johannesburg, late 1990s

Joel Stransky, the man whose drop goal won the rugby World Cup, told me years later: 'I was actually crap at drop kicks.' The highlight of his life hadn't been that goal anyway. It was a Sunday lunch that he and his wife had at Mandela's home afterwards.

Stransky's teammates had given him a big painting of his drop goal. When the Stranskys were invited to Mandela's, Stransky's wife insisted on bringing the picture for Mandela to sign. Arriving at Mandela's home, Stransky felt embarrassed by the stupid painting, so he hid it behind the front door.

They had a two-and-a-half-hour lunch, talking about politics, family, everything, while Mandela's grandchildren ran in and out of the room. Afterwards Mandela walked the Stranskys to the front door. That's when Stransky remembered: 'Shit, the painting.' Quick as a fly half, he picked it up and tried to smuggle it out unseen. 'Oh,' said Mandela, 'do you want me to sign it for you?'

The World Cup, France, June–July 1998

It still hangs in my wardrobe: a white, green and gold Bafana shirt, signed by every player, from the year they were going to win their first World Cup playing ticky-ticky.

Before the tournament, the young striker Benni McCarthy had said: 'I think we have a realistic chance to reach the quarter-finals, and after that don't write us off to reach the end too.'

The Bafana's preparations had been spotless. They had even got themselves a proper goalkeeper, the blond Dutchman Hans

Vonk. It was the South African journalist Peter Auf der Heyde who'd discovered that Vonk had been born in South Africa. He got the keeper's number from his Dutch club, and rang him to ask if he were willing to play for the Bafana at the World Cup. Vonk said, 'If I'm selected, I'll invite you to France and pay for your trip.' Auf der Heyde said he'd be happy with a match shirt.

South Africa's first game was against the hosts, France.* Pierre Issa, a South African-born Lebanese Frenchman recruited to strengthen the Bafana, said, 'I believe France is going to get an enormous warning.'

South Africa lost 3-0, with Issa scoring an own goal (or, by some counts, two). By then, Bafana's fans and players were growing fed up with their French coach Philippe Troussier and his boring sermons about tactics. South African footballers didn't need tactics.

Meanwhile, Troussier was growing fed up with his players. Taking advantage of their base in what they considered the ridiculously safe city of Marseille, ten of them had gone out after the defeat for drinks in a nightclub. Mark Fish said: 'We went to a restaurant, and came back a bit late.' Troussier had thrown an inexplicable temper tantrum, but that's what you got for hiring a Frenchman.

Puzzlingly, South Africa didn't win their second match either, drawing 1-1 with Denmark. That's when some South Africans began to suspect that they might not be the chosen football country after all. Then Troussier sent home two players who had been out till dawn. He said he sometimes felt he was leading a tour group on holiday.

The last group game against Saudi Arabia ended 2-2, with Issa giving away two penalties. Afterwards Auf der Heyde found Vonk under the stands of the Bordeaux stadium. The keeper gave the journalist the shirt and shorts he had worn against the Saudis. He told Auf der Heyde that it was true that his teammates hadn't all behaved professionally. Still, he would always remember the experience. 'Thank you,' he said.

---

* In chapter 6, I describe watching it in a Parisian café.

In 1998 Mandela was preparing to leave office. The miracle years were over. The chosen country had stepped into the world, and in football and some other domains it had fallen flat on its face. But the strangest thing of all is that the Bafana took Issa to the next World Cup.

Zurich, 6 July 2000

The old men of FIFA's executive committee (Exco) met to choose the host of the 2006 World Cup. Germany, England and Morocco were bidding, but everyone expected South Africa to be named the first-ever African host. Blatter, the FIFA president, was backing the country. He later told me: 'I wanted to go with the World Cup to Africa, and there were two African candidates, South Africa and Morocco, and for me Africa is south of the Sahara – not to speak about colour.'

Morocco was eliminated in the first round of voting, and England in the second. Weeks earlier, English hooligans had smashed windows and thrown plastic chairs at police during Euro 2000 in Belgium. 'I think our hopes of getting one or two European votes died the day the hooligans took to the streets of Charleroi,' said Alec McGivan, director of England's bid.

Germany and South Africa entered the run-off neck and neck. But the seventy-nine-year-old Scottish-born New Zealander Charles Dempsey had been instructed by his federation, Oceania, to back South Africa. His vote would make it 12-12 and give Blatter the casting vote. In South African cities, crowds gathered in front of big screens, ready to party.

Dempsey had other plans. Ignoring his confederation's instructions, he announced that he was leaving Zurich before the final vote. Mandela rang his hotel room to talk him round, but he refused to take the call. Dempsey said he had been put under 'intolerable pressure' by backers of the competing bids, some of whom had offered him bribes. (Indeed, officials of the German FA would spend many years wrapped in a court case over a payment of €6.7 million allegedly used to help buy votes. The case ended only in 2025 when the accused were ordered to pay fines, without the court passing a judgment.)

Germany won the run-off in Zurich by one vote. Some South Africans literally cried in the streets. Many people across Africa read FIFA's choice as a rejection by the white world. Their continent – 'the hopeless continent', a front cover of the *Economist* had called it two months before – still didn't count.

Letter from South African president Thabo Mbeki to Blatter, 2003

The successful hosting of the FIFA World Cup in Africa will provide a powerful, irresistible momentum to [the] African renaissance. We want, on behalf of our continent, to stage an event that will send ripples of confidence from the Cape to Cairo – an event that will create social and economic opportunities throughout Africa. We want to ensure that one day, historians will reflect upon the 2010 World Cup as a moment when Africa stood tall and resolutely turned the tide on centuries of poverty and conflict. We want to show that Africa's time has come.

I suspect Mbeki actually meant most of it. No previous would-be host had attached as much significance to a World Cup.

Johannesburg, March 2004

The South African World Cup would eventually morph into an overpriced extravaganza in new stadiums that became white elephants, but that wasn't the original intention.

The country's official bid book for 2004, 'South Africa 2010: Africa's Stage', laid out a sober tournament. Regarded as an embarrassment, copies were later 'disappeared'. Luckily, in March 2004 a South African football official had sat me down in his house and had let me take extensive notes from the document.

Rereading those notes twenty years later, I see that the bid book explained that South Africa already had perfectly good stadiums. There were five world-class rugby grounds (the traditionally white sport had always been well-funded) while 'Soccer City', never quite finished, never paid for, framed by the dumps from Johannesburg's gold mines, was one of the finest football grounds anywhere. The bid book proposed building only three new stadiums.

South Africa ended up building five and renovating five more. The ground in Polokwane alone, constructed for a city without a big football club, cost more than the entire sum of $158.5 million that had been budgeted in 2004 for all new stadiums, 'venue theming' and FIFA headquarters combined. South Africa's final bill for all the stadiums came to about $2 billion. That money, cement and construction labour could have been used to build several hundred thousand homes for people living in shacks.

FIFA *headquarters, Zurich, 15 May 2004*

When FIFA's executive committee gathered to choose the host of the 2010 World Cup, only African countries were allowed to bid, and South Africa was the favourite. Even Charles Dempsey, the New Zealander who had doomed the South African bid in 2000, said he hoped it would win this time.

By 2004, the main rap against South Africa was the country's homicide rate. Its own bid book called Johannesburg 'a tough city, an uncompromising city'. But, perversely, the best thing to happen to the bid was jihadi terrorism. After the attacks of 11 September, South Africa's Muslim rivals Egypt and Morocco looked scary to westerners. Johannesburg carjackings seemed soft by comparison.

South Africa's bidders were too tactful to mention the

Moroccans involved in the Madrid train bombings that killed 191 people two months before the vote. When I interviewed South Africa's campaign chief Danny Jordaan around that time, all he would say was: 'Since September 11 2001, South Africa has been ranked as one of the safest tourist destinations on earth.'

And the country had some handy lobbyists. Democratic South Africa's Founding Fathers still walked the earth in 2004, as if Washington and Jefferson could schmooze people at cocktail parties just a decade after the American Revolution. Archbishop Desmond Tutu offered FIFA's Exco members 'a guaranteed ticket to heaven, but not before they vote on May 15'. Mandela showed FIFA's inspectors around his old prison on Robben Island, something he'd been reluctant to do for anyone. He was such a presence throughout the bid that Blatter boasted to me: 'We met like two friends.'

Weeks before the vote, Tutu and a frail eighty-five-year-old Mandela even flew to the Caribbean to pay homage to the crooked Trinidadian Exco member Jack Warner. It would later emerge that South Africa had also paid Warner more literally: he, his American colleague Chuck Blazer and a co-conspirator received $10 million, disguised as support for the Caribbean's 'African diaspora'.

Mandela wanted to spend the rest of his life at home, but first he and Tutu flew to Zurich for the vote, as the warm-up act for South African actress Charlize Theron. They were selling the Rainbow Nation story that still seduced foreigners like me: the notion that sport could unite the country.

A member of South Africa's organising committee later recited for me their pitch to FIFA: 'Our democracy's young. It's being subjected to a lot of tests. This is just the right time to be pursuing a single pursuit by the entirety of the nation.' The man said, 'We needed a nation-building event, and there couldn't have been a better one.'

When FIFA chose South Africa, a large portion of the country took to the streets waving the national flag. It was the first time South Africans saw Mandela cry.

But not many of the black people celebrating regarded the World Cup as a 'nation-building event'. A decade into democracy, they were done with nation-building. They wanted the tournament to lift them out of poverty. Over a third of South Africans were living on less than $2 a day. 'The money is coming!' cheered people in Soweto.

No other host country had so fixated on the World Cup as an economic proposition. South Africa's bid committee forecast that the World Cup would create 160,000 jobs, boosting the economy by about £2 billion. Cheryl Carolus of South African Tourism said: 'The numbers of people coming here will be phenomenal.' Someone published a book about 100 ways in which South African small businesses could profit from the World Cup.

No serious economist believed this stuff. A country hosting the World Cup builds things that it doesn't need for daily life. For instance, a new highway to the port tends to create more long-term value than a highway to the stadium. True, some people get temporary work building these things, but it would have been better to give them more productive work. The World Cup would stimulate the South African economy, but not by much. In effect, South Africa was spending a £100 note to buy a £50 note – and that effort would swallow much of the government's time, attention and money for six years.

Yet throughout those years, South African leaders painted the World Cup as an 'economic bonanza'. It was the justification for the tournament that their voters wanted to hear.

Meanwhile, obscured by the hot air, a disaster was unfolding: a generation was dying of AIDS. In 2004, the year South Africa began planning the World Cup, its life expectancy bottomed out at fifty-two. Black life expectancy fell below fifty. Antiretroviral drugs were already available but they had not yet been rolled out in South Africa due to a mix of government incompetence, lack of money, and the conspiracy theories of President Mbeki, who had concluded from some googling that HIV didn't cause AIDS. The South African 'nation-building event' of the 2000s should have been putting AIDS clinics in every neighbourhood.

FIFA sponsors' workshop, Munich, 21–22 September 2004

FIFA's dealings with sponsors usually happen behind closed doors. I only got inside the relationship once, when FIFA invited me to give a talk to the sponsors about the South African World Cup.

Cunningly, FIFA had scheduled the workshop to coincide with Munich's Oktoberfest. We were taken to a pork dinner with the biggest beer glasses I had ever seen. The attendees worked for sponsors including McDonald's, Warner Brothers, Mastercard and Adidas. By the time we met in Munich, their companies had already paid up for the 2006 World Cup, but FIFA still had to persuade them to sign up for South Africa – a trickier proposition, on unfamiliar terrain, in the 'hopeless continent'.

We were greeted by Franz Beckenbauer, chief organiser of the 2006 tournament, wearing a headache-inducing outfit of brown jacket, orange tie, blue shirt and green trousers. He said, 'We call it "Oktoberfest" because it's held in September. Dat's Munich.'

An official from the German football federation talked us through the rise of sponsorship. He brandished the official programme of the previous World Cup in Germany, in 1974. In it, he marvelled, 'you will not find the word "marketing".' He played us TV ads from the era: German players making awkward statements to camera to promote a liquorice brand, or filling their cars with petrol to plug a chain of garages. Günter Netzer wore a spectacular white polo neck. A young Beckenbauer was shown eating branded soup.

We were promised that for 2006, FIFA's marketing would be souped-up beyond recognition. The tournament's mascot, a lion named Goleo, performed a rap for us that name-checked every sponsor:

Committed to the future, just like Toshiba
…
Making things better and better, like Philips …

The sponsors whooped.

A FIFA official cast the World Cup as the ultimate sales

opportunity: 'When people are emotional, they are much more susceptible to commercial [propositions].' And the sponsors were reassured time and again that their competitors would be fully excluded from the tournament. A rival company couldn't even put an ad on a billboard in a host city. All business would be reserved for FIFA's 'partners' and 'suppliers'.

That approach was going to nix the dreams of ordinary South Africans hoping to do something as low-end as sell sausages outside stadiums. A FIFA official told me that they should understand they wouldn't get many opportunities. South Africa's job was to pay for the World Cup's stadiums and infrastructure, while FIFA pocketed the TV and sponsorship money.

To my surprise, FIFA let me give a warts-and-all presentation about South Africa. I started by rhapsodising about the country's football culture. When I showed a video of Mandela dancing to 'Shosholoza' before the 1996 Nations Cup final, there wasn't a dry eye in the sponsors' workshop. I predicted that 'Shosholoza' would be the soundtrack of the 2010 World Cup. I quoted a French musicologist, who had told me that he had travelled the world but never seen a people with better dance and group singing than black South Africans.

Then I came to South Africa's warts. I showed a chart of murder rates in selected countries, and said, 'Broadly speaking, it shows that you are fifty-nine times more likely to be murdered in South Africa than in England, and ten times more likely than in the US.' The sponsors fell into a broody silence.

The next morning, one of them invited me to breakfast. He was trying to decide whether his company should sponsor the South African World Cup. They were inviting thousands of their 'top clients' to matches in Germany in 2006. The moment you invited someone on a trip, you were responsible for their security. If a client got killed or mugged or raped, they probably wouldn't give you more orders. This man said that whenever people at his company started getting enthusiastic about South Africa, someone would ask, 'What about security?'

Our conversation was a preview of the next six years: every

time the 2010 World Cup was mentioned, people talked about crime. Foreigners who had no notion of South Africa before it was named host now thought of it as a murderous place. South Africans had hoped the tournament would transform their country's image, but in fact it probably tarnished it. Whatever happened in the month of the World Cup would be outweighed by the coverage of the six-year run-up.

Moroka Swallows-Santos, Rand Stadium, Johannesburg, February 2005

The Swallows (slogan: 'Don't Follow Me, Follow The Birds!') were a fairly successful club, but you wouldn't have known that this midweek afternoon. I had got a lift from my cousin Jonty, a fellow football journalist, and we pulled up outside an almost empty stadium. We could park at once, as if we had come to watch a pub team. In the only food stall, a woman was hopefully frying *Boerewors* sausage.

Jonty had expected as much. By 2005, there were only three popular clubs in South Africa: the Pirates, the Chiefs, and Manchester United. New professional clubs were constantly being founded, while others died in silence.

Shortly before kick-off there were about 400 spectators. We could hear the teams singing downstairs in the changing rooms, accompanied by rhythmic clapping. When they took the field, fifteen minutes late, almost every player was black, but both coaches were white. The game was played in such silence that you could hear the Santos coach shouting 'Fucking!' There was a questionable penalty, a strange own goal, and then, happily, the final whistle, whereupon the assembled press corps (Jonty) rushed to the tunnel to interview both coaches.

When we drove out of the stadium at ten to six, Johannesburg was already almost deserted. The city died after dark, for fear of crime.

Hotel Adlon, Berlin, 7 July 2006

Beckenbauer, the tournament's chief organiser, was fighting his way through the lobby of the Adlon, once the favourite Nazi hang-out on the Unter den Linden. Two nights before the final, his World Cup was already a success. Nothing had gone wrong, the tournament had been a time to make friends, and the Kaiser could hardly take a step through the Adlon without an elegant woman strolling over to congratulate him. He had no bodyguards. You could just go up to him.

The scene didn't thrill everybody. A party of South African officials in green blazers was sitting around a table under the Adlon's glass dome, looking sullen. I spotted Irvin Khoza, president of the Orlando Pirates, and Albie Sachs, the judge, poet and ex-communist, recognisable by the empty sleeve of his jacket. (He had lost an arm and an eye to a car bomb planted by the apartheid regime.) Germany's perfectly organised World Cup had given the South Africans a fright.

Black South Africans had been told since childhood that they were inferior. Now they wanted to prove – including to themselves – that a black-run country could do everything that a white one could. They would have to match the Germans.

One South African official told me years later that it was in Germany that they decided to upgrade their World Cup. Playing matches in rugby stadiums and giving Soccer City a paint job wouldn't suffice. Anyway, South African cities had begun demanding new grounds for 2010. When the woman from Cape Town asked for a world-class stadium, the man from Polokwane demanded an even better one. And FIFA was worried about sponsors getting rained on in roofless stadiums. Germany's success gave South Africa's World Cup elephantiasis.

St Jakob-Park stadium, Basel, Switzerland, November 2006

The Bafana changed their manager almost every year. 'It's very irritating,' FC Basel's South African striker Delron Buckley told me. 'Every time for every game it's always a new team, with new players. They don't have a structure.' When I asked him if he ever felt that he didn't want to fly across the world to play in a disorganised team, Buckley said nothing, then grinned, and after a while said, 'Do I need to answer?'

Johannesburg for people who are afraid to go, February 2007

I'd flown here with my wife and one-year-old daughter to research the book I was trying to write about South African football. As a parent, your biological role is to protect your child. So it felt irrational to be taking her to a city of homicides, traffic accidents and disease.

A late-night Johannesburg taxi, February 2007

In 2007, AIDS helped kill about 350,000 South Africans. But most of these people died unseen, at home, from 'pneumonia' or 'tuberculosis' or 'a lingering illness'. Only occasionally did you glimpse the disease, like the night I took a taxi home through the sleeping city. When I got in, I thought I was alone in the back seat. Suddenly I noticed a toddler lying beside me, awake. His father, the driver, explained that his son always rode with him at night. I could imagine what had happened to his mother. I just hoped that the boy hadn't inherited her disease.

Kaizer Chiefs training ground, 16 February 2007

I'd been invited to watch the Kaizer Chiefs train. Early in the steaming African morning, my taxi driver drove me past the skyscrapers of downtown Johannesburg out towards Soweto. We turned off the highway just after Johannesburg Prison. My taxi driver used to work there. 'Why?' I asked. He shrugged: 'To see something different. It's not nice to work there all the time. It's a nice experience to work there a short time.' Then he described how inmates would rape fourteen-year-old boys.

Frank Eulberg, the club's German assistant manager, showed me around the Chiefs' complex, which looked like a luxurious golf club in Florida. Eulberg grinned: 'So that's the shabby Africa, about which we read so much.' He had never coached higher than the fourth Bundesliga when Ernst Middendorp took him to Iran as his assistant, and now they were at one of the world's most popular clubs. Eulberg loved seeing people on the street with Chiefs shirts.

Every foreign coach who lands here says that South African players have fantastic technique, and that he'll teach them discipline. Then his successor says the same thing. Behind closed doors, over coffee before training, the Germans were less diplomatic. Middendorp unleashed a rant against South African football. Fans and players here venerated ticky-ticky. The Germans were trying to teach them real football, but what thanks did they get?

Carlos Alberto Parreira, the Brazilian coach who had committed the sin of winning the 1994 World Cup with defensive football, had recently taken over the Bafana. I asked Eulberg whether Parreira would let South Africa play South African football in 2010. 'No,' he replied. 'Because there is no "South African football". What is South African football? Dancing on the ball? He'll have to defend, because they can't score goals.'

I was the only spectator at training. When the players arrived, each one said 'Good morning', or trotted over to shake my hand. Eulberg said every player was supporting dozens of relatives and acquaintances. While they passed the ball around, he called out rhythmically, in German-English: 'Vun touch! Vun touch! Vun touch!'

I took a taxi back to our rented flat feeling dissatisfied. You'd think that frank conversations in the coaches' changing room of a big club would be good material. You wouldn't get that access at Manchester United. But the Germans were outsiders like me.

They complained about South African football, but they didn't understand it.

Wits University-Kaizer Chiefs, Johannesburg, 18 February 2007

That Sunday, Chiefs played at Wits. That's how leagues all over the world work: you play opponents home and away. But in South Africa, 'home ground' isn't really a concept. You usually play the game in whichever stadium can fit the expected number of spectators, so the Chiefs almost always play in one of South Africa's biggest stadiums. They hadn't wanted to come to Wits' tiny university ground. It had no room for all the Chiefs' fan clubs, who normally drove hours from settlements around South Africa. Anyway, Chiefs hadn't been welcome at Wits since the time their fans broke the dome of the university's planetarium.

Other than a small Wits contingent, almost all the 5,000 spectators wore Chiefs' yellow and black. The future South African president Cyril Ramaphosa was going around shaking hands and waving. His smart striped shirt made him by far the most formally dressed person in the ground.

It was the first full South African stadium I'd seen that didn't sing. What I'd told the sponsors in Munich about 'Shosholoza' had gone out of date. A few years earlier, a guy called Neil van Schalkwyk had patented a plastic tooter called a vuvuzela, developed from a traditional horn used in ceremonies by a South African church. By 2007 the vuvuzela had become the only distinctive feature of South African football culture. The Chiefs fans at Wits blew them. Eulberg had imitated the sound for me: 'Zzzuuu! Zzzzuuuu!' The world's worst musical instrument, the vuvuzela couldn't play tunes, except the 'bapabapabapabapa' sometimes heard at cricket matches, though if necessary you could use it to bop someone on the head.

Ten minutes into the game, Chiefs' ungainly centre-forward Kaizer Motaung Jr, son of Kaizer Sr and a former pupil of

Harrow School in England, fortuitously scuffed the ball into the net. 'Zuuu! Zuuu!' A couple of dozen Chiefs fans wearing their trademark yellow and black miners' helmets broke into a dance, waving their vuvuzelas.

And then barely anything else happened all match. The Germans just wanted to scrape a win. Entertainment wasn't their concern. The Chiefs fans sat sullen and silent. Late in the game they started angrily blowing their vuvuzelas and whirling their hands, the universal gesture for 'Substitute!' They hadn't come to see offside traps and man-marking. They were fed up with these Germans, who could drop a guy just because he was drunk, when the whole stadium had come to watch him.

Café Europa, Norwood, Johannesburg, 19 February 2007

Dumi's father was a powerful man. He owned communal 'combi' taxis – the de facto public transport of black South Africa – and a professional football club. But only at his father's funeral did Dumi discover quite how mighty he had been: the deceased turned out to have fathered fifty-two children by eleven different women. In Dumisanu Phakathi's documentary film *Don't F*** with me, I have 51 Brothers and Sisters*, he travels South Africa to find them all.

Dumi told the story sitting among black and white Johannesburg hipsters at Café Europa in Norwood. Having risen to the middle class, he could describe his own origins with distance. But, he emphasised, 'I live in Soweto, I am from a disadvantaged background, I went to a shit school, I am a fucking real South African.' And as a real South African, he wanted to explain what soccer meant to black men from townships.

'Most average black men, 99 per cent of their conversation is about soccer. That's how they relate to each other,' said Dumi, imitating the 'click' sounds of a conversation in Zulu or Xhosa. He said these men rarely talked politics or poverty. 'They can't do anything about that. They feel powerless. They can't look after their families, so confidence is low. That's what poverty does: you can't read much, because you are so concerned about your life. And football becomes the one thing that is safe to talk about.'

Dumi said, 'Once you are well-off, being a fan is something else you can do. But when you are poor, there is not something else you can do. Every time I pass by and I hear a conversation about soccer, I think, "Shit, that's sad." Because these guys have brains. They could be talking about other stuff.'

A Thursday in Soweto, February 2007

When my taxi drove into Soweto, the flowers lining the streets formed the magic number '2010'. Many Sowetans lived in the township's characteristic four-bedroom brick bungalows, some of which had lovely gardens. Certain villas in the Thokosa Park neighbourhood could have been in Johannesburg's northern suburbs, while other Sowetan districts were slums. The township's true suffering, though, was on show in the ads for funeral homes painted on the roadside fences: 'Motaung Funeral Directors – We Salute the Spirit of Ubuntu!' There were the '21st Century Funeral Brokers', or you could have a 'rasta burial'.

Most Sowetans with jobs got up at 5 a.m. to board 'combi' taxis for the daily traffic jam to Johannesburg. When I arrived, only the legions of unemployed were still around. I'd come to see the former professional footballer Bongane Innocent Phakathi, one of Dumi's fifty-one siblings.

Bongane showed up in a pink fisherman's hat and a Bloemfontein Celtics shirt. We set off walking. After car-bound Johannesburg, Soweto's almost European street life was a joy. There were hardly any cars, and so people walked down the street, holding umbrellas against the sun. Many wore their finest attire – often special uniforms, one for each Christian sect – because Soweto's unemployed went to church on Thursdays as well as Sundays.

Bongane knew and greeted most people we passed. He had

been a talented footballer who once went for a trial at FC Copen-
hagen, but landed in Denmark to discover that the first team had
just left for a tournament in Marseille. He only had a two-week
visa, so in the end he could only train for about four days.

Today we were going to see unemployed footballers train on
a field that served three Sowetan neighbourhoods. It was full
all weekend, and Chiefs and Pirates sometimes came to scout,
because that saved them having to scour the countryside, the
veld.

After training, the exhausted players lay down in the beautifully shorn grass. One guy wore a vest adorned with a fake
newspaper headline: 'South Africa's Second Olympics A Huge
Success.' The players chatted in a mix of English and 'township
Zulu'. Some had played in South Africa's Premier Soccer League.

I asked, 'If you're seventeen and talented, how do you get into
the league?'

They shouted as one man: 'It's luck!' South African clubs
barely had youth teams. The best way to get scouted was to know
someone. That's why they were happy to meet an Englishman.
'When are you taking us to London?' one asked.

I asked what they expected from the World Cup. 'Italian girls!'
And Soccer City was only two or three 'combi' rides from Soweto.
'We will see men like Cristiano Ronaldo with the naked eye.'
Then they leafed through the photo book I'd brought, Hans van
der Meer's *European Fields*, with pictures of amateur grounds
around the continent. In their minds, they were already playing in
Norway or Hungary.

Rochester House, Johannesburg, 23 February 2007

The city was cleaning up its Central Business District for the
World Cup, so this morning I went with the police to raid gangsters. At 9 a.m. a ragtag platoon of about twenty-five men and
women, some in uniform and others in civvies, stood to attention at Jeppe police station in downtown Johannesburg. One man

wore a Chelsea shirt, almost certainly pirated. They chatted in African languages.

'Listen carefully,' said their leader, Director Louw, an Afrikaner with watery blue eyes and a smudge of grey moustache. When Louw joined the police on 3 January 1973, he wouldn't have imagined he'd end up commanding an almost all-black platoon. He said, 'We're going to do the building at number 36.' A tip had come in that gangsters were hiding there. We climbed into vans and drove to the address, about a mile from Ellis Park stadium.

Rochester House must have once been an office block for whites, but now poor people lived there. 'Gun Free Building', proclaimed a hopeful sign above an empty beer bottle by the front door.

Our raid was on! The police raced up the staircase waving guns. I ran after them, and was hit by a stench of urine so bad I could barely breathe. Pools of liquid lay on the floor. The windows were broken. We entered a room where a shirtless young man sat on the bed. A policewoman motioned at him to get off it, and searched under the mattress. Other officers rifled through his dirty laundry, while he watched us curiously.

Everyone here lived in one room, as if in a student dorm. Some had put a picture or Chiefs sticker on their room door. One woman, called Queen, was pleased that the police were searching her room. 'A copper is very nice,' she said, adding: 'This place is all right, but the toilet is not flushing.' That explained a lot. A sign outside the toilet read, in vain, 'Stop behaving like a child. This place is not for rubbish. It's a toilet please!!' Rochester House no longer had running water.

A policeman told me they had raided the place before. Like so many in central Johannesburg, it might have been abandoned by an owner who was dodging taxes. But perhaps now someone would buy Rochester House, clean it up, and put English fans in it during the World Cup.

Back on the street, we could breathe through our noses again. A little policewoman confessed, 'Unfortunately we did not find anything. Places like this, we must raid them at four in the morning when the criminals are relaxed.' I asked a sergeant at what time of day Johannesburg was most dangerous. 'Any time of the day is dangerous,' he replied.

The tenants were still savouring the raid: some entertainment in an unemployed day. Spilling out onto the street, they chatted about the World Cup. One promised, 'David Beckham and Ronaldinho are going to stay right here in this building.' Another said she'd rather share her room with Cristiano Ronaldo.

A young woman told us that she paid 500 rand a month (about €50) to live here. That was a lot. Perhaps she paid the building's legal owner, or perhaps the 'pirates' who had taken over many buildings around Ellis Park.

I told a white policeman that someone needed to fix the toilets. A simple intervention would revolutionise the lives and health of perhaps a hundred people. The policeman laughed. It was never going to happen. Why would anybody bother?

A sergeant with gold teeth toting a large gun (an R5, he explained fondly) gave the tenants a motivational speech. 'Listen man, the only thing you have to do is just work hard. The first time I failed my matric [school exams]. The second time I passed.'

Louw confided that an informant had told them that there were secret corridors in the building. 'But I think it was just a child's story, fantasy.' Another wasted morning. The raid had hauled in only a long rusty knife, unearthed in someone's room. Three minutes' drive later, we were back among the villas and tennis courts of white Kensington.

Norwood, Johannesburg, February 2007

This evening in our rental flat, I told my wife that I wasn't going to write the book about South Africa. Football here is mostly a sport of poor black people, I said. I didn't know them, and I couldn't tell their story.

I'd come to understand that, in a way, apartheid had succeeded. It had started from the absurd premise that people of different colours had nothing in common, and by keeping them apart, it created a country in which they had almost nothing in common. Each colour lived in its own neighbourhoods, grew to different heights, played different sports, and died at different ages. During apartheid, even the dogs belonging to the different colours were buried in separate cemeteries. Most Chiefs fans lived in townships I couldn't fathom, speaking languages I didn't know. Because South Africa was dangerous, I couldn't just hang out there and try to meet them. It was easier for me to reach the Chiefs manager. I wasn't saying that I didn't have the right as a white person to 'appropriate' their experiences. I just didn't know their experiences.

I didn't write the book. What I've written here isn't an account of South Africa. It's an account of my visits to the different South Africas. Most people whom I met along the way spoke fluent English, unlike the average South African, and were disproportionately well-off, male and white.

A restaurant in Sandton, February 2007

If the 2010 World Cup had a father, it was Danny Jordaan. He had been an anti-apartheid activist, schoolteacher and ANC member of parliament when in the late 1990s the ANC tasked him with bringing the tournament to South Africa. He travelled the world campaigning for nearly a decade, then ran the local organising committee.

I talked to Jordaan often, and grew to like him. This morning we were meeting in Sandton, Johannesburg's white business district, at a restaurant where breakfast cost more than the average South African daily income. I was shown to Jordaan's regular table. I'd arrived early, and the other seat was still empty.

I soon noticed that the grizzled little guy with the salt-and-pepper beard and skewed tie at the table behind me looked familiar. It was Danny Jordaan. He was having a breakfast before our breakfast (he was a touch chubby), talking football with two

Brits, a posh woman and a jowly bloke. I leaned back in my chair and eavesdropped.

Jordaan was explaining why West Africans were better at football than South Africans. Firstly, he said, they were poorer, which motivated them (which wouldn't explain why most World Cups were won by rich European countries). He added, 'Physically they are much stronger, the West Africans. You know, the Kenyan long-distance runners. [That's East Africa, Danny!] There is no public transport, so they run five miles.'

It was hard to imagine that people in other business sectors talked as much shit as people in football, but my colleagues at the *Financial Times* assured me that this was in fact the case.

The jowly Brit sounded like a world-class name-dropper: he referred to Klinsmann as 'my good friend Jürgen'. When the breakfast finally ended, he gave Jordaan a collage photograph of the last three Spurs captains to raise the FA Cup. There was Dave Mackay, Steve Perryman and the jowly bloke himself: Gary Mabbutt in 1991.

What did Spurs want from Jordaan? Everyone in football had their scheme for 2010.

I spirited Jordaan away for tea and biscuits in the atrium. He ignored both his constantly ringing BlackBerry and his phone, and talked about the World Cup, three years away. He admitted to worrying about the Bafana's quality: 'We cannot have a team that goes out in the first round.'

But before leaving on his usual journey to the airport to catch yet another flight, he wanted to tell me something: 'I think one is incredibly blessed. How many people have an opportunity to be part of the process to liberate their country? In 1976 and 1985, in those dark days, I was not sure that I would sit here today to talk to you. To see in 1990 Nelson Mandela walk out of prison, to see the elections go off peacefully in 1994, to see Bafana Bafana win the African Nations Cup in 1996, to be given the right to host this event – these are special events. Nobody decided for us to walk this road. We decided to walk this road. One is just blessed, I think.'

I'm sure he'd said it a thousand times before, but it was true.

Cape Town, February 2007

South Africa's two great cities relate to each other rather like Brazil's. Johannesburg, like São Paulo, is for work. Cape Town, like Rio, with its mountains dipping down to the beaches, is for play. In the aeroplane leaving Johannesburg for Cape Town, when the muzak played before take-off, my daughter danced on her seat.

Cape Town was not a football city. By 2007, the average Premier Soccer League match here drew just 5,000 spectators. In the posh white town itself – which as a Capetonian friend said, was 'really quite close to Africa' – hardly anyone went to games.

Yet Cape Town was building a 68,000-seater World Cup stadium in a prime white neighbourhood at Green Point. Capetonian officials grumbled that the trouble had begun when Sepp Blatter took a helicopter ride over the city. He had pointed to a spot beside the Atlantic, at the foot of Table Mountain, and said, 'You must build it there!' He could probably already picture the sponsors' brochures.

Why had the city agreed? David Hugo, who was overseeing the stadium for the municipality, explained to me that Cape Town had initially planned to freshen up the perfectly decent rugby stadium at Newlands for the World Cup. That would have cost very little. But Newlands' capacity was only 48,000, too small for a semi-final. Hugo said, 'We were advised by the "national organisers", let's say, that it was a semi-final or nothing.' In other words, Cape Town could only be part of the World Cup if it built Blatter's stadium.

The city had hoped it would get the opening match too. That didn't happen. So it was building the stadium effectively for one game, though I heard lots of talk about how Green Point would be used for pop concerts and suchlike after 2010, and anyway, the World Cup was going to 'put South Africa on the map'. The stadium ended up costing $600 million – way over budget, of course. Hugo told me that if they hadn't spent all that money in Green Point, it would have been channelled to 'poorer areas'.

De Tuynhuys, Cape Town, 27 February 2007

De Tuynhuys (Afrikaans for 'The Garden House') is a fine colonial building from which South Africa is run. But even here, the new country showed its unbuttoned personality. A lady at reception wearing a gardener's hat told me I couldn't come in without an ID. I hadn't brought one. She let me in anyway. I walked to the Tuynhuys itself. The guards there told me they were very strict, much stricter than the lady at reception, but they let me in too.

I had come to see a tall South African Indian named Essop Pahad, an old university friend of various Kupers. I found him in his office, long inhabited by apartheid ministers in black suits. He was wearing a pink shirt, without a jacket.

After apartheid, Pahad had mostly given up being a communist, and had risen to the apex of South African power. He was a minister in the office of President Mbeki, his chum during their exile at Sussex University in England, and also sat on South Africa's organising committee for the World Cup.

In 1959, Pahad and a few other anti-apartheid types had helped start professional soccer in South Africa, setting up a single league for blacks, so-called 'Coloureds' and Indians. They were desperate to find white players. Once Pahad even asked my dad to play a game, but he wasn't a football man and didn't feel like driving out to a distant township. (He now regrets not having done it.)

All right, but why did non-footballing towns like Cape Town or Polokwane need fancy new stadiums? Pahad said, 'If you take a longer-term view, not a short-term view, I think it's an unchallengeable fact that the popularity of soccer is just going to grow and grow, not just in South Africa but in the world. We were very mindful that we should not do what happened in Japan, in terms of putting up a few stadia which they did not require.' Japan was tearing down grounds from its World Cup, but that wouldn't happen in South Africa, oh no.

Pahad marvelled: 'We have a World Cup. I dreamed of liberating South Africa, but I never dreamed about that. When we started professional football in 1959, 1960, that one can sit back forty-seven years later and say, "My God, we're organising a

World Cup." And we will organise, I promise you, a world-class World Cup.'

Breakfast café, Green Point, Cape Town, February 2007

'A world-class World Cup' was the new cliché I kept hearing in South Africa. Jordaan had said, 'People will see that we are African, and world-class.' The Cape premier Helen Zille said, 'World-class is where we want to be.'

'A world-class World Cup' was a peculiar phrase. The Germans hadn't used it in 2006, nor the Japanese in 2002. But it expressed the anxieties of South Africa's elite. President Mbeki had spent twenty-eight years in exile, largely in the Soviet Union and Brighton. Former exiles instinctively compared South Africa to developed countries. That's why the World Cup had to be 'world-class', with stadiums as swish as the German ones.

South Africa's white English-speaking business elite shared the obsession with 'world-class'. Whites in Sandton often felt closer to white foreigners in Atlanta or London than to their black compatriots three miles away in Alexandra. They compared South Africa to the 'world-class' US or UK. Hosting a smooth World Cup would prove that South Africa was an adult country.

Not all South Africans were obsessed with being 'world-class'. Mandela knew he was 'world-class', so he assumed that his country was too – he didn't need a football tournament to prove it. And most black people who had never left South Africa didn't make comparisons with England or Germany. They just hoped the World Cup would create jobs.

But for the people who ran South Africa, the World Cup was, above all, a symbolic event. The political risk analyst Nic Borain explained this to me best. Over breakfast in Cape Town, just over the road from where the World Cup stadium was going to arise, he told me that if the tournament went well, and fans weren't murdered, and they got to games on time, that would somehow show that the new South Africa – and perhaps even the continent of

Africa – could hack it. Borain said, 'We worry that we can't do it. We represent Africa, we come after Germany, which in our minds represents the epitome of white on-timeness. We have invested the World Cup as an omen, a predictor of our future.'

Café in the El Corte Inglés department store, Madrid, November 2007

I was having coffee with South Africa's ambassador to Spain, Vusi Koloane, a cheery fifty-something raised in a township. He chain-smoked and raved about blossoming Spanish–South African trade.

Often, people only tell you the thing that's on their mind at the end of the interview. Strolling back through the expensive streets to the embassy, Koloane began talking about his tennis career. He had been a talented youngster. One day, the coach of the white South African player Johan Kriek spotted him and asked who his coach was. Koloane, who was studying to be a schoolteacher, replied that he'd never had a coach. He had learned tennis from books and videos that he borrowed from a library.

Kriek's coach wrote to fifty companies, asking them to sponsor the promising black player. Not one was interested. Soon afterwards, Koloane drifted out of tennis. What he'd learned from his own disappointment was that you always had to encourage other people. That's why he sponsored an annual golf tournament in his old township. He used to consider golf a white person's sport, but now he had a handicap of seven.

I asked if he was bitter. 'Very bitter,' he replied. He could have made the world's top twenty in tennis, become a millionaire. If even the ambassador to Madrid was bitter, how must other black South Africans feel?

Bois de Boulogne, Paris, 21 September 2008

Björn Borg was playing a veterans' tennis tournament in Paris, and I interviewed him on a lawn in the Bois de Boulogne. The Swede had morphed from ice god into an incredibly nice middle-aged man. He spoke with wonder about the young Björn Borg, as if he were a different person, but only grew emotional when he got onto Nelson Mandela.

When Borg and his old rival John McEnroe had visited Johannesburg for another veterans' tournament, Mandela had asked them to drop round. Borg said, 'I had the pleasure and the honour, me and John, we went home to Mandela. He told me and John: "I was listening to you when you played the final in Wimbledon."' In 1980 Mandela had somehow convinced his guards on Robben Island to get him a radio so he could follow the match on the BBC.

Borg and McEnroe had replied, 'Wow.' When Borg told me the story, I exclaimed, sincerely, 'Wow.' Borg said, 'Oh, that was unbelievable,' making a 'goosebumps' gesture across his forearm.

It was the ritual Mandela story – a story that maddened other senior ANC people. Essop Pahad told me, 'Whites are always talking about Mandela, "Mandela this, Mandela that, Mandela is a wonder-person." The only thing Mandela did was express non-racist ANC policy.'

A New York recording studio, February 2010

The South African band Freshlyground spent much of the early 2000s travelling around Europe and the US as 'the face of the new South Africa'. Each time they took the stage, the happy new post-racial country existed. The secret was in their positioning. Two small women danced at the front of the stage: the black singer Zolani and my white cousin Kyla. Directly behind them stood two handsome male guitarists, one black, the other blond. The band's surplus of white men was tucked away at the sides of the stage.

Four months before the 2010 World Cup, Freshlyground were recording in a studio in New York when they got lucky. A few floors below in the same building, the Colombian singer Shakira was producing her World Cup song. Her producer thought it needed 'something South African'. Freshlyground were summoned downstairs to jam with her. Their joint creation, 'Waka Waka (This Time for Africa)', became the Official 2010 FIFA World Cup™ Song.

FIFA took a huge slice of the royalties. Kyla says, 'I never made any considerable money from one of the world's most played songs of all time.'

Freshlyground were booked to play the World Cup's opening concert, and the closing ceremony at the final. They weren't paid for either appearance. Still, when Kyla visited India a few months after the tournament, every time she said she was from South Africa, people would spontaneously reply: 'Waka waka!'

South African billboards, March 2010

As the officials at the Munich workshop I attended had promised, FIFA obsessively protected the World Cup's sponsors. It banned the tiniest South African mom-and-pop outfits from putting the words '2010' or 'World Cup' on their products. It pushed the country into passing a law that made 'ambush marketing' a criminal offence, for which you could be jailed. FIFA even seemed to think it had trademarked South Africa's flag. The federation's screwing of South Africa became a parable for centuries of screwing of Africans by whites.

That's why the South African airline Kulula.com came up with a slogan to tease FIFA: 'Unofficial National Carrier of the You-Know-What'. Naturally, FIFA fell into Kulula's trap. It took the airline to court, arguing that 'the You-Know-What' obviously referred to the 2010 FIFA World Cup™. In March 2010 a judge made Kulula pull the ads.

Days later, Kulula had a new slogan: 'Not Next Year, Not Last Year, But Somewhere in Between.'*

---

* Kulula folded in 2022, not because of FIFA.

Johannesburg, 11 May 2010

A month before the tournament, the twenty-eight-year-old dribbler Emmanuel 'Scara' Ngobese died in hospital of 'tuberculosis',
a common consequence of AIDS. Ngobese, who won the league
with Kaizer Chiefs in 2005, played once for the Bafana. How
many South Africans who might have played at the World Cup
were dead instead?

11

World Cup 2010: Did South Africa Win?

This wasn't the finest hour of my life as a father. I said goodbye to my twenty-two-month-old twin boys, my four-year-old daughter, and my poor wife, and left Paris for Johannesburg.

My hotel was on Empire Road, just up from Wits University – my parents' alma mater. It was fifteen minutes' drive from Ellis Park, fifteen minutes to my granny in Houghton, and even less to my Aunt Ruth in Killarney. In other words, the World Cup was being played in white South Africa – not in the black South Africa where the country's football culture originated.

True, not all stadiums were in white areas. The neighbourhood around Ellis Park had morphed since apartheid from white to almost entirely black. But white South Africa was where fans, journalists, sponsors, FIFA officials and players were encouraged to hang out between games. Almost all the hotels, shopping malls and official 'fan parks' – along with the tens of thousands of security guards protecting the visitors – were in overwhelmingly white neighbourhoods. The organisers didn't want people wandering off in search of the other South Africas.

Houghton, Johannesburg, 8 June 2010

My grandmother had been looking forward to death for years. But the day I landed she was still there, morbid, negative and ninety-two years old, but not even ill.

I visited her in her art deco block of flats full of elderly white widows. The black security guard at the front door seemed to wave through anyone who could prove they were white. Once inside, it wasn't immediately obvious that apartheid had been abolished. There were still two lifts, one smart and one rickety, although they were now marked 'Residents' and 'Staff' instead of 'White' and 'Black'. Other than the *sangoma* (or witch doctor) in the flat next to my granny, and Mandela down the road, there still weren't many black people living in Houghton.

The *Financial Times* had given me an amazing new device that when plugged into a laptop created instant Wi-Fi anywhere. From my grandmother's flat I skyped home to Paris. When the three kids appeared on screen and said shy hello's to my grandmother, she froze in disbelief. Then she called over her black carer and her cleaner to see; they couldn't believe it either. But what to do with this miracle? The children weren't yet brilliant conversationalists, especially not with a bewildered nonagenarian at the bottom of the planet, so they sang her a French nursery song.

Early June 2010

The economist Stefan Szymanski and I had recently published a book called *Soccernomics*, which used data to explain football. Eager for publicity, we'd agreed to a request from a website to simulate the outcome of the World Cup. Using a complicated formula that predicted the result of each match, we showed that Brazil would beat Serbia in the final.

Look away now if you don't want to know who won the 2010 World Cup, but we were wrong. I also wrote an article early in the tournament saying that France (who were headed for disaster) might win, and another headlined, 'Spain are the best team by far – they will probably fail'.

These exercises confirmed an obvious truth that I took years to learn: so many chance elements affect the result of a single football match that it's pointless even trying to forecast a World

Cup. The winner of the tournament plays just seven games, most of which will be decided by a single goal or on penalties. In such a short random walk, almost any plausible team can get lucky. Only once you accept that the World Cup is held together by flukes (a bit like life itself) does the whole thing start to make sense.

Today, having learned from my humiliations, if I were forced to predict the world champion, I still wouldn't. I've noticed from messages I get from friends during World Cups that fans love making predictions. Journalists, on the other hand, use mealy-mouthed formulas to avoid it.

Hillbrow, Johannesburg, 9 June 2010

The Dutch team in South Africa had decided to ditch the national tradition of glorious defeat and moral victory. The new thinking was summed up in an advert for Nike, showing grim-faced, sweating Dutch players during a training session. Military drums played as the players marched along a corridor. 'Football is not total without victory,' said a slogan that evoked Goebbels's 'total war' as much as Cruyffian 'total football'. And: 'A beautiful defeat is still a defeat.' The ad foretold *Oranje*'s World Cup better than any pundit had.

The Dutch were staying in the Hilton in Sandton, seven miles and infinite demographic categories removed from inner-city Hillbrow, where immigrants from Nigeria and Zimbabwe lived many to a room. Businesses had fled the district, to be replaced by muggers, sex workers and drug gangs. By 2010, the word most often used to describe the neighbourhood was 'warzone'.

That afternoon, before the first ball or opponent had been kicked, the Dutch team bus pulled up in Hillbrow. The Dutch FA, as a gift to South Africa, had paid for an all-weather, floodlit football pitch to be built on what had been a concrete wasteland. The players had been sent to open it. In the stands around the pitch, dozens of children sat waiting in the winter sun, while curious residents thronged the stairwells of the surrounding apartment blocks.

The World Cup was encountering poor South Africa, and things began awkwardly. Some Dutch players wore watches that could have funded a Hillbrow child for life. They pulled out their phones and photographed the kids, but they didn't greet them. Gathering in the centre circle, the Dutch turned away from the children towards each other. Khalid Boulahrouz giggled with Robin van Persie.

Then a mini-tournament started, and the local kids were divvied up into teams led by Dutch multimillionaires. For a while things stayed awkward: the players could barely acknowledge the children they were playing with. It was Dirk Kuyt of Liverpool who saved the day. He gathered his team in a pre-game huddle, in which kids and stars put their arms around each other and gave a communal cheer. When a small girl scored the team's opening goal, the internationals formed a circle around her and danced with her. Kuyt's team danced together after every goal. I'm guessing those kids still remember it today.

South Africa-Mexico, World Cup opening match, Soccer City, Johannesburg, 11 June 2010

On the highway from Johannesburg, our 'media shuttle' bus sat almost motionless in a traffic jam for over an hour. Would we miss the opening game? I ended up walking the last half hour to the stadium. It looked that day as if the sceptics were right, and the South African World Cup would become an African disaster.

Most stadiums had been completed late and in a rush, leaving little time to test them beforehand with friendly matches. This was dangerous. An international security official working in football told me that people in his profession barely worried about hooliganism, which might look spectacular on TV but rarely killed anyone. They worried about crushes in stadiums.

My uncle and some of my cousins had tickets for the game. Inside Soccer City, they got stuck in a tunnel full of people. There was some sort of obstacle at the front, so nobody could move forward. Thing got claustrophobic. The doors on the sides of the tunnel wouldn't open. Then, just as people began to panic, somebody unlocked a side door and everyone was able to pour out. Nobody died.

All the different South Africas turned on their TV sets to see the Bafana literally dance onto the field. Rugby-loving white Afrikaners had, as far as I could tell, never supplied a single Bafana player, yet viewing figures for the game on the Afrikaans channel were three times the previous record for a football match. The Grace Bible Church in Pimville Zone 1 in Soweto screened the game to 4,000 congregants, many of them tooting the vuvuzelas that had spread far beyond South African football. 'We have vuvuzela celebrations every Sunday,' the church organiser, Edwin Tshabalala, told the *Financial Times*.

Ten minutes after half-time, another Tshabalala from Soweto, the Chiefs' midfielder Siphiwe, smacked a left-footed drive into the top corner of the Mexican net. It was the kind of goal that everyone who ever kicked a football has dreamed of scoring at a World Cup. Tshabalala would spend his career in the South African league, bar a brief unsuccessful spell at a small Turkish club. In most people's memories, his life is forever condensed into one shot. He had given the world a glimpse of the black South African football tradition, nurtured on all those Saturdays in Orlando Stadium.

Soon after, there was one last tribute to the old style: 'Tico' Modise feigned to pass but instead swept his boot back and forth in the air over the ball. The pointless 'shibobo' slowed down a Bafana attack, but it drove the crowd wild.

Otherwise, South Africa's manager, Carlos Alberto Parreira, had succeeded in replacing 'ticky-ticky' with adult international football, meaning that the Bafana had become as boring and almost as competent as everyone else. In the stands, too, South Africa had buried its football tradition. The 'Zuuu!' 'Zuuu!' of the vuvuzelas droned all match. The unvarying sound switched off the game's emotional thermostat, because you couldn't tell whether the fans were approving or booing the action. The vuvuzelas would remain the ambient sound of the tournament, so much so that spectators were soon being offered earplugs.

In the closing minutes, Mexico equalised, and the game finished 1-1.

SABC TV studio and Garden Court hotel, 12 June 2010

I rose at dawn to go to the South African Broadcasting Company TV studios. The public broadcaster had invited me onto a morning show to talk about an article I'd written, in which I argued that the non-white Bafana were still handicapped by apartheid.

South Africa's white sportspeople were, in the beloved phrase, 'world class'. The rugby team (who would come to cheer on the Bafana in their match against Uruguay) were world champions. The cricketers were winning in the West Indies. White golfers like Ernie Els were world-beaters. No wonder, because they had all been nurtured on far more resources than the Bafana. The most basic resources are food and healthcare. Every player in the squad had been born during apartheid. Half the starters against Mexico were 1.75m tall or shorter – a freakishly undersized team by international standards.

Poverty hurts sporting performance in myriad other ways. Poor countries tend to underinvest in grassroots sport. Many talented South African footballers were spotted late, and received little good coaching. Modise, for example, had played for tiny and now defunct clubs in the poor Limpopo region until he was twenty-three. With better early coaching, he would have been better.

Apartheid also isolated black South Africans from global best practice. Imagine if they had learned perfect English at school, travelled abroad, and been able to benchmark themselves against the world's best athletes. Those divides hadn't magically disappeared with Mandela's inauguration in 1994. In 2010, white kids still received dedicated coaching on well-groomed school playing fields.

SABC received such a flood of emails for and against my

argument that they invited me back the next Saturday. The emails seemed to divide fairly neatly along ethnic lines. Most black South African commenters agreed with me, even if they thought I was stating the obvious. Most white viewers were outraged. One man with an Afrikaner name wrote to SABC:

> Luckily the majority of SA was sleeping this morning when Simon Kuper was on air … How can he make a statement on apartheid and the size of Soccer players on air. We in SA sit in a very tender situation regarding the apartheid issue as well as politics and he makes a ridiculous statement on the size of players.
>
> I have personally done research on the size of athletes and sports people (The revolution of Athletes). Simon Kuper's statement is the biggest load of nonsense I have ever heard!!!

Many whites believed that sixteen years after the abolition of apartheid, it was absurd to whine about its legacy. They certainly didn't want to hear this garbage at a moment of national unity. I spoke to several South African whites who placed the Bafana's shortcomings in the context of the country's long-running argument over 'standards'. Conservative whites liked to say that there were absolute, colour-blind standards. You had to meet them, whether you were a student, a civil servant or a footballer. These people assumed that they themselves met standards; the Bafana didn't.

Some black South Africans dismissed white talk about standards as 'racism'. Others made a different point: true, the Bafana didn't meet international standards but that was because they hadn't been given the resources even to know what those standards were.

I returned from that first appearance on SABC to another allegory of South African race relations. My seventy-six-year-old aunt Ruth had come to meet me for breakfast in my hotel. She was possibly the most old-fashioned person in South Africa. She didn't have a TV in her flat, nor almost any other item post-dating

1960. She had never used the internet. She quietly disapproved of black rule and usually tried to pretend it hadn't happened. She had never watched a football match in her life, not even (obviously) on TV.

I found her in the lobby staring at a group of black cleaners and other female hotel staff, who were dancing with the grace of a professional troupe. Possibly on their own initiative, they had dressed up in Bafana gear and were singing South African harmonies, pitch- and word-perfect. Nowhere in Europe could a randomly assembled group of twenty women have matched the performance. Several foreign TV crews were filming them. (Journalists love 'colour' that conveniently happens inside a media hotel.)

I expected Ruth to be scornful. The only culture she respected was made by dead white writers. But when I kissed her hello, she barely glanced at me. Eyes fixed on the women, she said, 'I want to burst into tears.' When she said, 'I want to join in', I was even more surprised. Then, when the women sang the national anthem, 'Nkosi Sikelel' iAfrika', with lyrics in five languages, despised by conservative whites as a revolutionary song, she sang along.

The World Cup was turning Ruth into a new South African. She had adorned her car with a South African flag, and when she drove around town, black people cheered her on with cries of, 'Gogo, gogo!' ('Grandma, grandma!') They appreciated her embracing their shared country.

Ruth was as wealthy as a European, whereas the cleaners were probably almost as poor as Mozambicans. Somehow, though, the World Cup was connecting these people. The tournament was shaping up to be what South Africans called a 'rainbow moment': one of those tableaux of reconciliation that the country did so well, when all colours of their 'Rainbow Nation' briefly mixed. Once it ended, some people would still live like Europeans and others like Mozambicans, but perhaps a little of that brief experience of togetherness might stick.

Argentina-Nigeria, Ellis Park, Johannesburg, 12 June 2010

After breakfast, I took the media shuttle to Argentina-Nigeria.

So much for an 'African' World Cup: we were a short walk from Hillbrow, which was practically a Nigerian fiefdom, yet the stands were full of Argentinian flags. Well-off South Africans who never watched Chiefs or Pirates but followed European football on cable TV had come out for Leo Messi.

During Argentina's 1-0 victory, my eye kept being drawn to a little figure by their dugout: Diego Maradona, who was cavorting like a well-oiled fan cheering on his team over an *asado* with mates back in Buenos Aires. He sprinted along the touchline with dribbling players, held his head after every Argentinian chance or illegally appealed for a yellow card when Messi was fouled.

Maradona had appeared here in a new incarnation. He looked like a bearded hermit who had just been discovered after forty years living off cheeseburgers on a desert island, then washed, given several watches, poured into a posh grey suit and made coach of Argentina.

He wasn't really a coach. Someone in the press box remarked that Argentina played like an NFL team: an 'offense' and a 'defense' that performed in splendid isolation from each other, plus a quarterback, Messi, who was forever getting 'sacked' by massive opponents.

The sight of Maradona meant more to me than the game itself. The World Cup is an unending story that accompanies us through our lives. Maradona had been one of the main characters since 1978, when the seventeen-year-old controversially wasn't picked for Argentina's home World Cup. He was supposed to star in 1982, but exited with a red card after kicking the Brazilian Batista in the balls. In 1986 he won the tournament almost single-handed. In 1990 he accused FIFA of rigging it against him. In 1994, he was banned for drugs. In 2006 he was reborn as an ordinary supporter, an Argentinian shirt strained across his belly, bouncing up and down on the terraces as he sang along to 'If you don't jump you're an Englishman'. (The peculiarity of Argentinian fans is that they live the game with their entire body.)

It was a comfort to see him back. Usually it's only teams and their idiosyncrasies (a hapless England letting down an over-excited nation) that recur at every tournament. Maradona, along with his enemy Sepp Blatter, was practically the only ever-present character. Everything around you in life changes, people die, but the World Cup always returns, in an eternal cycle, with the same team shirts and a new version of Maradona, and when you're watching you become a child again.

Johannesburg, June–July 2010

Every World Cup, I'm awed by fans who have spent fortunes to experience what we journalists are paid to do – but in South Africa, I was especially awed by people who travelled to a danger-ous country at the bottom of the earth in midwinter.

There weren't many of them, even if you counted the Chinese people flown in by North Korea to pose as its supporters. (The only genuine fan of the Hermit Kingdom I spotted was a South Korean journalist urging them on from the media stand.) The largest single group of visiting fans were from the US. Then there were surprising numbers of Latin Americans, benefiting from the first World Cup in the southern hemisphere since 1978. Many stayed in cut-price Soweto, just down the road from Soccer City. Mookho Lebelo, owner of Mookho's Bed and Breakfast in Soweto, reported that business was up 50 per cent.

Latin Americans found South Africa instantly recognisable. As in Brazil or Mexico, light-skinned people lived in big houses while dark-skinned people generally didn't. Just as at home, socialising occurred in shopping malls. And like much of Latin America, South Africa didn't feel safe.

Visitors from the northern hemisphere rarely ventured outside white South Africa. Even in the rich business district of Sandton, whose whole *raison d'être* was its safety, some American journal-ists went around with bodyguards. To the Japanese, arriving from the world's safest country, all of South Africa felt terrifying.

In stadiums, fans of opposing teams sat together blowing vuvuzelas in unison (if not in harmony). But there was one thing missing from the tournament. At my previous World Cups, the party had generally been better than the football. After a match, people would catch another game in a bar, or walk the streets gawking at all the fans from everywhere. Bulgarians would run into Australians or Chileans, and they'd chat with immediate understanding, because everyone cared about the same thing.

In Johannesburg, I never found the party. Wandering crime-ridden streets at night wasn't an option, and the city had barely any public spaces beyond a few thinly populated 'FIFA fan parks' for lovers of Arctic weather. So after matches, South Africans mooched home in their winter 'beanie' hats, while visitors went back to their hotels and thawed out.

There were empty seats at most games, especially in the VIP zones reserved for sponsors. Thinking back to my breakfast with the sponsor in Munich in 2004, I suspect that companies like his hadn't dare invite clients to South Africa. Many seats seemed to be filled by local school groups, who had presumably been given free tickets. The promised tourist invasion didn't happen.

France-Mexico, Polokwane, 17 June 2010

In the changing room at half-time during France's hopeless 2-0 defeat, the forward Nicolas Anelka shouted at his coach, Raymond Domenech: '*Enculé*! [roughly, 'bugger']. Do it yourself then, with your shit team! Me, I'm quitting.' Since all those involved were French, what shocked Domenech most was that Anelka addressed him with the familiar '*tu*' instead of the formal '*vous*'.

France Football magazine had fretted beforehand that the French World Cup would be an 'awful, awful, awful remake of a calamitous Euro 2008' – but it was much worse than that. After Domenech and France's football federation expelled Anelka from the squad, the players, in a quintessentially French response, went on strike, in the middle of the tournament. The phrase, 'The bus of shame' – the bus that the team sat in one day, refusing to train – entered the French language. The affair was instantly racialised. Many white French people felt that their long-standing suspicions had been confirmed: these mostly non-white expat multimillionaires didn't love their country.

Domenech then blundered by reading out his players' declaration of the strike to the TV cameras – thereby associating himself publicly with a reviled act of which he disapproved. (His first reaction, on seeing the declaration, was to wonder who had written the long words for them.)

Next, France contrived to lose 2-1 to the Bafana, and were knocked out (together with the South Africans) in the group stage. The captain, Patrice Evra, fought with the fitness coach. And all this was just what became public. Imagine what happened in the privacy of their hotel (which was castigated by the French sports minister Rama Yade as too expensive, until it was revealed that her own cost even more). Rarely had a team offered so little entertainment on the pitch but so much off it. France were undisputed winners of the *Financial Times* worst team award, succeeding the US (1998), Saudi Arabia (2002) and Serbia (2006).

Domenech could have won the 2006 World Cup had Trezeguet's penalty in the shoot-out been an inch lower, yet he had long been disliked in France for his maddening ironic smile, his team's tedious football, and his quarrelsomeness. (In an 'only in France' episode, he once squabbled with a football magazine about deontology.) He returned from South Africa so despised that his three-year-old son asked him: 'Papa, are you going to go to prison?' But his players were even more despised. In 1982, the 'enemy' for most French fans had still been the Germans; now it was their own team.

After France's elimination, President Nicolas Sarkozy instituted an inquiry into *les Bleus*. The bitterness between population and players would last for years. In a poll in 2013, 82 per cent of French people said they had a negative opinion of the team. The French side of 2018 achieved something even bigger than winning the World Cup: they more or less won over their own country.

A conference centre in Sandton, 26 June 2010

A group of Brazilian government officials was on a 'study tour' of South Africa, hoping to get some tips for hosting the 2014 World Cup. In Sandton, South African organisers gave their guests a frank briefing. Dawn Robertson, a senior official of Gauteng province, which includes Johannesburg, told them: 'There are a lot of mistakes we made that you hopefully won't make.'

Gauteng is South Africa's economic powerhouse. Robertson said that in early 2009, she had reviewed the projected economic bonanza from the tournament for Gauteng, and realised that it wasn't going to bring the benefits that South Africa had been promising its citizens. The World Cup wouldn't make the country richer. In the end, the province had tried to make the best of things by treating the tournament 'almost like a thirty-day advertisement for Gauteng'.

I asked Robertson why the economic legacy hadn't materialised. She said, 'If you look at all the research about mega events, all the findings are that the economic returns are highly inflated by people hoping to profit from the events.' Yes – that's what almost any sports economist would have told South Africa before it bid to host the event.

Farouk Seedat was chief financial officer of the South African World Cup's local organising committee. A Brazilian from the Minas Gerais state government asked him whether South Africa had thought about the 'sustainability' of stadiums after the tournament.

Seedat laughed. 'That's a very difficult question.' He said the host cities had been made to draw up detailed business plans for the future of their stadiums. 'I guess the reality of that is: we will see in the next year or two or three whether in fact they have been realistic plans.' He admitted that a sustainable future would be especially 'challenging' for 'smaller host cities such as Nelspruit and Polokwane'.

A house in Oaklands, Johannesburg, 27 June 2010

The South African writer Njabulo Ndebele had grown fed up with the government's boasts about 'world-class' stadiums. What made the country 'world-class', he said, wasn't stadiums or a good football team; South Africa was world-class because it had talked its way out of civil war and into freedom – and had kept talking ever since. There was an endless national discussion in which everyone disagreed with everyone else but in which every person of every colour was respectfully heard.

It was in that spirit that the *Financial Times* gathered five smart South Africans around a table one morning to answer the question, 'Did South Africa win the World Cup?' Over coffee and pastries, we witnessed a world-class debate. One of our guests, Sanza Tshabalala, the DJ who had sold apples at Orlando Stadium back in the 1980s, put it best: 'I think we will always remain a talking nation.'

Our guests had come not as experts, but as South Africans. They were critical of their country, but never cynical. And there was one point all five kept returning to: pride.

'I think expressly black people feel proud,' said the black academic William Gumede. 'Sorry that I'm using "black". You can't talk that way in a sense, but there is the element of pride: the World Cup is being put together successfully, and black people predominantly could be seen as putting it together. Even if you don't have a job or a house, even if the new transport infrastructure is not serving you, there is still that sense of reverence around it.'

Ferial Haffajee, a newspaper editor of Indian-Malay origin, added: 'The subtext of the South African narrative is one of how [blacks] can't do it, "Look how they are messing up the government." And in fact, [during this World Cup] I see great moments of pride: "We can do it."'

This talk might have made no sense to Europeans. They never doubted that they could organise World Cups. But apartheid had told non-white South Africans from their first day at school that they were inherently less intelligent than whites. They were educated only for jobs as servants or unskilled labourers. They were taught to lack confidence. Now there was pride around the kitchen table because Africans had defied age-old stereotypes.

Had the World Cup been worth it? Haffajee said, 'I think rationally and fiscally, absolutely not. But emotionally, I wouldn't have missed it for the world.'

Stadium media centres and late-night highways, June–July 2010

I was forty, and no longer the wide-eyed young journalist of earlier World Cups. Most days in South Africa, I'd wake up tired, write my first article, board the media shuttle, spend hours crammed among hundreds of colleagues at the office – here called the 'stadium media centre' – catch bits of the early game on TV, queue for canteen food that was straight out of a British boarding school circa 1957, and then freeze on the 'media tribune' (as FIFA called the press stand) during a game like Paraguay-Japan (0-0, Paraguay winning on penalties).

I was also losing patience with my colleagues. During the group stages, half the media tribune would spend entire games catching up on emails. During one match, the Latin American journalist next to me made a long Skype call to his wife, without using headphones. I could barely hear the vuvuzelas. Finally I closed his laptop.

Many journalists weren't there for the match. They didn't know how to watch it. They only saw the action on the ball, whereas most of football happens off it. They had come to report the result and, above all, the post-match press conference.

There, the man of the match would be wheeled out by FIFA for about one and a half questions, which he would try not to answer. The coaches, because they had the only speaking parts in the drama, were treated as the main characters, their words and emotional states weighed as if they were Soviet and American leaders meeting at a Cold War summit. Journalists who didn't have a head for football tactics interrogated them about 'team spirit', 'motivation', 'momentum', or a team's supposed quest for 'revenge' for some ancient defeat.

Then there was the 'mixed zone', the place where ageing journalists would shout questions at passing footballers wearing big headphones. Often they didn't share a language anyway, though the Swiss players, the stars of the mixed zone, spoke about five each.*

The chief consolation was that with all the articles I was selling, it was the highest earning month of my four-year work cycle. I cracked on, knowing I'd be able to prioritise kids over work for months afterwards.

My German colleague Christoph Biermann, who sometimes chauffeured me to matches (one of my many handicaps is that I don't drive), told me that we were the lucky ones. Most Chinese journalists who were here couldn't get into games, he said. There weren't enough press tickets, and priority went to journalists from countries that were playing in the tournament. China hadn't qualified, but it had sent hundreds of journalists, so most of them were reduced to watching games on TV in the stadiums' media centres. One day, Christoph had seen the Chinese gather in a huddle just before kick-off. Then they suddenly stormed the staircase together, hoping to overwhelm the stewards and break into the stands. They failed, but Christoph admired them nonetheless.

He and I were driving down another late-night highway. I asked, 'Why are we here, watching mostly crappy football? What good does it do?' He said something like, 'Well, we're here, so we see more than people back home. We write what we honestly think, we're not trying to bullshit anyone, and we help our readers understand the World Cup a little bit better. That makes them

---

* The tournament's champion linguist was my old Dutch contact Boudewijn Zenden, who had gone from player in 1998 to pundit. One day, I saw him sitting in the stand at Wits University watching *Oranje* train, when an Asian TV crew came up and asked him for an interview. 'Where are you from?' asked Zenden. When they said, 'Indonesia', he switched into Bahasi Indonesian.

happier. So I don't think we're doing any harm, and perhaps it's even worthwhile.'

A dinner in Melville, Johannesburg, 1 July 2010

It had been billed as 'Africa's World Cup', but by this point, as the quarter-finals loomed, all the African teams but one had already been knocked out. The Bafana had become the first hosts in the tournament's history to be eliminated in the group stage. Only Ghana survived. They would face Uruguay the next day.

Over dinner, the great Cameroonian keeper Joseph-Antoine Bell tried to explain Africa's problem. As a teenager in Cameroon, he said, he had often played four matches a day, ferried on the back of someone's scooter from one to another. In those days there were plenty of open spaces in African cities to play football. But as the cities got built up, the spaces disappeared. That wasn't a problem in Europe, Bell said, because European kids played football in organised clubs. Africa, though, had very few clubs. (China and India had the same problem: there was almost nowhere in their new megacities to kick a ball.)

Look at the best African players, Bell continued. Didier Drogba had moved to France aged five. Samuel Eto'o had arrived in Europe as a teenager. Increasingly, African national teams were staffed by players who were born or at least raised in Europe, because only there could they learn top-class football. Barely any players in Cameroon's squad had even played a league match in Cameroon. Most African teams fielded players discarded by European countries. Cameroon's hapless left-back Benoît Assou-Ekotto had been born and raised in France. If he had been any good, France would have capped him. How, asked Bell, could Africans beat Europeans with European rejects? Africa might win a World Cup, he joked grimly, if it was allowed to field a single team, 'Africa'.

Uruguay-Ghana, quarter-final, Soccer
City, Johannesburg, 2 July 2010

In the last minute of extra time, with scores tied 1-1, a Ghana-ian header was flying towards Uruguay's goal. The ball travelled through the air long enough for everyone in Soccer City to realise the magnitude of the moment. If it went in, an African team would be in the last four of a World Cup for the first time. Almost the entire stadium was willing the ball into the net.

But Uruguay's brilliant young forward Luis Suárez threw up a hand and blocked the header on the goal line. The referee sent him off and awarded Ghana a penalty. Their captain, Stephen Appiah, handed the ball to Asamoah Gyan, saying: 'Make the whole of Africa proud.'

But Gyan's penalty pinged off the crossbar. On the touchline, Suárez erupted with joy. The game immediately went to a penalty shoot-out, and Uruguay won.

Suárez's handball encapsulated the injustice of football. It also summed up both Uruguayan and African football history. It remains one of the richest, most resonant moments I've seen at a World Cup.

Crowning a champion is just one of the tournament's many subplots – and one that concerns only five or six countries. Every World Cup is also about establishing several lead characters beside the Champion. There's the Clown – often England, striding in to strains of 'Rule, Britannia' and then slipping on a banana skin. There's the Beautiful Loser (the title for which Holland usually compete), the Worst Team, and the Cinderella, which in 2010 was Ghana.

In World Cups, as in cinema, the most compelling character is usually the Villain. Often the president of FIFA enters the tourna-ment as frontrunner for the title, and sometimes wins. But think of Toni Schumacher torpedoing Battiston in 1982, or Materazzi and Zidane competing for the role in 2006. In 1986 Maradona, beautifully, became Villain and Champion rolled into one, thanks to his 'Hand of God' goal against England.

Now Suárez, with his handball, had made himself the Villain

of 2010. A well-structured drama pits the main characters against each other, and here we had the Villain slaying Cinderella. Satisfyingly, Suárez embraced the role. 'I made the best save of the tournament,' he boasted.

And Uruguayans embraced him. Singing crowds welcomed him home to Montevideo. The great Uruguayan writer Eduardo Galeano praised his 'act of patriotic insanity', adding: 'He was expelled but his country wasn't.'

A nation of 3.5 million people that only impinges on international consciousness during World Cups, Uruguay expects its footballers to display an unironic willingness to die for the shirt. Uruguayans feel they can only beat bigger nations thanks to their fighting spirit – '*la garra charrúa*', as they call it, after the Charrúa tribe that once inhabited the territory of today's Uruguay and fought off foreign invaders. Suárez's handball embodied this spirit. Uruguayans felt that he had done the right thing. In fact, his teammate Jorge Fucile had tried to do it too, but his outstretched arm missed the Ghanaian header.

For Africans, the moment encapsulated their eternal disappointment in World Cups. After Cameroon reached the quarter-finals in 1990, it became a cliché to predict that one day an African team would lift the trophy. With hindsight, 1990 turned out to be not the beginning of the continent's rise, but the end.

Germany-Argentina, quarter-final, Cape Town, 3 July 2010

Impressively, Argentina had reached the quarter-final stage while playing without tactics. Maradona had built a system in which Messi typically received the ball on the halfway line, with nine opponents between him and the goal, and none of his teammates moving. Germany loved it. The last image of Maradona in South Africa was the obese little man weeping beside the dugout in his magnificent suit as his team went out 4-0.

Postscript

That match would prove the end of Maradona's high-level managerial career. What followed, over several months, was an embarrassing, desperate and tawdry cycle of rejections and what British tabloids call 'Come-And-Get-Me Pleas'.

For instance, the Socceroo Robbie Slater suggested, for reasons known only to himself, that Australia should appoint Maradona as head coach. 'Are you really serious?' responded Australia's technical director Han Berger. 'You only have to take a look at YouTube, where there is a clip of Maradona at the World Cup at training, participating in a small-sided game with some players while smoking a cigar.' Australia didn't hire Maradona.

In October 2010 he turned fifty. 'It is the saddest birthday of my life,' he told Argentina's sports daily *Olé*. 'The best gift would have been [continuing with] the national team.'

Rumours in the media linked him with Boca Juniors. He said, 'I would die to be Boca's coach,' but Boca appointed someone called Falcioni instead. Maradona tried to respond gracefully: 'I wish him the best, but for me, he shouldn't be there.' He added that Boca's president 'cannot tell a football from a rugby ball, and he chose Falcioni – a *keeper*. I thought they were going to call me.'

Next, Blackburn Rovers didn't hire Maradona. Anuradha Desai, chairwoman of the club's Indian owners Venky's, clarified: 'He is not being considered, not now and forever in the future.'

Aston Villa, Iran and every other mooted destination didn't want Maradona either. He ended up spending a few peaceful years in a house packed with TV sets in the provinces of the United Arab Emirates. After stops at small clubs in Belarus and Mexico, in 2019 he returned to Argentina, where he was treated for alcohol dependency. Early in November 2020 he underwent brain surgery. On 25 November, aged sixty, he suffered a fatal heart attack while asleep – in a collapsing country, during the coronavirus pandemic. His lawyer said later that the ambulance had taken more than half an hour to reach his house. Argentina's dysfunction may have helped kill the country's greatest son. His wake was abandoned prematurely when some of the tens of thousands of mourners clashed with police.

Netherlands-Uruguay, semi-final, Cape Town, 6 July 2010

The semi-final in Cape Town was the match for which the South African authorities had decided to build a World Cup stadium across six city blocks on the oceanfront. I'm not sure it was worth it: neither team was world-class, and there were many empty seats. I sat in the media tribune watching my team, *Oranje*, win 3-2 to reach the World Cup final, and I was so anxious that I spent the whole game wishing it was over. I had become a fan again – and it sucked.

Watching your team play at the World Cup is like watching your child sit a test that you are sure they will fail; you know your own players too well to have faith in them. Khalid Boulahrouz, to any Dutch fan, was the caveman who had sat on the bench at Chelsea and then at Seville, and by 2010 was sitting on the bench at Stuttgart. John Heitinga thumped clearances like a Sheffield United centre-back in 1983. And after thirty-five-year-old Gio van Bronckhorst opened the scoring against Uruguay with a screamer into the top corner from thirty yards, Dutch fans struggled to recall him ever doing that for sorry Feyenoord Rotterdam. Meanwhile Uruguay's Diego Forlán looked to me like an infallible force from a more advanced universe.

The other reason why life is anxiety-inducing for fans of teams like *Oranje* – for almost all teams, in fact – is our history of failure. In the end, something always goes wrong. I watched Uruguay-Holland with all of Dutch football history in my head. I had flashbacks to West Germany-Holland in 1974, Argentina-Holland in 1978, Brazil-Holland in 1998, Russia-Holland in 2008 and so on.

This time, *Oranje* somehow clung on. The coming Sunday would probably be the only time in my life that I'd sit in the stands watching my team play in a World Cup final. It was going to be horrible.

Bilbao and Johannesburg, 8–11 July 2010

A Basque economist I knew, Ignacio Palacios-Huerta, was the world's leading expert on penalties.* He maintained a database of thousands of kicks by different penalty takers, and he ran complicated statistical tests to predict each taker's next kick: left or right side, high or low, waiting for the keeper to move or not, and so on.

When Holland reached the final, I emailed a Dutch FA official I knew. I said Ignacio was willing to write the Dutch a penalty report on Spain, for free. Was the official interested?

Ignacio – who, as a Basque, was perfectly happy to scheme against Spain – pulled two all-nighters to write the report. I emailed it to the Dutch. Their goalkeeping coach Ruud Hesp wrote back, the day of the final: 'It's a report we can use perfectly.'

A gated villa in northern Johannesburg, 10 July 2010

On the morning of the final, I went for breakfast at the house of Essop Pahad, the government minister and member of South Africa's local organising committee. Three years earlier in De Tuynhuys, he had told me: 'We will organise, I promise you, a world-class World Cup.' This morning, over Indian scrambled egg and English tea, I asked him whether they had done it.

It had started badly, he admitted, with the traffic jams to the opening match, South Africa-Mexico. The bus drivers carrying fans and journalists for some reason didn't use the special fast lanes that the planners had reserved for them, and ordinary traffic filled the lanes. Travelling to the stadium from central Johannesburg took nearly three hours. Worse, by that point two Portuguese journalists and one Spaniard who had come to cover the tournament had been robbed at gunpoint in their hotel.

But after that, said Pahad, the glitches were mostly sorted out. For the next month, the fast lanes worked. So did almost

---

* There is a longer account of this story in my book *Soccernomics*, written with Stefan Szymanski.

everything else. There was only one report of shots being fired at a foreign visitor to the tournament: the American David James Bueche was shot and wounded in Sandton as he walked to his hotel one night. That was less carnage than expected, given South Africa's estimated fifty murders a day.

By that last weekend of the tournament, almost every foreign observer agreed: South Africa's World Cup, the planet's most public logistical challenge, had been a success. It may not have been worth it, it had distracted the government from bigger issues, it had been sold to the population with economic lies, and it had cost too much, but South Africa had pulled it off.

Netherlands-Spain, World Cup final, Soccer City, Johannesburg, 11 July 2010

The Dutch friend with whom I'd watched Belgium-USSR on TV in 1986, and with whom I'd sworn to go to the 1990 World Cup, was landing in Johannesburg this morning in an orange suit to watch the final. The trip was costing him €3,500, and he was flying home straight after the game. I didn't have a minute free to meet him, but I hoped that *Oranje* would make it worth his while.

I went to say goodbye to my grandmother, and found her lying in bed as usual. She told me she had given instructions that if she died during the World Cup, she wanted an unobtrusive funeral. I said, 'If you're planning to die during the World Cup, you'd better hurry up. You've only got about ten hours left.'

I was flying home straight after the final, with no plans to return to South Africa. She and I were close, and I didn't know how to part for probably the last time. She said, 'Don't mourn me.' I tried to sidestep the emotion. 'Maybe I'll see you again,' I said.

'You won't,' she said.

She was quite right. She died four months later.

I went back to my hotel, packed, checked out, and took the

media shuttle to Soccer City. Near the stadium it got stuck in an endless jam, and I had to walk the last few minutes.

When I got to the media stand, I witnessed what may have been the most South African moment of the tournament: a fat middle-aged English journalist who couldn't find his seat was screaming abuse at a young black steward. (It's common for journalists to crack up towards the end of a World Cup.) The steward didn't respond and led him to his seat, but then returned a minute or two later with her supervisor, an older black woman.

The supervisor addressed the journalist: 'I hear that you were not polite to my colleague.'

He tried to argue, but she rapidly defeated him. He admitted that he had misbehaved. Then she told him: 'Now you will apologise to my colleague.'

And the Englishman literally got on his knees before the young woman, and said, 'I am very sorry.'

Black South Africans had learned to value dignity.

The point of the Dutch team isn't to win trophies – it's to play Dutch football. And so the final turned into a national argument about what kind of nation the Netherlands should be. Everyone involved took sides, including me.

The Dutch had bored their way to the final playing counter-attacking football – the new International Style, as it were. Ditching their traditional system of wingers, they fielded two defensive midfielders. It was as if seventeenth-century Dutch Calvinists had decided to drop predestination because it no longer worked.

Confusingly, the team that were exhibiting the most traditional version of fast-passing, attacking Dutch *totaalvoetbal* were Holland's opponents in the final, Spain. The Spaniards had begun cross-breeding with Dutch football in 1988, when Johan Cruyff, father of the Dutch style, became manager of Barcelona and instituted the system from the club's first team all the way down to the under-eights. Barça's youth academy, the Masía, provided about half the Spanish team that played in the 2010 final. David Winner, author of *Brilliant Orange: The Neurotic Genius of Dutch Football*, diagnosed the match as a case of 'Jungian mirroring': 'Holland's path to the world title is blocked by the more authentic version of their better selves.'

Admittedly the Spaniards hadn't produced much high-grade *totaalvoetbal* during their subpar World Cup, but at least they were trying to, whereas the Dutch, as foreshadowed in that militaristic Nike ad, had abjured their tradition. They didn't even seem to want to be morally superior any more.

That night, the Dutch played such an ugly game that I gradually stopped supporting them. I no longer wanted them to win. When I explained this later to fans from other countries, they found it absurd: how could you not support your team in a World Cup final? But Holland were a style of football. When they stopped being Holland, I stopped being a fan.

The players did show that they were still the masters of one element of Dutch tradition: the intellectual understanding of passing and positioning. They delivered a masterclass in how to neutralise a better team. At times, I couldn't help but be proud of a little country that had reached its third World Cup final in thirty-six years with several mediocre players. Even their clogging was intelligent (leaving aside Nigel de Jong's karate kick in the chest of Xabi Alonso, for which he somehow wasn't sent off). The Dutch disrupted Spain's passing with constant fouls in midfield, hardly ever giving away free kicks in dangerous areas. They alternated their fouls so well that almost every Dutchman ended the game with a yellow card of his own; only in extra time did one player, Heitinga, get his second.

Journalists hate extra time. How to write a report on a World Cup final that's still tied 0-0? My editors in London kept imploring me to file before the game ended. They said they'd add the result afterwards. I couldn't do it, so I missed the paper's main deadline.

There were only minutes left to play before a penalty shoot-out. Sitting in the stands, I reread Ignacio's report on my laptop. He wrote that Fernando Torres, who was the only recognised Spanish penalty taker still on the field, hit three-quarters of his penalties along the ground. Whichever corner the Dutch keeper

Maarten Stekelenburg chose, he had to get to ground immediately. What would the other Spanish kickers do – the ones who never normally took penalties? Ignacio wrote that inexperienced right-footed penalty takers tended to shoot to the keeper's right, because that was the most natural penalty to hit. Skimming the report, I fantasised about helping my team win the World Cup.

Then, with four minutes left in extra time, Andrés Iniesta scored. I reacted not as a fan, but as a journalist: thank God. Finally I could file the damn match report, race to the plane and see my family after five weeks of nonstop work. I was done with the South African World Cup.

Postscript

It turned out that many other Dutch fans had also withdrawn their support during the final. They felt that Nigel de Jong had delivered a karate kick to the chest of a great tradition. Most significantly, the father of Dutch football agreed. 'I thought my country would never dare to play like this and would never give up its own way of playing,' Johan Cruyff said afterwards. 'Even without great players like in the past, a team has its own style. It saddens me that I was wrong and Holland chose this awful way to bring home the title. This nasty, vulgar, hard, closed game that wasn't watchable and was barely football any more, yes, with that they could trouble Spain. If that satisfies them, OK, but they lost anyway. They played anti-football.'

That was true, but lots of Dutch people embraced anti-football. Two days after the final, over 600,000 fans gathered in Amsterdam to welcome the dirty losers home. Most of them were under forty, people who knew Cruyff only as an old whinger on telly. They didn't see why Holland should play holier-than-thou football. They thought a World Cup was about winning.

Years after the final, I interviewed the Spanish defender Gerard Piqué. He had broken into the first team at Barcelona, his home-town club, in 2008, aged twenty-one. By 2010 he had won the Spanish league, the Champions League and the World Cup. He told me, 'It all happened so quickly that I found winning normal. When I began to lose, I started to understand everything I had won. It was as if you'd go to play a competition like the World Cup or the league, and you were going to win it. You start winning everything and you think, "You're the best and you must win. You can't waste this opportunity." Because we were going at such a speed that we'd beat any team put in front of us.'

'The money is coming!' Sowetans had cheered when South Africa was awarded the World Cup in 2004. Now it was time to tot up what the tournament had done for the country.

In 2009, the management consultancy Grant Thornton – a serial producer of upbeat economic forecasts about the World Cup – had predicted that the tournament would draw 483,000 foreign visitors. A retrospective study based on official South African statistics, co-authored by my co-writer Stefan Szymanski with his fellow economists Thomas Peeters and Victor Matheson, estimated that the country had received only 220,000 additional visitors in June and July 2010. That was less than half Grant Thornton's forecast. But it was almost precisely the total of 221,000 'international' visitors predicted in South Africa's original 2004 bid book for a frugal World Cup that had later been 'disappeared'.

The tournament had only one great financial beneficiary: FIFA. The federation reported a profit of $631 million from the 2007–2010 World Cup cycle, having expected a loss. Sepp Blatter told me: 'Interestingly, the World Cup in South Africa was a very big economic success for FIFA too, better than the World Cup in Germany.'

FIFA didn't shower that windfall on South Africa, or on poor kids anywhere else in the world who dreamed of playing on an actual football pitch. Ken Bensinger writes in his book *Red Card*: 'By some estimates, FIFA donated less than one-tenth of one per cent of its profits from the tournament.'

South Africa had few football fields for ordinary people, but it was now saddled with ten 'world-class' stadiums – at least eight more than it needed, given that only Chiefs and Pirates could draw large regular crowds. In October 2010, the French company SAIL Stadefrance announced that it was pulling out of its thirty-year lease to operate Cape Town's stadium at Green Point, even before the lease had taken effect. The company admitted it had under-estimated the cost of running Green Point. The stadium didn't seem capable of paying its own way, but it would be sitting there by the ocean for decades to come.

South Africa's president Jacob Zuma offered reassurance: 'There are a number of plans in place to make the stadiums profitable after the last whistle blows.' For instance, South Africa was thinking of bidding to host the 2020 Olympics. Even more excitingly: 'We are also looking into getting foreign soccer stars, especially during the European league season, to come play here.' What did the 2010 World Cup leave behind? I would have to come back one day and find out.

*

Istanbul interlude, September 2010

The first surprise of my visit: Guus Hiddink, coach of Turkey, was in Turkey! That didn't happen often, according to Turkish media, but I found the Dutchman in a five-star hotel, his natural habitat, drinking his traditional beverage, a cappuccino, dressed in his usual polo shirt adorned with a national flag. This morning, it was Turkey's. A Dutch magazine had sent me here to interview him.

Hiddink had watched the recent World Cup with family and friends at home in the Netherlands. I asked where he stood in the argument about *Oranje*'s play. He admitted: 'I watched, but I realised I wasn't watching eagerly. Around me in the house, I saw disappointed people. I had no feeling with it at all.'

Then the Turkish press arrived for his press conference, and Hiddink delivered his message: Belgium, the next day's opponents, were a fantastic team. Admittedly, they hadn't qualified for the 2010 World Cup, or for Euro 2008, or in fact for any tournament since 2002, but nobody should underestimate their practically unknown players.

The clash of titans was scheduled for the Fenerbahce stadium, in the Asian part of Istanbul. Crossing the Bosporus by ferry is football's most scenic journey, providing you aren't a poor commuter from Asia for whom this is part of your daily four-hour odyssey. The one bit of Istanbul where there are no traffic jams – for now – is the river.

The stadium was packed with Turks, plus thirteen visiting Belgian supporters. That was a decent turnout: at some away games, the Belgian contingent consisted of Ludo Rollenberg, the Red Devils' only diehard fan. Some of the national team's matches in this era weren't shown live on Belgian television because hardly anyone was interested. In Istanbul, when the Belgian anthem was played, some Turks whistled through it, but the Belgian fans and players listened politely.

The English saying was, 'If they're good enough, they are old enough.' The Belgians had taken this a step further: even if they weren't good enough, they were old enough. Players like Vincent Kompany, Jan Vertonghen, Mousa Dembélé and Thomas Vermaelen had been losing with Belgium for years. Fresh-faced youngsters such as Marouane Fellaini, Toby Alderweireld, and seventeen-year-old Romelu Lukaku looked set to be part of Belgian failures for years to come. Against Turkey, the Devils were hanging on at 1-1 when Kompany was sent off. The dictum that ten men sometimes defend better than eleven didn't apply to the Belgians; with barely an hour gone, they looked shattered. Vast gaps opened all over the field, like in an amateur game. Two minutes after Kompany's dismissal, two Belgians mowed over a Turkish cross and Semih Senturk made it 2-1. A minute later, Turkey's keeper came running out of his goal for a dead ball as if he had an urgent appointment at the other end of the field, and Daniel van Buyten nodded it into the empty net.

Twelve minutes from time, a Turkish shot took a deflection

off Fellaini's leg or hair and into the net: 3-2. Belgium were going to miss another tournament. At the press conference, their coach Georges Leekens lamented, in English: 'The happy sight of the world and in heaven is not coming to us at this moment.'

Then it was Hiddink's turn. How had he managed to beat this top team? 'They are dangerous on corners and free kicks,' he revealed. 'For the rest, not so much.'

I wrote a piece for a Dutch magazine mocking the poor Belgians. I didn't realise that I'd seen the future. Ten of the squad who lost that day in Istanbul, including young Axel Witsel and Eden Hazard on the bench, ended up amassing eighty or more caps each. Vertonghen reached 157. Add on Thibaut Courtois, Dries Mertens and Kevin De Bruyne, who all debuted for Belgium in 2010 or 2011 and each accumulated over a century of caps, and this became the most experienced generation of any international team in history. These men, born in one little country between 1985 and 1993, played together so often, from national youth teams onwards, that they developed the understanding of a club side. The Belgian team that finished third at the 2018 World Cup – and could have won it – featured eight of the losers of Istanbul.

12

In Search of the World Cup 2010: Return to South Africa, 2024

Johannesburg, November 2024

Driving from the airport into the city, I passed a flowerbed at Settlers Park whose flowers still spelled out the magic number: '2010'. Somebody remembered.

My hotel was around the corner from my late grandmother's flat, in the northern suburbs of Johannesburg. The tranquil avenues overhung by trees hadn't changed much since my childhood visits during apartheid. True, there were some ugly new office buildings, housing white businesses that had fled the now almost entirely black former central business district. But otherwise, the northern suburbs still looked like they did back in 1984: low-slung houses with pools and gardens and mostly white inhabitants sheltering behind security walls in glorious sunshine. As in 1984, almost everyone puttering past in cars was white, while the maids, cleaners and security guards walking along the pavements, often for miles, were black.

I had come back to look for the legacy of the 2010 World Cup. My googling beforehand hadn't revealed much. Almost every South African government report or newspaper article that mentioned the tournament's 'legacy' had been written before the World Cup ended.

I couldn't see any legacy in international league tables. In September 2010, after the World Cup, the Bafana stood 58th in FIFA's men's rankings. By the time I landed in 2024, they had risen to 57th. In the Anholt-Ipsos Nation Brands Index, which measures the 'soft power' of different countries, South Africa had ranked 35th in 2009. By 2023, it was 42nd. Nor had the World Cup made the country a more attractive destination: foreign investment in 2023 was below the annual average for the 2007–2014 period.

I wanted to find South African officials whom I'd talked to in the years to 2010, and ask them how they now saw the tournament. Essop Pahad had died in 2023, but Danny Jordaan, chief organiser of the World Cup, was still president of the South African Football Association. He had always helped me out. I sent him a WhatsApp asking to meet, but he didn't reply. I phoned and messaged him repeatedly, but he still didn't get back to me.

I finally understood when I read that he had been arrested and charged with fraud a week before I'd landed in South Africa. Jordaan stood accused of spending R1.3 million of SAFA's resources for his own use, including hiring a public relations firm to protect his image a month after a former ANC MP accused him of rape. He denied all charges. Released on bail, he continued to run SAFA. His PR campaign claimed that Irvin 'Iron Duke' Khoza – by this time seventy-six years old, but still running both Orlando Pirates and the Premier Soccer League – was colluding in a plot to unseat him. Meanwhile, South Africa's sports minister Gayton McKenzie, a convicted former gang boss who had spent seven years in prison before remaking himself as a motivational speaker, announced that he was investigating SAFA.

The South African economy had barely grown since 2010, and life for most South Africans remained tough. I had kept in touch with a granddaughter of Nester's, my grandmother's late maid. She told me about her struggles to find decent-paying work, put her child through school, and traverse Johannesburg without a car. She said that she sometimes felt like giving up.

Polokwane, late November 2024

From Johannesburg I travelled 200 miles north-east to the 2010 host city of Polokwane, to see what the tournament had left behind there. I'd timed my visit to coincide with two league games being played in the city's World Cup stadium, including a visit from the Kaizer Chiefs.

Polokwane (known during apartheid as Pietersburg) was a faded town baking in the heat of the rural Limpopo province. The town centre was mostly white, and the outskirts black. The region was dry at the best of times, but when I arrived it was suffering its worst drought in a century. Many people were going hungry. Driving around, I saw the herds of goats that were replacing cows because their willingness to eat almost anything made them more climate-resistant. Climate change had become South Africa's new challenge, and the government was doing about as little to adapt to it as it had done to tackle AIDS. These issues weren't priorities, as the World Cup had been.

Polokwane, a low-slung city, was overlooked by one large, even magnificent structure: the Peter Mokaba Stadium, built for the World Cup. It could seat 46,000 people, though its full capacity hadn't been needed during the tournament. It had hosted four matches, all group games: Algeria-Slovenia (0-1), France-Mexico (0-2), Greece-Argentina (0-2), and as a grand finale, Paraguay-New Zealand (0-0). The largest crowd, drawn by Messi's Argentina, had been 38,891. I suspect that even that wasn't an economic bonanza to Polokwane, as most of the spectators probably drove up from Johannesburg for the day.

The stadium had since been handed over to club football, but the problem – foreseeable in 2010 – was that the Limpopo didn't have any popular football clubs. Like almost everywhere else in South Africa, most fans here supported Chiefs or Pirates, and you couldn't lure them up to the Peter Mokaba every week. Polokwane's stadium authorities offered the Chiefs financial sweeteners to play there, but stadium authorities around the country were doing the same thing.*

---

* Cape Town, a much bigger city than Polokwane, had managed to find more diverse uses for its World Cup stadium. As of 2025, Green Point, renamed DHL Stadium, is a regular venue for sports and concerts in large part because

In Polokwane I visited a football official called Abel Rakoma in his municipal office. He drove me two minutes to his other government office, where he reminisced about the city's World Cup: 'It was awesome!' At one match, a guy had climbed a floodlight pylon to watch, refusing entreaties from the police to come down. 'I think he was simply driven by excitement,' reflected Rakoma.

I told him that South African football looked to me much like it had twenty years earlier, before the country got the World Cup, still with only two clubs that anyone cared about.

'It is,' agreed Rakoma.

I said that South Africa still wasn't even a leading African football nation.

'No, it's not,' he agreed.

Then he closed his eyes. After a while I realised that he had fallen asleep, so I left.

Sekhukhune United-TS Galaxy, Peter Mokaba Stadium, Polokwane, 26 November 2024

Over two successive nights, the stadium was hosting league games. The four teams involved were staying at the little Dorp Inn opposite the ground. I went to the hotel bar to meet a football official named Ndahve Ramakuela, and during my long wait for him, I watched a team of merry young footballers splash around in the swimming pool. I presumed they would be playing in the next evening's match, not the one kicking off in just over an hour.

When Ramakuela showed up, he explained why Polokwane had needed a World Cup stadium. Admittedly, he said, the city already had a stadium before 2010. In fact, it was still standing – he jerked a thumb at a floodlight pylon, visible from the hotel bar. But that ground seated only 15,000, enough for the demands

---

it exists. If it hadn't, these events would have been held somewhere else in town. But when local football teams play at the DHL, the stands are usually almost empty.

of local football but not for a World Cup. So they had built the Mokaba about a mile away. In an alternative universe, they would have spent the money on homes, or schools.

Ramakuela told the same upbeat story about the World Cup that I'd heard from other officials: a happy time of nation-building for South Africa, and of personal development for themselves. He called the tournament 'one of the most valuable experiences I ever had'. The Mokaba stadium was still heavily used, he said, hosting eight matches in just the last month. In short, it was all good.

Before I crossed the road to the game, I asked if there was anything in particular I should look out for in the stadium. Suddenly he changed tack: 'You'll notice that it looks like a misfit to have small teams playing in a big facility in front of 3,000 people, when they could have played in a smaller stadium.' He pointed again at the old ground behind us, and asked rhetorically: 'So is there value in it?'

Smaller South African clubs continued to be born and to die like fruit flies, and tonight's match was between two new creations. Sekhukhune had emerged from an older club in 2020, while TS Galaxy had been founded in 2015, and were named for their owner Tim Sukazi.

In theory the game was a Limpopo derby, but when I walked up to the vast stadium twenty minutes before kick-off, there was barely another spectator in sight. I remembered Essop Pahad's prediction in 2007, when I'd asked why towns like Polokwane needed big stadiums: 'I think it's an unchallengeable fact that the popularity of soccer is just going to grow and grow, not just in South Africa but in the world.'

Maintaining the vast stadium, and opening it for games, cost money. Tonight there were police cars, security guards, and a medical team with stretchers on the touchline. In fact, it would have been economically smarter for South Africa not to have built the Peter Mokaba at all, and instead to have flushed the $175 million it cost straight down the toilet. That would have saved decades of pointless maintenance costs.

The stewards, who seemed to outnumber the spectators, assumed that as a white man I must be looking for the VIP section. In fact, I had paid forty rand (about £1.75) for a 'general ticket'. Only one entrance had been opened that evening; the stewards weren't sure where it was, but I eventually found it.

The stadium looked as smart as anything in Germany or Japan. But minutes before kick-off, it contained perhaps a thousand spectators, all sprinkled across the main stand – the only one with a roof, which FIFA had made South Africa build to keep the sponsors dry. On the field, the Galaxy players warming up looked suspiciously like the guys I'd just seen in the hotel pool.

I sat next to a brass band of musicians and dancers whose members wore identical red shirts branded 'TS Galaxy Supporter'. They struck up at kick-off, and played a kind of upbeat jazz, heavy on trumpets, without stopping for the whole match. Their leader, a bearded man with a silver dandy's cane, sashayed back and forth along the seats. Spectators continued arriving throughout the match – the final attendance was perhaps 5,000 – and some came over to dance with the band.

When an own goal gave TS Galaxy the lead, no band member cheered, or even missed a note of the song they were playing, confirming my suspicion that they were a paid claque. Presumably the club owner had realised that without them there'd be no atmosphere at all. As it was, TS Galaxy looked like a band with a football team attached.

The football itself was much faster and more direct than the show-offy ticky-ticky style I remembered from the 2000s. I was told that daily exposure to European football on TV, plus regular encounters in the African Champions League, had rubbed off on South African players. Galaxy won 3-1. Nobody seemed to care.

Kaizer Chiefs-Richards Bay, Peter Mokaba Stadium, Polokwane, 27 November 2024

Chiefs were no longer much good (they'd finished tenth the

previous season), yet they remained the most popular club in southern Africa. Their owner was still Kaizer Motaung, now eighty years old. And they still operated like travelling minstrels, without a fixed home ground. I'm not clear on what terms they'd agreed to play this game in Polokwane. Ramakuela had tried to explain how these deals typically worked: 'It's what we call – not bartering, but each person will get something out of it.' For instance, the stadium authorities might pay Chiefs but then get to keep the gate money.

Even Chiefs couldn't fill the Peter Mokaba, though. By half-time, perhaps a third of the seats were taken, meaning about 15,000 spectators. Almost all were Limpopo fans of Chiefs – men, women and children, many sporting the traditional Chiefs yellow and black miners' helmets. I didn't see a single spectator supporting Richards Bay (founded 2017).

South African football remained a creation of black culture. I counted only three other white people in the stadium: a hefty defender on each side (the traditional role of whites in South African teams was to act as the muscle) and one spectator, wearing an Arsenal shirt. I saw him again at the airport the next evening, so he was probably a British tourist. Nobody seemed to notice me, or care that a white man was there.

The dominant noise during the game was the angry-bee sound of the vuvuzelas. Vendors walked around selling biltong, beer and more vuvuzelas. As I watched Chiefs win 2-1 in the hot night, I traced the line of descent: not from the 2010 World Cup, but from Orlando Stadium in the 1970s. The eternal elements of South African football – the people who ran it and the clubs that mattered – seemed to have survived the World Cup untouched. The local drama rolled on, in front of the same select but devoted audience. The only residue of the tournament was the stage itself: the 2010 FIFA World Cup South Africa™ stadium, two-thirds empty but world-class.

13

Qatar, Russia, Sepp Blatter and How a World Cup Vote Explained the World

'The politics of soccer make me nostalgic for the politics of the Middle East.'

Henry Kissinger, 1983

On 2 December 2010, FIFA's executive committee (Exco) gathered in their luxury underground bunker at FIFA House in Zurich to choose the hosts of the 2018 and 2022 World Cups. Exco at this point consisted of twenty-two mostly elderly men; two others had been suspended prior to the vote for alleged corruption. This group was about to make the most momentous decision in FIFA's history.

I had been following the bidding race for years. Between 2007 and 2010, you'd run into officials from bidding countries in bars and hotel lounges at every football conference or major tournament. From chats with these people, mostly off the record, I had absorbed the view that Exco was going to choose Russia for 2018, and the US for 2022.

But as I wrote my preview of the vote for the *Financial Times*, I checked the odds offered by the bookmaker William Hill, and got a surprise: the runaway favourite to get Exco's nod for 2022 was not the US but tiny, boiling Qatar, a country that many people in 2010 hadn't even heard of. Qatar had no football culture to speak of. I phoned a contact at William Hill to find out what was going on. He advised me not to read much into it. Very few punters had bet on the 2022 race, which meant that just a couple of largeish bets on Qatar would be enough to skew the odds.

He and I both knew that Qatar wasn't really going to get the World Cup. So I wrote in the *FT*, with some overcaution to avoid being sued for libel:

> Don't put too much faith in William Hill's odds that show Qatar as the massive favourite … the oil-rich mini-state has suffered from the recent scandals to afflict the bidding process. There's no suggestion that Qatar offered any illegal inducements to FIFA Exco members, yet if, after this scandal, the Exco anoints Qatar then FIFA risks looking tacky … Qatar's biggest disadvantage is its weather – 'a potential health risk for players, officials, the FIFA family and spectators,' says FIFA's evaluation report.

On 2 December, Exco first chose Russia as host for 2018. Then FIFA's eternal president Sepp Blatter opened an envelope and pulled out the winning name for 2022: Qatar. 'I am a happy president,' he said with a grimace.

Few observers had seen Qatar coming. Theo van Seggelen, president of the international footballers' trade union Fifpro, told me later: 'For me – and I was reasonably close to the fire – the vote was a complete surprise.'

Other journalists have retraced the murky trail by which Russia and Qatar got their World Cups. A majority of the Exco members who voted in Zurich were subsequently charged or accused by US authorities of criminal wrongdoing, or sanctioned by FIFA's ethics committee. My question in this chapter isn't who paid what to whom. It's how did that day in Zurich illuminate the shift in global power and the decline of the West? I've explored these questions with, among other people, Sepp Blatter.

A friend of Blatter's, a businessman based in Zurich, had put us in touch. Blatter's email address turned out to be a homage to a legendary German footballer (not Beckenbauer). On a January morning in 2024, a taxi deposited me in front of an empty restaurant beside a hay barn on the rustic outskirts of Zurich. I'd been told that the restaurant was practically Blatter's living room. The 'legends' of Grasshopper Club Zurich met here, and Blatter was their honorary president. It was the last post he still held, quite a comedown for a man who had hobnobbed with Mandela and Vladimir Putin. Blatter had been ousted as FIFA president in 2015, after seventeen years in Jules Rimet's old seat. Now he was an irrelevant former power broker – the ideal interviewee, because he knew a lot and was now free to say it.

A fancy car pulled up, and a fragile, birdlike eighty-eight-year-old in an impeccable suit and waistcoat was helped out of it by his personal press officer. Almost the moment we sat down, I realised I would have to work hard not to be seduced. Blatter was a people person, a born politician. His eyes twinkled, he talked with his hands, he was fully present, and he treated me as a trusted companion. He told me, correctly, 'I think I have this quality to convince people. I'm positive. I am always smiling. I'm not crying.'

We started in German, because I thought he would express himself best in his mother tongue. But when he switched to his inimitable Swiss-English, I realised that, contorted though it sounded, he spoke it with equal fluency.

It was hard to know which stories to believe. Talking me through his early career, he said,

> I had once the chance to become a professional with a club in Switzerland, Lausanne-Sport. I was eighteen years old. This was in '54. They said, 'You have a talent, you are fast and you go for goal.' But at eighteen, at that time, we had no civic rights in Switzerland. You must be twenty. So, I needed the signature of my father. And my father, a very good prophet, he took the paper, he crushed it and said, 'My son, you will never earn your living by football.' He could just realise before he died in a car accident in '76 that I have started in my football career in FIFA as a development officer.

FIFA, when Blatter joined, was still a tiny organisation, not much bigger than the one Rimet had left behind in 1954. Its president from 1974 onwards was the haughty Brazilian João Havelange, an autocrat known for flying suitcases full of cash first class between Zurich and Rio. Since Havelange wasn't in the office much, a lot of the actual work was done by a caste of multilingual Swiss administrators. Blatter – a friendly workaholic who was a master of detail and first into the office each morning – was a good man to have around.

When Havelange retired in 1998, FIFA's congress in Paris had to elect his successor. The president of each national soccer federation has one vote in congress – Montserrat, with its population of 5,000, the same as China. Many presidents proved corruptible. David Yallop, in his 1999 book *How They Stole The Game*, recounts how the emir of Qatar flew $1 million in cash on a private jet to Paris, where twenty voters were each handed envelopes stuffed with dollars. This was Qatar's debut as a force in global football. Blatter was elected president – or as a FIFA document of the era describes the role, 'supreme leader'.

Those envelopes set the template for his rule by patronage. Blatter's thing wasn't money, but power – and that made him the eunuch in the harem that was FIFA. He wasn't personally chasing bribes. A man who worked with him told me he'd been surprised how unspectacular Blatter's house was. It was a nice place, in Zurich, but it didn't have great art or anything else you'd notice. By the end of Blatter's presidency, his secret basic annual salary was three million Swiss francs, but I suspect that he valued this chiefly as a marker of status.

He kept power by funnelling chunks of FIFA's income to national and continental football barons. The funnelling was typically shrouded in the language of 'development': a grant, often handed over personally in an envelope on the eve of a FIFA presidential election, was supposedly meant to fund facilities in the official's country. Some national federations were so poor they didn't have a phone line. However, if the baron slipped the envelope into his jacket pocket, nobody would complain. Corruption was Blatter's system. He made sure that the people around him were corrupted. If anyone dared challenge him, then FIFA's ethics machinery – which he controlled – would reveal the challenger's wrongdoing.

The champion milker of this system was Jack Warner, the Trinidadian alcoholic's son who had risen from schoolteacher to footballing power broker and who had the status to summon Nelson Mandela across the Atlantic. Warner controlled a voting bloc of thirty-one mostly tiny Caribbean national associations, which in a congress of a little over 200 countries was often the swing vote. And so, as David Conn documents in *Fall of the House of FIFA*, Warner received at least $26 million from FIFA to build a Dr João Havelange Centre of Excellence in his home country, on land that later turned out to belong to him. (Banned from football for life in 2015, Warner still lives peacefully in Trinidad.)

Little of FIFA's money was spent on fields for ordinary Trinidadians to play on, or safe stadiums where they could watch games. Warner preferred to use his Centre to host more profitable 'weddings, dinners, shows', writes Conn. It was a pattern replicated in many national federations.

Nobody troubled them much. I'm not sure that a single journalist in the Blatter era had a full-time assignment covering FIFA. The reporter who devoted most energy to the organisation was the English freelancer Andrew Jennings, who posted his findings – unchecked by any editor – on his personal website in fonts of many colours. I was on Jennings's email list but eventually stopped opening his missives, which typically intermingled unverifiable claims with narcissism:

EXCLUSIVE! World Cup in trouble as fans in England, Germany, USA, Holland, Denmark and many more countries, disgusted with extortionate prices charged by Sepp Blatter's family and business friends, boycott South Africa. Even the touts are sobbing as they clutch bundles of unwanted tickets.

Brazil Fans Honour Andrew

Andrew Jennings' presentation 'The Truth about FIFA Corruption and Ricardo Teixeira' to the Brazilian Senate's Education, Culture and Sports Committee on October 26 was a media sensation. Federal President Dilma Rousell's office called asking for a copy. And fans at one of the country's top clubs – Internacional of Porto Alegre – created a massive banner begging Andrew to save the 2014 World Cup!

Like the media, the Swiss authorities mostly left FIFA alone. They treated it as a simple sports association, barely subject to regulation, almost like a village hunting club. Dozens of other sports federations, including the International Olympic Committee, had set up their headquarters in this forgiving and efficient country.

FIFA's biggest barons sat in Exco. For many of these men, bribes were the whole point of choosing World Cup hosts. Annoyingly, the votes on the 2010 and 2014 tournaments hadn't been especially lucrative. Blatter had reserved 2010 for African bidders, which cut down the number of would-be hosts and therefore the bribes. The 2014 tournament was earmarked for South America, and Brazil ended up the only bidder, so nobody on Exco got rich from that one either. The votes for 2018 and 2022 looked more promising. Every country on earth was free to bid, and two hosts would be chosen in a single day.

Most of the bidding nations were established developed countries: England, the US, Australia, Japan, South Korea, Spain and Portugal (as a joint bid), and the Netherlands and Belgium (also joint). The bidders understood that Exco wasn't a gathering of utilitarian philosophers who would decide in the interests of football; it was more like a horse fair in the Wild West. And yet, rereading the notes from my conversations with the losing western bidders, I see now that they each misunderstood the world in their own way.

My journey began one day in 2007 when a public relations executive named Peter Hargitay – debonair moustache, pinstriped

suit, imposing bulk – buttonholed me on the sunny terrace of
FIFA House. We were attending the International Football Arena,
an annual conference for the unseen rich men who run the sport.
Hargitay was blessed with the advantage, in international football, of being Swiss. He handed me a business card that declared
him 'special adviser' to his close friend Blatter. Hargitay and the
Swiss former FIFA official Markus Siegler were setting up a business together as lobbyists. Three countries bidding for 2018 had
asked them to represent them, and the duo were going to choose
one of the three as its client. That choice, Hargitay told me, could
determine the destination of a World Cup.

I asked why. He said, 'Forget marketing, forget promotion.
The target audience is not the world. The executive committee of
FIFA is twenty-four men, one of whom is Sepp Blatter.'

Hargitay went on: 'It's very important to be close to Blatter, to
make sure he values the bid that comes his way. I don't think that
in the consulting business anybody has better access and better
knowledge of the twenty-four men than Markus and me. Over the
years you develop, you might even say, friendships.'

I said, 'So you sit down a committee member—' Hargitay
interrupted: 'I don't know if I sit him down. I don't want to go
into details of how this is done. It's a classic lobbying job. Totally
above board.'

He said the winning bid had to be technically excellent, but
that several bids would be. The US, for instance, would 'make
a bloody good bid. Maybe the country that will not be the best
bidder can pull it off. That is where a good adviser will come into
it. You see, football is just a product like anything else. It goes
without saying that I love the game.'

His message was that just as Mandela had been the star lobbyist for 2010, for 2018 it was Hargitay. 'It's twenty-four men,' he
kept repeating. He referred to Jack Warner as 'Jack'. I said that if
that was how the World Cup would be awarded, it was depressing.
He grinned: 'Why is it depressing? It's a selling opportunity for
me.'

Next thing I heard, Hargitay had joined England's bid, but

like a club-hopping star centre-forward, he soon moved on. By the 2010 World Cup, he was working for the Australian bid. I found him in a luxury hotel in the white-flight district of Sandton, where most visiting dignitaries had holed up. He took me to the suite of the shopping-mall magnate Frank Lowy, chairman of the Football Federation Australia, and introduced us. Then Hargitay asked me, 'Do you speak Hungarian?' When I said, 'No', Hargitay and Lowy conferred in Hungarian. They had both left Hungary as child refugees.

After I interviewed Lowy, Hargitay and I sat in the smoking section of the hotel restaurant and gossiped about the bidding race in low voices, to avoid being overheard by Exco members at surrounding tables. Hargitay pointed out one of them, a man, he said, who was 'totally in Qatar's pocket', before paying for our espressos with a 'FIFA Club' card attached to the accreditation badge around his neck.

With hindsight, I see that Hargitay was an example of how each western bidder imagined that the world worked in the way he did. As a lobbyist, he assumed that the vote would be decided by lobbying. The Spanish-Portuguese bidding team followed their own logic: they thought the vote would be won by their friendships inside FIFA. Latin American Exco members were going to vote for them out of cultural kinship. After all, wasn't that how the world worked?

The English and American officials I spoke to made a different mistake. As instinctive capitalists, they assumed that FIFA would reason like a capitalist corporation: its goal must be to maximise profits, so it would choose the biggest sports markets with the shiniest stadiums.

Both the US and England also put faith in their stables of global celebrities. The American bid fielded Barack Obama and Bill Clinton. The English dream team of Prince William, David Beckham and prime minister David Cameron was going to dazzle Exco members in one-on-one meetings.

Meanwhile, the Dutch and Belgians believed in their environmentally friendly bid for a compact World Cup. They even cycled into Zurich to present it. Surely, in a time of climate change, FIFA would want to reward the greenest bid? And wouldn't Exco members from small countries back other small countries?

I was so impatient with these arguments that I told the Dutch bidding chief: 'I just don't believe Exco care about all that. I think they'll decide for selfish reasons.'

The Dutchman was irritated to be taken for a naïf. He said, 'Don't you think I know that? There'll be much harder stuff going on behind the scenes. We have plans for that, but I'm not going to tell them to you.' However, an Englishman told me that nobody thought the Low Countries had a chance. The proof, he said, was that no rival bidder bothered to bad-mouth them.

The great unknown of the European bidding race was Russia. You didn't hear much from it, but long-legged Russian ladies were stalking football conferences, and the bid seemed to be rolling in money. Russia's bidding chief Alexei Sorokin, who had excellent English and a perennial smile, said he didn't know whether a Russian World Cup would cost $180 billion or $500 billion. In any case, it wasn't a 'cost' – it was an 'investment'. One English official remarked to me that $180 billion was the size of the UK government's budget deficit. I watched Sorokin give a presentation, set to stirring classical music, of a series of as yet unbuilt futuristic stadiums. Russia, he told the room, was 'the new modernising society'. Its bid was 'in many ways about hope'.

Russia had its own feared lobbyist: Putin. By this point, he had a track record. In 2007, the International Olympic Committee had chosen the snow-free subtropical Russian city of Sochi to host the 2014 winter Games, after Putin personally showed up at the IOC's vote in Peru and made a speech in hard-won English. His own favourite sports were judo and ice hockey, but he probably conceived of the World Cup as his coming-out as an admired member of the 'international community' – his version of China's 2008 Beijing Olympics.

Putin flattered Blatter by treating him as a president of equal status. Blatter told me, 'I've met him since years, we had good contacts together', and he recounted the time in St Petersburg that

Putin invited him to join him in a game of ice hockey. (Blatter, who at the time was in his seventies, declined.)

Putin met half a dozen Exco members in the months before the vote. He was able to promise them big state-to-state deals, whereas western bidding teams could only offer relative peanuts: England, for instance, agreed to pay Bryan Robson's salary as manager of Thailand.

Certain backers of England's bid hired the former MI6 agent and Russia specialist Chris Steele to collect intelligence on rival bids. Steele is the man who in 2016 would warn the FBI about purported collusion between Donald Trump's presidential election campaign and Russia. Digging into the Russian bid, he heard 'troubling rumours'– stories, for instance, of bid officials offering Exco members paintings from St Petersburg's Hermitage Museum. Westerners were starting to understand that Russia under Putin played the international game by its own rules.

Some western bidders thought that Russia's unabashed corruption would backfire: surely FIFA cared about its own image, and would want to choose a 'clean' winner?

But that wasn't how many Exco members saw it. In fact, they were outraged by the impudence of the 'English' media, led by Andrew Jennings, which kept uncovering FIFA's scandals. When an English bid team member visited the Exco member Nicolás Leoz at his house in Paraguay, Leoz came out waving a piece of paper and shouting, 'What are you going to do about this?' It was a letter he'd received from Jennings. Leoz, incidentally, had declared himself open to voting for England, provided the English could give him a knighthood and name the FA Cup after him.

Exco members were horrified that British media were allowed to wiretap, secretly film and entrap targets. If the members were to spend the next few years visiting England to prepare the World Cup, it could happen to them, too. Many of them had grown up in autocracies. They respected the Qatari and Russian systems, which had short lines of decision-making, and no shabby journalists running around shouting vulgar nonsense. By 2010 autocracy was looking like a viable alternative model to the West, which had been wounded by its self-inflicted financial crisis of 2008. FIFA itself functioned like an autocracy – except that given its control of international football it felt superior to any mere government.

Sepp Blatter was quick to grasp the shift in global power. That's because he was an eternal Swiss type: the hotel concierge, '*der Portier*' in German, is friendly, multilingual and unideological. He always remembers his guests' names. Above all, living in a country that money flows through, *der Portier* knows which of them can afford the hotel bills: in the nineteenth century the British, later the Americans, and, in the twenty-first century, Russians and Gulf Arabs. *Der Portier* never asks where they got the money; as long as they have it, he treats them with respect. Blatter spotted early that wealth was moving eastwards, and that it cared about football.

He wanted to give a World Cup to Russia, but not to Qatar. He realised how corrupt his organisation would look if it anointed a boiling hot microstate without a football culture, whose bid had been criticised in FIFA's own evaluation report. That's why, in the weeks before the vote, he corralled Exco's members into agreeing to back the US over Qatar for 2022. 'That was a general acceptance,' he told me in the empty Zurich restaurant. 'It was not written down, but everybody was happy. Everybody was happy until, less than ten days before the decision is taken, there was a meeting in Paris.'

This 'meeting' was the legendary lunch at the Elysée Palace in Paris on 23 November 2010, involving French president Nicolas Sarkozy, the Qatari crown prince and Michel Platini – the French former playmaker, president of the European association UEFA, and Exco member. Platini led the bloc of four European Exco votes, and had walked into the Elysée planning to vote for the US. The next day, however, he phoned Blatter. This is how Blatter recounted the call to me.

Platini: Uh, Sepp, now we have problems. Perhaps it will not work as we agreed.
Blatter: Why?

Platini: My president has asked me that we should, I should, vote for Qatar.

Blatter: He said you have to?

Platini: No, it was not even a recommendation. He only said, if you and your fellows could vote for Qatar, it would be nice.

Blatter: What did you say?

Platini: What would you say if your head of state would ask you such a question?

Blatter: This question is not feasible in Switzerland because we have no head of state in Switzerland.

Platini: It is now possible that you cannot count on four votes.

That was when Blatter realised, to his horror, that Qatar was going to win. He told me, 'This was an error to go to Qatar. It was not – let's say, in my opinion – the destination of a World Cup.'

The lunch in Paris, as much as the vote in Zurich nine days later, dramatised the shift of global power from west to east – 'easternisation', as my *Financial Times* colleague Gideon Rachman has labelled the process. For centuries, France had been one of the western countries that ruled the world. After the 2008 financial crisis, it was reduced to sucking up to Qatar. The Qataris bought French stuff ranging from fighter jets to Parisian mansions. That day at the Elysée, it was agreed that they would buy into French football too. The emirate would take over the ailing club Paris Saint-Germain (which President Sarkozy supported) and create a broadcaster (the future beIN Sports) to pay fortunes for the rights to the French league, which nobody else wanted. Just to make sure everyone was happy, Platini's son Laurent was later given a job at the Qatar Investment Authority.

The deals demonstrated the decision-making speed of autocracies: Qatari royals, just like Vladimir Putin, could hand out fortunes without asking anyone's permission, whereas western leaders were hamstrung by rules and voters.

The lunch at the Elysée was an allegory of our times: eastern autocracies were co-opting western elites. It was happening in London as much as in Paris. Russian oligarchs had flooded into the UK, and splashed cash on British universities, art museums, Chelsea Football Club and the ruling Conservative Party.

Legitimate economic power alone probably won Qatar the World Cup. However, the country also deployed its cash in murkier ways. When I said to Blatter, 'Some Exco members took money to vote for Qatar,' he replied, 'I don't know that. I don't know … People said they have given money.'

Qatar did. I'll cite a couple of examples. In 2017, the Garcia report on World Cup bids, kept secret by FIFA's ethics committee for over two years, was leaked to Germany's *Bild* newspaper. FIFA then immediately published it, claiming 'transparency'. The report, by American judge Michael Garcia, alleged that Sandro Rosell, a consultant for Qatar and former president of FC Barcelona, had sent $2 million to the ten-year-old daughter of the Brazilian Exco member Ricardo Teixeira, Havelange's former son-in-law. Still, the report noted: 'No proof exists linking Qatar and this $2 million.' Garcia also found that just after Qatar was named host, a former Exco member thanked Qatari officials by mail for a transfer of several hundred thousand euros. British MPs tabled evidence in Parliament suggesting that Qatar paid two Exco members $1.5m each.

Qatar denies any wrongdoing. But one senior Qatari official gave me a more nuanced account: FIFA's bidding process was designed to elicit bribes, and every bidder paid them in some form or another, yet Qatar alone was scapegoated. That was partly because western bidders tried to pay only 'legal' bribes. England, for instance, donated large sums to 'football projects' in Warner's Trinidad, and elsewhere. The English sought to oversee these projects, but the receiving Exco member would often say, 'It's so much easier if you give me the money directly.'

The brazenness of the request always threw the English. They didn't know how to respond. They somehow had to do business with crooks without becoming crooks themselves. One man who worked for England's bid told me: 'Everyone knew that FIFA was corrupt, but we didn't realise quite how bad it was. Something we did not factor in was that the voters were so old. Other than their reputations, which most of them didn't give a shit about, they just wanted to get paid one last time.'

Qatar and Russia were willing to pay the most. As outsiders in a western-made world, they followed strategies that played to their strengths.

The night before the vote on the two World Cups, Prince William, David Cameron and the Olympic runner-turned-sports admin-istrator Sebastian Coe went around the Hotel Baur au Lac in Zurich, lobbying Exco members. At various points, eight Exco men told either William or Cameron, 'You have my vote.' In the final days of any bid, bidders tend to get overexcited and over-estimate their chances. It happened to the English.

On 2 December 2010, a snowy day in Zurich, the twenty-two men of Exco (twenty-four minus the two who had already been suspended for corruption) met in their underground bunker at FIFA House – built by Blatter with a big chunk of the TV income from World Cups. (His take on architectural transparency was, 'Places where people make decisions should contain only indirect light.') Geoff Thompson, the English Exco member, reported that just before the vote, Blatter told the twenty-two men: 'Please remember how we have been treated by the English media.'

Exco watched the presentations from the different bidding teams. Then the twenty-two men went one by one into a booth, placed their votes in sealed envelopes, and handed them to KPMG consultants to count. The results would be announced in Zurich's Hallenstadion.

The bad news for England's bid came unexpectedly fast: it was knocked out in the first round, having received just two votes, one of which was presumably Thompson's. Even the Low Coun-tries had managed four.

Blatter told me that when the results were announced, 'England was very unhappy. I remember that the prime minister, would he have had the power, they would have hung me in the morning in this famous prison in England.' (He meant the Tower of London.)

In Blatter's telling, Cameron hissed at him, 'You promised!'

and Blatter replied, 'I did not promise, I have received all the delegations, and I wished them well.'

The English bidders were outraged. It seemed that Exco members had deliberately led Cameron and William to expect victory in order to inflict maximum humiliation on the arrogant English, with their disgusting media and their super-rich Premier League that drained all other leagues of players and TV money. England's massive football economy wasn't a strength, as the bidding team had imagined, but a provocation. Exco members felt that England didn't need the World Cup.

The wounded English bidding team retired to a Zurich bar, where the mayor of London, Boris Johnson, who had flown out to help them, made a proto-Brexit speech along the lines of: 'Frankly, I think we should burn down FIFA House and take our ball home. Why don't we just organise our own World Cup?'

While Cameron had blundered by making himself the face of a losing bid, Putin was shrewder. He watched the voting from Kaliningrad, the Russian enclave in Europe that is a short flight from Zurich. When Russia won, Blatter recalled, 'he took a plane and he was here. He came to the Hallenstadion, and he had a press conference there.' In the eyes of most Russians – and many foreigners – Putin had personally won the World Cup.

While Russians and Qataris celebrated, an English bidder texted Jérôme Valcke, FIFA's secretary general: 'Surely the whole game is going to hell?' Valcke replied: 'Soon, my friend, very soon.' He had told the English beforehand that Russia plus Qatar would be the 'doomsday scenario'. If that were the outcome, Valcke had said, 'we are finished.'

Blatter felt the same. He knew that Exco's choice of two autocracies – and especially Qatar – would confirm everybody's suspicion that voters had been bribed. Self-enrichment hadn't been merely a factor in the vote. It turned out to be *the* factor – the main reason, in fact, for holding the vote. Valcke wrote in a leaked memo that Qatar 'bought' the World Cup. (He said he'd been misinterpreted. FIFA later banned him from football for ten years for breaches of its ethics code.)

After the vote, Blatter sensed that American justice and the mighty British media were going to come after FIFA. He would always blame the FBI's assault of 2015 (see chapter 17) on the American defeat of 2010. Straight after the vote, though, the dominant sentiment among the defeated westerners was impotence. They had discovered that they were now last in line at the concierge desk, behind the new spenders. Their protests were in vain. The revelations of corruption by western media had been worse than pointless; they had goaded FIFA into rejecting England.

Meanwhile, many Latin Americans, Africans, Middle Easterners and East Asians were gleeful at the West's humiliation. After all, westerners had humiliated everyone else for centuries. Exco members in the so-called 'Global South' enjoyed backing Russia against the West in 2010, just as many heads of government in these countries would enjoy backing Russia in 2022 after Putin invaded Ukraine.

FIFA's ethics committee did try later to investigate the allegations of Russian bribery. But when it asked to see the Russian football federation's computers, the Russians explained that they had been destroyed after the bid. Meanwhile, the gifts kept flowing. Franz Beckenbauer, who had reportedly voted for Russia, was appointed ambassador of the 'Russian Gas Society' in 2012.

At the FIFA Congress a few months after the vote on the World Cups, England proposed to delay Blatter's re-election until claims of corruption had been investigated. In response, Julio Grondona, Argentinian vice president of FIFA, told the assembly: 'We always have attacks from England which are mostly lies with the support of journalism.' He urged the English, 'Please leave the FIFA family alone. Say what you have to say but with truth. Say it clearly and without upsetting our family.' His speech was greeted with applause. England's motion lost by 172 votes to 17.

Most non-westerners in football dismissed the English and Americans (with some justification) as hypocritical whining losers. Richard Attias, a French communications consultant who advised Qatar, told me: 'Only a microcosm is interested in how World Cups are attributed – a very British microcosm.'

The West, if it still existed, was weaker than it had imagined. I was privy to conversations in the months after the vote about assembling a bloc of western countries – including Germany, England, the US and the Scandinavians – to boycott the World Cup unless FIFA reformed. A boycott would have weakened the tournament and impoverished FIFA.

But western countries never attempted it. Characteristically, they weren't willing to make any sacrifices for their supposed principles. In the same way, outside football, they tutted about the wrongdoings of the Russian and Saudi states while continuing to do business with them. And so FIFA sailed on unreformed. Its dysfunction didn't noticeably harm the World Cup's popularity; corruption was a blemish that the tournament could bear.

I discussed the case study of FIFA with Roger Pielke Jr, then a political scientist at the University of Colorado. Given waning western power, he asked, 'How do you effect global change? It turns out it's really difficult. If we can't reform FIFA, my goodness, how can we deal with nuclear proliferation or carbon emissions or trade?' It turned out, in the post-2008 world, that 'we', the West, couldn't deal with those issues either.

14

Interludes in Donetsk, the Vatican and Soho

June 2012, Donetsk and Kharkiv, Ukraine

I had come to eastern Ukraine to cover Euro 2012. Checking into my hotel in Donetsk, I discovered that the place was literally still being built. Some outside walls on my floor were missing, but at least my room was finished.

Donetsk had never had tourism before, and even a European Championship hadn't set things rolling. One day on the city's main boulevard, I passed a 'Tourist Information Center', staffed by two young women who had taken off their shoes and were lying stretched out on plastic chairs, because there were hardly any tourists wanting information. At most games, vendors outnumbered the fans.

I travelled between Donetsk and Kharkiv in the special new Euro 2012 trains. We'd whoosh through vast steppes dotted with dilapidated farmsteads, while Russian soap operas blared from the train's TV screens, and conductors jokily practised their English: 'It's nice!' At the time, before Putin's first invasion of their country, most eastern Ukrainians spoke Russian as their mother tongue, and felt some sort of kinship with Russia. When I think back to that fortnight in the two doomed cities, I remember the mosquitoes in the Donetsk park, the security guards outside restaurants, the Ukrainians with graduate degrees who could barely make a living, the giant Lenin statue at Kharkiv's fan park, and the chants of 'Rossiya!' at every match, from Russians who had popped across the border.

As I write in summer 2025, Donetsk is under Russian occupation and Kharkiv is under Russian attack. Donetsk's stadium hasn't been used since 2014. The host cities of Euro 2012 arguably no longer exist.

The Vatican, 13 August 2013

Before an Italy-Argentina friendly in Rome, the two teams had an audience with Pope Francis, who warned them: 'Football has become a business. Take care that it does not lose its sporting nature.' On display were the grip that football had on Francis, and the grip that Catholicism had on the World Cup.

For a nine-year-old boy in lower-middle-class Buenos Aires in 1946, there were three towering influences: Catholicism, Argentina's new president, Juan Domingo Perón, and football. Jorge Mario Bergoglio, the future pope, absorbed them all. In that magical year, he and his father, an immigrant Italian railway worker, watched their team San Lorenzo win the Argentinian league. Seventy years later, Bergoglio could still recite San Lorenzo's 1946 line-up plus substitutes.

Any virgin bachelor leading 1.4 billion people will struggle to seem a regular guy, but football helped. San Lorenzo had been central to Bergoglio's image since he was a priest in Buenos Aires exchanging football chatter with parishioners. As pope, he continued to pay his club membership fees every month.

San Lorenzo suited him: it was a neighbourhood club, founded by a priest and too small to irritate fans of other Argentinian clubs. For similar reasons, in the 1940s, just as the child Bergoglio was becoming a San Lorenzo fan, the writer Jorge Luis Borges was becoming a fake one. Borges was then a librarian in Buenos Aires, and his colleagues talked football for six hours a day. When Borges admitted he knew nothing about the game, they advised him to say he supported the club near the library, San Lorenzo de Almagro. Borges later recalled, 'I learnt that by heart and always said I supported San Lorenzo ... But I noticed that San Lorenzo de Almagro almost never won.' Indeed, that was part of their charm.

Francis 'was' San Lorenzo, but he kept his distance from modern football. Having renounced watching TV in 1990 after accidentally witnessing a smutty scene, he had never seen Leo Messi play. In any case, he couldn't support Argentina because he had his whole flock to think about. The World Cup is a peculiarly Catholic affair: although only about one human in six is a Catholic, majority Catholic countries won eighteen of the twenty-two tournaments up to 2022. The former West Germany, which was split about fifty-fifty between Protestants and Catholics, won three more. The only undeniably non-Catholic world champions were England in 1966.

One consequence is that the iconography of World Cups is Catholic. Substitutes make the sign of the cross before coming on. A player penalised for a foul will often clasp his hands together to beseech a referee for forgiveness. Lincoln Harvey, an Anglican vicar in London who wrote *A Brief Theology of Sport*, explains: 'It's a posture of humility, of recognizing where the power lies.' It also shows the ref that you aren't going to hit him.

Century Club, Soho, London, 2 October 2013

My allotted hour for lunch with the Football Association's chairman was up, and Greg Dyke had the FA and the British Film Institute and the Ambassador Theatre Group to go and run, but two men arguing about football are hard to separate. So we sat for another twenty-five minutes debating the great question: why did England lose?

Dyke had been canvassing expert opinions. 'The guy who owns Brentford is Matthew Benham, right? He's made his money gambling on football. He does everything on statistics. He says: the single biggest factor why England haven't done well is because they've been unlucky. He says you can alter the chances of winning on penalties, but not by a lot. So when you get knocked out four or five times on penalties, which is what's happened to England, he says if luck had gone the other way, we'd have won one or two of those.'

15

World Cup 2014: Brazil Shows Its Game to the World

The dominant Brazilian mood heading into the World Cup was anger. People were raging against the '*Padrão FIFA*' – the 'FIFA Standard' that the host country was being told to apply to everything, from stadiums to the shape of goalposts.

Meeting 'FIFA standards' cost money, but it also dashed the Brazilian dream of staging a truly Brazilian World Cup, complete with, say, the sensuously long, loose, low goal nets in which shots had nestled throughout the Maracanã's history.

João Philippe de Orleans e Bragança, a Brazilian investment manager (and direct descendant of Brazil's last emperor), told me: 'We had to build these European stadiums in place of the typical South American *caldeirão* ('cauldron'), which is packed, warm and vibrant. It was not a Brazilian World Cup, but a FIFA World Cup in Brazil.' Brazilians feared that the tournament would prove a case study of cultural colonialism: a northern organisation imposing its rules on a southern country.

Nothing Brazilian seemed to meet the '*Padrão FIFA*'. Nobody with power over the tournament cared about the country's traditions – or as FIFA saw it, it's markers of backwardness. A single family – João Havelange and then his son-in-law Ricardo Teixeira – had ruled Brazil's dreadful football association, the CBF, for almost the entire period from 1958 to 2012. The initial organising committee for the 2014 World Cup, wrote sports historian David Goldblatt, consisted of Teixeira, his daughter, 'his lawyer, his press secretary, his personal secretary and factotum, and the man who had advised him during the 2001 congressional investigation into football'. Though Teixeira decamped to Miami in 2012 following some embarrassing revelations, the World Cup remained mostly his baby.

In June 2013, a year before kick-off, the biggest protests in Brazilian history broke out. People demonstrated against everything from bus fares to homophobia, but what galvanised their anger was the wasteful spending on the World Cup. They demanded schools and hospitals that met 'FIFA standards'. One banner said, 'A teacher is worth more than Neymar.'

The World Cup became the symbol of the state's corrupt incompetence. Triggered by the tournament, Brazilians were debating, more publicly than ever before, what sort of society they wanted to live in. Going into the World Cup, the rage was directed chiefly at Brazil's left-wing president, Dilma Rousseff, pre-scripted by Brazilians as Villain of the tournament.

But they still hoped to show the world their finest creation: *jogo bonito*, the style of play that represented something more than football. It stood for the triumph of the free Brazilian spirit over the '*Padrão FIFA*', or even over global capitalism itself. The template was 1970, when Pele's 'Beautiful Team' won Brazil its third World Cup – the country's peak of global status, its equivalent of the American moon landing of the previous year. In 2014, a Neymar-led Brazilian team was tasked with recreating 1970 at home.

Barcelona, 8 May 2014

A painfully thin little chap walked into our meeting place, an old industrial loft in Barcelona converted into a studio. Here was the first great Brazilian footballer to emerge in over a decade, just twenty-two years old. Everything was scripted for Neymar to be not merely the winner of the World Cup, but the incarnation of *jogo bonito*. I got the sense that he himself fully bought into the story. He saw himself as the tournament's main character.

He greeted us with the magical smile that he used to charm and ward off the world. Then he changed clothes for a photoshoot, and we were granted a sight for which some would kill: the shirt came off. Beneath the tattoos, he looked slight, not a typical modern muscle-pack footballer. The camera loved Neymar. He wasn't beautiful, but his smile was, and he had '*ginga*' – that peculiarly Brazilian rhythmic, jaunty way of moving, almost like dancing.

He told me his memories of the Brazilian team, the Seleção, winning the World Cup, in 2002, when he was ten. 'I woke up before dawn to watch the final at home. I even had Ronaldo's haircut. I watched with my parents and sister, everyone together. Then we went to my granny's house, we had a barbecue, everyone shouting "We're Champions!" like real fans. The World Cup has always been my goal in life. It's funny that today it's nearly come true.'

Was he going to win it?

'It's what I want more than anything.'

I had tipped the Seleção to win. In my defence, so did almost everyone else.

Paris, May–June 2014

I still have my Panini sticker albums from the 1978 and 1982 World Cups. My childhood friend Edward and I spent entire afternoons in my bedroom in Leiden playing gambling games for stickers.

By 2014, my daughter was eight years old and my twin sons were five. I knew their first World Cup would be a landmark in their lives, so I bought them each a Panini album. I intended it as a gateway drug, to get them into football.

My plan worked too well. Footballers replaced cartoon super-heroes in their brains. Soon, the boys were spending family dinners reciting the weights of 'Korea Republic' players, always using each country's full name as given by Panini.

One evening, Leo proudly declared a truth he had just

discovered: 'Most people in Brazil are Brazilians.' The albums were teaching him about the world. Another time, he asked, 'What's the name again of the team that invaded Mozambique?' 'Portugal,' replied my wife. 'It's not a team, it's a country.'

He brought his most treasured possession, a sticker of the French winger Franck Ribéry, to nursery school to show his teacher. She studied it solemnly, then pronounced: 'Ribéry, he is the ugliest. I detest him.' It was Leo's first glimpse of the thorny relationship between the French and their team.

When I flew to Barcelona to interview Neymar, the children were confused: so he wasn't just a sticker? A few mornings before I left for Brazil, I was dropping them off at school when a teacher asked me: 'Are you really a sports journalist who is going to the World Cup?' She had assumed it was just a child's fantasy.

Every time I Skyped home from Brazil all they talked about was the World Cup. As far as I could gather (though my wife denied it) the kids seemed to be staying up till 11 p.m. to watch two matches a day, before falling asleep clutching their albums.

My wife asked Joey why he was obsessed with the World Cup. 'Because it's the biggest thing in the world,' he said. The tournament had connected a little boy to something gigantic.

It was also reshaping their identities. The boys had been disappointed to realise that, through my wife, they were American. 'But America has never won a World Cup!' Leo complained. As native Parisians, they wore France shirts pretty much daily, though Leo, keen to back a winner, was also supporting Brazil, and briefly tried to get us to call him Cristiano Ronaldo. (We refused.)

I realised that I'd forgotten what it was like to idolise footballers, or to believe that the result of a match really mattered. I was happy for the kids, but I wanted to believe that Panini stickers were a passing phase of childhood, like losing your milk teeth.

Maybe they weren't, though. The young Costa Rican forward Joel Campbell was so excited to be in the album that he went out and bought 100 packs of stickers, hoping – in vain – to find one of himself. And when Holland somehow beat Spain 5-1 in their opening match, my childhood friend Edward and I exchanged triumphant transatlantic text messages. For a moment, we were eight years old again.

São Paulo, 10 June 2014

I think it was Alex Bellos who wrote that the cliché that Brazilians love football wasn't quite right. More precisely, they love watching Brazil play in World Cups. Workplaces close for the Seleção's games. People watch in family clans, often over barbecues, as Neymar had in 2002. Some could still recite decades later what now-dead Daddy or Grandma had said about a particular goal.

Yet as my taxi from the airport crawled into São Paulo two days before the opening game, almost the only trace I saw of the World Cup was on the billboard ads. Brahma beer's slogan was strangely familiar: 'Football's coming home.' I did pass a favela where a few homes were flying Brazilian flags, but in the rest of the megacity, there was barely a painted street. This was not how Brazil was supposed to look just before a World Cup, let alone one at home. What had happened was that this tournament had become political.

A poll by Datafolha had found that most people in São Paulo opposed hosting the World Cup. The middle classes, in particular, weren't going to toot their horns for what they saw as a festival of Brazilian government propaganda, waste and corruption. They also feared a shoddily organised tournament. The government had abandoned many planned infrastructure projects. The one time in history that the world was paying attention to the country, Brazilians feared looking like an international joke.

A friend who had come over from Rio said that the only sense you got there of an impending World Cup was hordes of people trading or selling Panini stickers in public places. It was their way of expressing love for the World Cup without endorsing the government or paying a corporation.

Brazil-Croatia, opening match, São Paulo, 12 June 2014

Apparently, it was Brazil's left-back Marcelo who came up with the idea. He told his teammates that when the national anthem was played before the match, they should keep singing after the music stopped.

A World Cup is the one football competition in which players are expected to present themselves not just as professionals, but as fans, citizens and patriots – and the requirement was especially strict for a Brazilian team at a home World Cup. In this festival of Brazilianness, the Seleção had to prove they were members of the national family, not expat multimillionaires driving around their former homeland in a team bus with tinted windows.

In the São Paulo stadium, the plan worked. Fans and players roared out the words together a cappella for nearly a minute. It was a series of statements: this is our country, not any politician's, we won't make our singing fit into the 'Padrão FIFA', and São Paulo loves the Seleção too. It was an anthem of defiance.

This rendition of the anthem would remain a Brazilian ritual for the whole tournament. It was the one moment when the nation was made flesh. But looking around the São Paulo stadium, you saw how tricky it was to call Brazil a nation. In this city of endless skin hues, almost all the spectators were white: they were the people who could afford the tickets.

President Rousseff was there too, but she couldn't make a speech or even have her name announced for fear of being jeered out of the stadium. People chanted, 'Dilma, shove it up your arse!'

Three doves were released before kick-off, as a symbol of peace, but instead of flying off they fluttered above the field for a while to watch the *jogo bonito*. An own goal from Marcelo was an unfortunate start, but on the half hour, Neymar scored the goal of a great footballer: a roller on the run, hit from twenty yards with his weaker left foot, in off the Croatian post. The nation exploded: the script was being followed.

Neymar understood his role as bearer of Brazilian tradition. He was the only player who could provide *jogo bonito*, so almost every time he got the ball, he'd try a dribble or a back-heel. The tricks weren't always functional, but functionality wasn't the point. The crowd chanted his name. When the referee gave Brazil the softest penalty, Neymar made it 2-1, before Oscar scored a third. After the game, Brazil's coach Luiz Felipe Scolari triumphantly told the press conference: 'Never again can you say São Paulo doesn't support the national team.'

Tostão, a star of Brazil's 1970 team, a former medical doctor who now wrote a thoughtful newspaper column, asked: 'Has anyone yet considered the possibility that Brazil won't win the Cup?'

Manaus, The Amazon, 14 June 2014

I was the only *Financial Times* journalist covering the football in a country the size of a continent. Today I took a six-hour flight from São Paulo to Manaus, a small city marooned in the middle of the Amazon. The endless rainforest started on the verge of the two-lane road into town. Although Manaus didn't have a serious football club, Brazil had built a stadium to host four World Cup matches. I was flying in for England-Italy.

It was probably the only time I'll ever visit the Amazon. I spent thirty hours there, working almost nonstop, mostly watching matches in bars. The only other people watching tended to be my fellow English football journalists. Most Brazilians only watched Brazil. To them, the World Cup was a one-team tournament. Or to quote the Brazilian government ad: 'This is our cup. This is the cup of cups.' The rest of the world was welcome to watch.

The Amazon, 15 June 2014

Manaus was an ugly industrial city that had turned its back on the infinite expanse of nature around it. There was barely a flower or park to be seen. The humidity was so dehydrating that you had to drink water constantly, and you could smell everyone's armpits. Alice Roberts, an anatomist at the University of Birmingham, had suggested that England and Italy adapt to the conditions by playing naked except for ice vests.

On my one free morning, I went for a walk, turned off a main street, and suddenly, at the end of a cul-de-sac, there it was: the mighty river. A man in shorts was standing in the clear water, shampooing his hair. Roosters pecked through rubbish by the shore. I dipped my fingers into the lukewarm Amazon, and communed with the scene for five minutes. Then I had to go and watch the game. The best moments at World Cups often happen away from the football.

England-Italy, Manaus, 15 June 2014

The Brazilian shirt count in Manaus was higher than in São Paulo, but this hadn't required either a big outlay or surrender to global capitalism. Pirated team kits, almost all of them bearing Neymar's name, were on sale around town for about 15 reais (€5) each. I bought my kids one each.

That evening at England-Italy, a crowd full of locals in pirated shirts sang, 'I am Brazilian, with much pride.' The inhabitants of one of the world's most isolated cities, many of whom had never left the Amazon, were claiming membership of the nation.

Mario Balotelli headed Italy's winning goal. Afterwards, he posted a picture on Facebook of the Italian pages of the Panini World Cup album: he had filled all fourteen spaces allotted to his teammates with stickers of himself.

Salvador, 17 June 2014

This poor northern coastal city was marketing itself as a tourist resort, and its beachfront had a lot going for it. In the evening, the sun set spectacularly over the palm trees, the Portuguese colonial forts – and over the leaky Portaloos, installed to service visiting supporters and the homeless people who lived on the beach.

Unfortunately, the sun also set over the brigades of labourers who were still digging up the beachfront several days into the World Cup. Presumably someone from the city council had told the construction company, 'This has to be done before the tournament. Get all your people on it.' But in the seven years they had to prepare, they never got around to it.

At least the stadium was finished. The previous evening, I had watched Germany hammer Cristiano Ronaldo's Portugal 4-0 there. Brazil seemed to have decided in the end that all you needed to host a World Cup were stadiums. Even signs to the stadiums were optional extras.

Spain-Chile, Maracanã Stadium, Rio de Janeiro, 18 June 2014

This was an encounter between a falling team – the reigning Spanish world champions – and a rising one. The early energy of the World Cup was with Chile. Not having a superstar like Neymar, their tattooed little men had been obliged to master fast

European passing football, and they had blown away Australia 3-1 in their opening game.

They also had an entire nation behind them. Banco de Chile's TV advert for the World Cup drew on a potent national symbol: the Chilean miners who had spent sixty-nine days trapped underground in 2010. In the ad, the miners line up like a football team, Chilean flags flying, and their leader Mario Sepulveda asks: 'Spain is difficult? Netherlands is difficult? We don't fear the "group of death", because we have beaten death before!'

The commercial elicited a Dutch parody, in which a few men line up in a meadow and their leader intones: 'We Dutchmen have been trapped all our lives. In the Netherlands.' The men enumerate the struggles of Dutch life: shopping trolleys with missing wheels, smartphones with poor reception, etc. The climactic speech is: 'We're not afraid of death! We're just afraid that we'll be eliminated in the first round'; and the closing slogan is, 'And otherwise, after the first round we'll support Belgium.'

Chilean fans didn't do irony. You saw thousands of them trooping through airports yelling, 'Chile!' Others had driven to Brazil, slept and ate in their cars, washed in the free showers on Rio's beaches, and communicated with locals in the Spanish-Portuguese mix known as 'Portunhol'.

Today at the Maracanã, hours before kick-off, dozens of Chileans stormed into the media centre, shattering glass and damaging walls. One chap, who looked about seventy, had to be removed by stewards. I hoped I'd be like that at his age. I asked Brenda Elsey, expert on Chilean football at Hofstra University on Long Island, to explain the logic behind storming a media centre. She thought it made sense: 'I'm from Detroit, and when we win anything, we burn it.'

Part of the needle around the Spain match concerned which team got to call itself *'la Roja'*, 'the Red'. Both sides used the moniker, but a Chilean online campaign had proclaimed, *'La Roja is Ours'*. A video explained, 'Some years ago, a team lacking an identity appropriated our name, our heart ...'

The match settled the matter. Spain fielded probably the

world's most successful generation of international footballers, men like Xavi, Iniesta and Iker Casillas who had won Euro 2008, the World Cup 2010, Euro 2012, Spanish titles and Champions Leagues. But, after getting hammered by Holland in their opener, they were passed apart by the Chileans, who won 2-0.

Spain's coach, the Marquess Vincente Del Bosque (ennobled for winning in 2010), sat watching in the dugout, fiddling with his nose. At one point, a wry smile spread across his aristocratic moustache. It was the correct response. When world champions screw up, it's not tragic but hilarious.

Spain had done what winners of World Cups usually do: they had stopped learning and had picked players based on past performance. By that logic England should have sent their 1966 team, while Diego Maradona would have been in Brazil as Argentina's number ten, not as a TV pundit who couldn't always even get into the stadium.

In fact, most players who win a World Cup should instantly retire from their national team. Those who hang on tend to grow arrogant, sated or just plain old. Few top-class players survive for more than five years at the summit of football. The modern World Cup is a mountain that any generation can climb only once. No country has won two in a row since 1962, and the only player since 1970 to win two is Brazil's Cafu. Football evolves so fast that a team cannot succeed by playing the way it did four years earlier. In 2014, Spain became the fourth reigning world champion out of five since 1998 to exit the World Cup in the group stage.

The beach at Fortaleza, 21 June 2014

Happily for my World Cup experience, England were knocked out after two games. This meant that I didn't have to spend an entire day taking two flights to their now pointless match against Costa Rica. Through a benevolent realignment of the universe, I instead contrived to spend five days in a Costa del Sol-type resort tacked onto the poor coastal city of Fortaleza.

One morning I sat working in a beach café overlooking the placid Atlantic. The café's sound system blared out Dutch evergreen pop hits, while the mostly German clientele listened impassively, served by waiters in *Oranje* shirts. The evening's game was Germany-Ghana.

I was eating a bad lunch when the Ghanaian squad wandered past, making the slowest of promenades down the beachfront, accompanied by a few military policemen. The German drinkers gawked. Here were the tournament's main characters, descended from the TV screen for a moment, and they turned out to be just a bunch of ordinary young men far from home. Ghana held Germany to a 2-2 draw.

Uruguay-Italy, 24 June 2014

Luis Suárez taking a bite out of the shoulder of Italian centre-back Giorgio Chiellini was the first unforgettable moment of the tournament. The Uruguayan had made himself Villain of the previous World Cup by stopping a Ghanaian goal with his hand; now once again he was displaying his dysfunction to the world.

As in 2010, only his compatriots defended him. Uruguay's captain, Diego Lugano, accused the victim, Chiellini, of 'crying' and added: 'As a man he disappointed me totally.' The coach, Oscar Tabárez, blamed the 'English' media. Uruguay's *El Obser-vador* newspaper said of the apparent bite mark left on Chiellini: 'It could just be a mole.'

That day, Suárez seemed to have become the first person to be Villain of the World Cup twice. Soon, though, as everybody reflected on his act – truly a global topic of conversation – it came to appear more bizarre than evil. I watched a late-night Brazilian TV show in which guests took turns to make jokes about it. The bite didn't even help Uruguay: with Suárez suspended, they were immediately knocked out. Chiellini forgave him. Suarez morphed from Villain of the tournament to early frontrunner for Clown.

Brazil, June–July 2014

A World Cup meant spending a month surrounded by other men, who kicked your seat on the plane, or left you with a dirty toilet at the Stadium Media Center. Exhaustingly, you had to deal with most of them either in a foreign language, or in the strained English ('media tribune') that was the tournament's lingua franca. It was particularly hard for a misanthrope like me who spent the rest of the four-year cycle working in a room by himself. (I was only slowly discovering the solution to most human problems: earplugs.)

At least a journalist's life at the World Cup was simple: no universe outside the tournament, no childcare, nothing but travelling logistics and work. On mornings when I woke up in Fortaleza or Rio, I tried to walk on the beach for half an hour after breakfast. I'd feel the Brazilian winter sun on my neck and the dirty ocean water between my toes, I'd drink a tiny *cafezinho* or a sliced-open coconut in a deserted beach bar, and then I'd be good to work sixteen hours until I fell asleep in yet another city.

Brazil 2014 was the hardest I'd seen journalists work at a World Cup. I'd speed-walk through a media centre hours before the match, spot a colleague I hadn't seen in years, and what would we do? We'd exchange nods, I'd speed on, and he'd continue typing, because the writing here never stopped.

Many journalists were funding their own travel because their newspapers were nearly broke, having lost readers and advertisers to free websites. People might bash out five articles a day for different publications for tiny fees, trying not to lose money covering the World Cup. A respected journalist told me that he'd been offered £8 for an article by the *Guardian*. In media, the old days really were the best.

Copacabana Beach, Rio, 27 June 2014

There is so much on Copacabana that bounces more entrancingly than any football, as the Scottish journalist Hugh McIlvanney once wrote, but there were footballs bouncing too. Some were kicked by foreigners: I watched Arsenal's manager Arsène Wenger, aged sixty-four, diving for a header, limbs everywhere, his every fibre striving to win a point at football tennis. But almost all the players were ordinary Brazilians. Walking the length of the beach, I saw what they could do with a ball.

Mostly, they juggled it in groups, kicking, heading, chesting or shouldering the ball to each other. The only country where I'd seen higher-skilled casual football was Cameroon, in 1992. But the Brazilian game was about show, not scoring. Even the few mini-matches where goals had been set up were primarily aesthetic displays: almost every pass was a lob or back-heel. It wasn't about function. It was the Brazilian idea of *jogo bonito*. It was the way Brazilians played in sports halls, on bumpy playgrounds, and, for a few lucky or wealthy people, on beaches. (Proper grass pitches barely existed here.) It was the style of football they demanded of their national team.

Brazil-Chile, Belo Horizonte, 28 June 2014

In the second-round game, the Chileans outplayed Brazil as they had Spain. The Brazilians' game plan seemed to be a) somehow get ball to Neymar; and b) hope he does something.

It took me a while to work out why Brazil reminded me of England. Eventually I realised that it was their habit of passing vertically forward – the easiest pass for opponents to read. They had never learned (or possibly even thought about) the diagonal pass that characterises modern football.

Brazil's centre-forward, Fred, spent attacks loafing near the back post, hoping defenders would miss the ball. He built ami-cable relationships with his markers, often holding up a hand in contrition after a clash. By this stage of the tournament he had scored once, against Cameroon. The Brazilian sports daily *Lance!* calculated that he was Brazil's worst centre-forward at a World Cup ever, worse than the legendary Serginho in 1982.

Lance! interviewed Serginho, who offered a piece of advice: 'He should be thinking, "I need to score a goal".' Presumably Fred had worked that out. The question was: how?

As the Seleção laboured in the second half against Chile, the home crowd fell silent. FIFA, too, must have been terrified that Brazil would go out. There were so few foreign fans that the elimination of the self-absorbed hosts would have pulled the plug on the event.

A minute from time, with the score tied at 1-1, the Chilean substitute Mauricio Pinilla crashed an unstoppable drive against the crossbar. Brazil hung on to win on penalties. Afterwards Neymar wept in relief. Brazil's keeper, Julio Cesar, gave a TV interview in tears.

Pinilla wasn't heartbroken. In fact, he immortalised his moment. He got a tattoo on his back showing the ball hitting the bar, with the words, in English, 'One centimeter from glory'. Chile flew home as the Cinderellas of the tournament, which was probably all they wanted.

A swimming pool in Brasilia, 29 June 2014

My team, *Oranje*, had just completed an unlikely victory over Mexico, and I was floating in the swimming pool of the house where I'd watched the game. Tropical birds chirped in the trees above, and friends chirped in the water around me. That's when it struck me: 'This is the best World Cup I've been to.'

It was an unbiased Olympian judgement. As Nigeria's coach Stephen Keshi said straight after his team's elimination: 'So far it's been wonderful.' But why?

The first element was attacking football. With ten matches left to play in Brazil, there had already been more goals than in the 2006 or 2010 World Cups. My theory was that since the early 1990s, live televising of matches had pushed football to create more entertaining content. The game had gradually become more attacking. (Every World Cup from 2014 to 2022 averaged between

2.64 and 2.7 goals per game, noticeably above the 2.23 and 2.3 of the borefests of 2010 and 2006.)

The second reason this tournament worked: Brazil. Partly it was the hot sun, especially after the South African Highveld winter in 2010. Partly it was the beaches – the one thing the Germans didn't provide in 2006.

A third element that no World Cup should be without: Brazilians. Living in Paris as I did, I felt disoriented going around a country where almost everybody was nice. In Brazil, even military policemen gave you a friendly backrub as you passed (if you were a white foreigner, anyway). Mixing with Brazilians, you learned to take setbacks with grace. The taxi to the airport that you ordered didn't come, and now you're sitting in a traffic jam? Sit back and relax. Also: everyone in Brazil cared about the World Cup, or at least about the Seleção. This wasn't Japan 2002.

Another pleasure: it was a World Cup almost without fear. My first tournaments had been overshadowed by the obsession with hooligans. After 9/11 it was terrorists, and, in South Africa, crime. True, Brazil's murder rate was high, but Brazilians didn't seem to internalise fear the way South Africans did. At night, Rio and São Paulo were humming with people, whereas Johannesburg pretty much closed down. I wasn't sure if that meant Rio and São Paulo were safer, but it was joyous anyway.

The big worry before the tournament – perhaps especially among Brazilians – had been incompetent organisation. But everything was going smoothly. Admittedly, Brazil had got lucky. Early in the World Cup, I took a metro train to a game at the Maracanã. I had never been in such a packed carriage. For minutes it was hard to breathe. When we got to the stadium, everyone tumbled out alive. It could have been different.

The stadiums were perfectly fine and didn't fall down (though a walkway at the Maracanã nearly did before Argentina-Bosnia), the airports coped, and the traffic wasn't too bad, even if Brazil had to close schools and universities and proclaim public holidays in order to achieve that.

True, an overpass in Belo Horizonte built for the tournament collapsed, killing two people. Overall, though, Brazil managed what every modern host did: a professional World Cup. (The unromantic truth is that FIFA knows how to organise these tournaments, and if the hosts follow its rulebook they'll be OK.) President Dilma's reputation was rebounding from its opening-day low.

Brazil had staged a wonderful World Cup. Now it just had to win it.

Brazil-Colombia, quarter-final, Fortaleza, 4 July 2014

Probably the player of the tournament going into this match was Colombia's James, a clean-cut twenty-two-year-old with perfect balance who had scored five in his first four games.

Brazil couldn't pass like Colombia, but they had Neymar. All tournament, he had been quoting Brazilian tradition. Against Cameroon, after scoring twice to ensure victory, he began doing sombreros: the lobs over opponents' heads made famous by Pele in 1958. Neymar's penalties against Croatia and Chile were *paradinhas*, with a slight pause in the run-up – again, quotations of Pele's oeuvre. One thin little chap with *ginga* was keeping the national tradition alive.

So Brazil versus Colombia was supposed to be Neymar versus James – until the Spanish referee Carlos Velasco Carballo intervened. Referees in this tournament had followed a new directive: 'Let them play', meaning, don't keep interrupting games with free kicks and cards. Velasco Carballo took this policy to its absurd extreme.

Brazil confronted Colombia with a classic old-style orchestrated kicking plan: take out the opponents' best player, the way Pele had been kicked out of the 1966 World Cup and Maradona provoked out of 1982. James, assaulted every time he got the ball, usually by Brazil's Fernandinho, did what any sane person would have done: he retreated ever further back down the field, staying away from the Brazilian goal. By the end, Fernandinho (who never even got a yellow card) only had to look at him and he'd pass.

Then Colombia's Juan Camilo Zúñiga kneed Neymar in the back, breaking a vertebra and (according to the Brazilian team doctor) coming within two centimetres of paralysing him for life. Brazil won the gang fight 2-1. Thanks to the referee, two geniuses had been eliminated from the tournament in one evening. I left the stadium feeling sick.

Breakfasts with tears in São Paulo, July 2014

Every morning in São Paulo, I'd buy a couple of Brazilian newspapers, go for coffee and rolls in a café on the Avenida Paulista, the city's main drag, and force myself to read the local World Cup coverage in Portuguese. With total knowledge of every ball that rolled at the tournament plus a dictionary, I usually could do it.

Eventually I realised that most of the specialised vocabulary I had built to understand coverage of the Seleção had to do with crying (*chorar* in Portuguese). The newspapers spent little time on the team's tactical deficiencies. Instead, they and Scolari, the coach, were forever debating the players' weepiness. Was the crying causing the Seleção to play badly? Or was the crying their secret strength, the thing that had carried them through to the semi-final despite mediocre football?

The tears poured in unprecedented quantities after Neymar broke his back. Brazilian TV, always mawkish, had morphed into a morbid personality cult. Half the time you saw the same old commercials of Neymar pushing innumerable products; the other half, you saw him on news broadcasts being helicoptered to hospital; Neymar, trying not to cry, addressing the Brazilian people; Brazilians keeping a vigil outside his clinic, et cetera. He had become a Catholic hero: the saviour who sacrificed his body to redeem his people. He couldn't play the semi against Germany, but his teammates promised they would win the game for him.

Brazil-Germany, semi-final, Belo Horizonte, 8 July 2014

I had chosen the wrong semi. I was in São Paulo for Holland-Argentina, and so I watched Brazil-Germany on TV in a bar on the Avenida Paulista. When the teams lined up for kick-off, the weeping Brazilian players held up a giant effigy of the absent Neymar. Twenty-three minutes later, with Brazil 0-2 down, an editor at the *Financial Times* rang: 'The hosts are going out. We'll need you to write a news story.'

By the time we'd finished talking, five minutes later, it was 0-5. The hosts' defence was everywhere, except in front of its own goal. David Luiz and Marcelo kept making forward runs at the wrong moments. The space in front of Brazil's penalty box was occupied by Germans, pressing with an intensity that Brazilians had never encountered. The TV cameras showed people in the crowd weeping, even collapsing.

At half-time I walked down the Avenida Paulista to see how the wider Brazilian public was coping. In every bar I passed, hordes of people in canary-yellow shirts were laughing their heads off. The Brazil team had become Clown of the tournament.

The 1-7 victory was the most surprising result of all 833 World Cup matches played since 1930, as calculated by the American statistician Nate Silver. It was Brazil's first defeat at home in a competitive match since 1975. As the German team bus drove through Belo Horizonte to the airport after the match, thousands of Brazilians lined the streets to applaud. Joachim Löw, Germany's coach, said later that the ovation was possibly the highlight of his career.

The 1-7 was an unrepeatable one-off, but Brazil's tactical backwardness wasn't. Without Neymar, Brazil offered neither *jogo bonito* nor fast European passing nor a defensive wall. They only had passion and tears. The 1-7 marked the end of a road for Brazilian football. They needed to bury their tradition and start building a new one.

Argentina-Netherlands, semi-final, São Paulo, 9 July 2014

When Argentina won the penalty shoot-out after a goalless draw, their fans were still thinking of Brazil: they raised seven fingers in triumph. The 1-7 would forever remain a highlight of Argentinian football history.

At the press conference afterwards, Argentina's coach Alejandro Sabella repeatedly explained that his team had drawn the match we had just seen, and had won on penalties. He then drifted into a long reminiscence about a game that his old club River Plate once played against Gremio.

Watching him, I was reminded of Peter Sellers' 1979 film *Being There*. Sellers plays a simple gardener who through a series of accidents becomes a political star in Washington. His gardening clichés are received as profound wisdoms. In the film's last scene he is shown walking on water.

Sabella had yet to provide any evidence that he knew what he was doing. His Argentina were a classic 'broken team': the defenders stood watching attacks, while the forwards scarcely defended. The forward line was much better than the rest, as if Manchester City's attack had been tacked onto Barnsley's back eight.

The only strategy seemed to be *Messidependencia*. The little man had scored four of Argentina's eight goals, while another was an unprovoked own goal, and one had flown in off Marcos Rojo's knee. But Messi looked exhausted. All tournament, he had walked the field in an apparent torpor, hoping his teammates could beat the likes of Bosnia and Iran without him, and he had twice performed his match-winning interventions only in the last minute.

He was also doing an unofficial second job as Argentina's chief selector. The eleven with which Sabella entered the World Cup had lasted for only the first half of the opening match against Bosnia. After that, the line-up was frequently rejigged according to Messi's wishes. Sabella, unbeknown to himself, seemed to have been appointed chiefly for his willingness to subordinate himself to Messi. Since Messi almost never spoke, Sabella usually asked the player's companions since boyhood, Angel di María and Sergio Agüero, which line-up he wanted. On the field, midfielder Javier Mascherano handled tactics.

Argentina's players certainly didn't treat Sabella as their omniscient leader. While he was instructing Ezequiel Lavezzi on the touchline during the game against Iran, the little forward squirted a water bottle over him. Yet Sabella was now one match away from glory.

A beach café in the Gaza Strip, 9 July 2014, 11.30 p.m.

About a dozen Palestinian customers at the Fun Time Beach café (Waqt-al-Marah) were watching Holland-Argentina on Israeli TV, when an Israeli missile fell through the roof, killing nine of them, including three sets of brothers and a cousin.

What happened here was what often happened during World

Cups: Israel took advantage of the world's distraction to fight a quick war that it had been planning for a while. This one would last seven weeks and kill more than two thousand people, overwhelmingly Gazan Palestinians.

Governments everywhere try to use the World Cup to their own advantage, but Israel was an unusually skilled practitioner. As a small country that was often at the centre of global news, it had evolved an unmatched media savvy about military operations (at least until 7 October 2023, when it lost interest in foreign opinion). Israel always had enemies that it wanted to kill – 'cutting the grass', Israelis called this – and the time to do this with minimal publicity was during the world's biggest media event.

The 2014 war followed an old template. A week before the 1982 World Cup, Israel had invaded Lebanon. During the 2006 World Cup, it launched Operation Summer Rains in Gaza. The World Cup didn't cause these conflicts, but it shaped their timing.

Xingu region of Brazil, 10 July 2014

Until the 1-7 defeat, the great Brazilian football trauma was always considered to be the defeat to Uruguay in the de facto World Cup final of 1950, witnessed by Jules Rimet – the so-called 'Maracanaço'. Brazilian writers have labelled that match the country's 'Hiroshima' or 'Waterloo'. However, historical revisionists suggest that the defeat was a trauma chiefly if you happened to be a male living in Rio de Janeiro. Many illiterate rural Brazilians in 1950, beyond the reach of wireless, didn't even know there was a World Cup on. This time, I wanted to find out: did the 1-7 resound across Brazil?

The anthropologist Carlos Fausto spent the 2014 World Cup with the isolated Kuikuro indigenous group deep in Brazil's Xingu region, far from anywhere. The Kuikuro loved football, and Carlos watched the tournament with them. The day after the 1-7, he sent me the following email. I have made only minor edits to improve the English:

From the beginning, the Kuikuro were not happy with Felipão's choice of team. Bernard [the midfielder] is too small, they said, it's not going to work. After the third goal some people left, and stopped watching the match. Some 20-year-old girls went to the football field in the center of the village ring, and started playing. People were not crying, or too shocked. The Kuikuro do not react too emotionally to things like this.

But in the early evening a new event drew the attention of the whole village. A 35-year-old man disappeared and was found walking some 5 km from the village. The shamans diagnosed him as a victim of a spirit attack. They have spent the whole night treating him. Again, we were all miles away from the World Cup.

... Most say they don't care about the World Cup anymore. For them, the match against Germany proved that Neymar was our sole 'kindoto' or 'ojotse', which are their words for the best wrestlers here ... They said all other Brazilian players were 'talokito' (of no value).

Copacabana beach, Rio, 11 July 2014

A European diplomat I knew had flown down to Rio from Brasilia. We went for a walk on the Copacabana, which two days before the final was filled with beer-drinking Argentinians, dressed in a rich variety of Argentinian club shirts. The diplomat loved Brazil. I asked him how he had experienced the 7-1.

He said, 'It was awful. I felt so embarrassed for the Brazilians.' Brazil, he explained, felt inferior to the developed world in almost every sphere of achievement. It had a so-called 'stray-dog complex'. Its one source of international pride had always been football.

Germany-Argentina, World Cup final,
Maracanã, 13 July 2014

Four forwards had a chance to decide this match. One did.

Twenty minutes into the game, a backward header by Toni Kroos, a moment of madness from a star of the tournament, put Argentina's Gonzalo Higuain through alone against Manuel Neuer. The Maracanã froze as the great finisher steadied himself – and half-volleyed wide. I'm guessing that moment still often plays in his mind.

Ezequiel Lavezzi was the player of the first half, leading Argentina's rapid breaks. Yet at half-time, his coach substituted him. Was Lavezzi injured? No, replied Sabella afterwards. Had the accidental manager really punished his star player for squirting water in his face live on TV a few games earlier?

The man expected to win the game was Messi. But he hadn't scored since the group stage, and once again looked spent. Just before the final whistle, he smacked Argentina's last chance, a free kick, high into the stands. It looked then that he would go down in history as a great player who failed in World Cups.

The forward who did win the match was the little German Mario Götze, who came on as a sub after eighty-eight minutes. In extra time, the son of a technology professor chested down a cross, swivelled, and volleyed home the game's only goal. Just twenty-two years old at the time, Götze didn't go on to have the great career that his goal seemed to herald. But he saved Dilma Rousseff from the photo op she had been dreading: handing Brazil's World Cup to the Argentinians.*

---

* Thanks partly to the smooth World Cup, Dilma won re-election that October, but in 2016 Brazil's Senate impeached her for breaking budgetary laws.

16

Jules Rimet Still Gleaming: Hunting the Lost Cup

One peculiarity of the modern World Cup is that the physical cup itself isn't very alluring. The FIFA World Cup Trophy, featuring two human figures holding up the earth, was introduced in 1974 to replace the original Jules Rimet Cup, which Brazil were allowed to keep after winning it for a third time in 1970.

FIFA's sponsors used the new trophy in endless commercial campaigns. This had 'degraded' the cup, admitted a FIFA official at the workshop I attended in Munich in 2004. Before the 1998 World Cup, for instance, Coca-Cola took the trophy on a world tour. I'd watched as the thing was paraded through the Ajax stadium in Amsterdam at half-time of a league match. A poor idiot with a microphone ran alongside it screaming: 'A BIG HAND for the prize that WE ALL KNOW will be coming back to Holland in July!' Nobody in the stadium clapped.

The new trophy never matched the mystique of the Coupe Rimet. That was the piece made by the Parisian sculptor Abel Lafleur for his friend Rimet before the first World Cup in 1930: the thirty-five-centimetre-high golden statuette of the winged Nike, the Greek goddess of victory, on a blue base of the semi-precious stone lapis lazuli.

'The Jules Rimet trophy was the people's trophy,' the FIFA official told the workshop. It was burnished by mythical stories. The Italian football official Ottorino Barassi had supposedly hidden it from the Nazi occupiers in a shoebox under his bed in Rome. The cup had been stolen from a stamp exhibition in London in 1966, and then found by a dog named Pickles. In 1983 it disappeared one final time, in Rio de Janeiro, stolen by thieves from its glass case in the Brazilian football federation's headquarters. It has never been seen since, but I suspect it's still out there somewhere.

In 1983, the Brazilian police found the thieves but not the trophy. They later said it had been melted down into gold bars in the foundry of the crooked Argentinian goldsmith Juan Carlos Hernández in Rio, but there are holes in this theory. For a start, the Rimet couldn't have been melted into gold bars because it wasn't solid gold. Moreover, the police had no evidence that the trophy had been melted down. In fact, Hernández (admittedly a liar) testified that he *hadn't* melted it down. A chemical analysis of his foundry found traces of gold of a different quality to the trophy.

At my request, the journalist Andrew Downie put these points to Pedro Berwanger, the Brazilian police officer who had led the original investigation. Berwanger admitted: 'Nobody really knows what happened to the cup. I wouldn't sign a document swearing it was melted down.' He said the trophy would be worth most intact: 'It'd almost be like having the Holy Grail, owning this trophy.'

I spent years pursuing the Rimet Cup. To me, it was the Maltese Falcon of football. I thought there was a good chance that it was still sitting around somewhere intact. Perhaps it had been swapped long before that theft in Rio for one of the several unauthorised replicas that had been made of it, by the Uruguayan FA, the German FA, the English FA, and probably others. If that were so, the Brazilian thieves had made off with a worthless copy.

Or perhaps the thieves had stolen the real thing, and then, instead of melting it down, had sold it to a collector. The goldsmith Hernández once told Brazilian police that the theft had been commissioned by an Italian millionaire. He was probably lying, but it's plausible that some collector did buy the trophy. In that case, they most likely kept it in a private place in their house. The collector or their heirs couldn't easily have shown off or sold such a famous stolen item. My hypothesis was that someone in the family still had the original Jules Rimet at home.

I wasn't the only one hunting for it. So was FIFA. At an auction at Sotheby's in London in 1997 it paid a staggering £254,500 for a lot titled 'Copy of the Jules Rimet Cup used as the World Cup Football Trophy Between 1968 and 1970'. This was supposedly the replica commissioned in 1966 by the English FA after the theft in London. However, FIFA secretly hoped that the cup would prove to be the real Rimet. It wasn't – it was just a cheap bronze gilded replica, after all.

FIFA confirmed the story to me in 2006:

Dear Simon,

Thank you for your enquiry.

Yes, FIFA took the decision to buy this trophy as it was thought to be the original one.

We trust this will be of use to you.

Best wishes,
FIFA

Media Department

I eventually gave up looking for the real Rimet. I accepted that it was the cup that had been stolen in Rio in 1983, and that it might have been melted down into gold bars. But in 2014, a companion of mine in the hunt found a chunk of the original trophy.

Four of us Rimet obsessives searching for the cup had pooled our efforts: me, the historian Guy Oliver from the FIFA Museum in Zurich, and an investigative duo, Jim Lynch and Joseph Coyle. One afternoon in May 2014, in a quiet corner of the tea room of the Ritz in London, I filled Guy in about an intriguing discovery. Coyle, a photojournalist, had analysed news photographs and spotted that the Rimet trophy had changed appearance between 1954 and 1958. Certainly the base was visibly bigger.

Guy went back to FIFA in Zurich, studied about fifty pictures of the trophy, and grasped what must have happened. Abel Lafleur's original lapis lazuli base had been small and four-sided. By 1950, each side was filled with one winner's name: 'Uruguay 1930', 'Italia 1934' et cetera. When the West Germans won in 1954, Guy told me afterwards, 'They get home and think, "Where do we put our name?"' There was no space left.

And so, he deduced, either the West German FA or FIFA had replaced Lafleur's base with a new, larger eight-sided one, which could fit more winners' names. Only Coyle seemed to have noticed the switch.

But where was the original base? Guy guessed that FIFA wouldn't have chucked it out. On 23 September 2014, he and Dominik Petermann of FIFA's documentation department found it, Guy told me, 'unnoticed and unlogged, hidden away on a shelf in FIFA's vast archives'. Guy emailed me a picture of the side that honoured the first champion: '*COUPE DU MONDE DE FOOT BALL ASSOCIATION _____ URUGUAY CAMPEON 1930.*'

The Uruguayans must have engraved their own achievement, which is why the language switches from FIFA's French to Spanish.

Guy wrote: 'It was one of those moments when you just stand there and you feel all funny. You daren't even pick it up, because it's a priceless work of art. The thing is, it was among a load of cheap and nasty imitations made over the years, all with weird bases.' How was Guy sure that this base was the original? 'I had looked at a whole lot of photos. The "Italia 1934" – under the "1934" there is a very big white splodge. The first thing I did was look for that and say, "Hallelujah, we've found it."' Closer inspection confirmed his judgement.

I'm still hoping that one day we'll find the winged Nike herself.

17

The Fall of Sepp Blatter

Hotel Baur au Lac, Zurich, 27 May 2015

At dawn, Swiss police raided the five-star hotel and arrested seven senior international football officials. As the men were led away, hotel staff held up Baur au Lac-branded bed sheets to shield them from photographers.

The police were acting jointly with the FBI. 'The defendants fostered a culture of corruption and greed,' said the FBI director James Comey. 'Undisclosed and illegal payments, kickbacks and bribes became a way of doing business at FIFA.'

The fall of Sepp Blatter's iteration of FIFA had been initiated by the American soccer official Chuck Blazer. I had met Blazer in 2010 at a soccer film festival in Manhattan. Perched on a mobility scooter, he was an obese, smiling, white-bearded figure who looked like Santa Claus, or, as Vladimir Putin once observed, Karl Marx. At a loss for a conversation starter, I asked brightly, 'So what's it like to be Chuck Blazer?' He reflected for a moment, and replied, 'Pretty good, actually.'

That was correct. Blazer had discovered the sport in the 1970s as a 'soccer dad' in Queens, New York. By 2010, he inhabited an entire floor of Trump Tower in Manhattan, keeping one apartment just for his cats, as David Conn recounts in his book *Fall of the House of FIFA*. Blazer liked to suggest that he had got rich inventing the ubiquitous smiley faces. In fact he had got rich as the corrupt secretary general (under President Jack Warner) of Concacaf, the Confederation of North, Central America and Caribbean Association Football.

But one day in 2011, as Blazer trundled his mobility scooter down East 56th Street, the tax authorities tapped him on the shoulder. He hadn't filed taxes for at least seventeen years. Soon he was back on FIFA's luxury-hotel circuit, but now as an FBI informer, carrying a recording device in his key fob, writes Conn, 'reportedly because he was too obese for a wire to be run in the standard way up his stomach'. Blazer also educated the FBI in how corruption works in international football: an official sells a marketing agency a set of TV or sponsorship rights on the cheap and in return pockets a kickback.

The FBI soon discovered that other corrupt soccer officials from across the Americas were foolish enough to do their banking in the US. That brought them under US jurisdiction. The FBI began investigating whether FIFA was, in American legal parlance, a RICO: a 'racketeering influenced criminal organization'. Most RICOs are mafias.

The FBI and British journalists uncovered corruption in World Cup bids far into the past – sweeteners paid by Germany for 2006 and South Africa for 2010, even before the all-you-can-eat bribery buffet of the 2018 and 2022 bids. Blatter would always see the FBI's investigation as American vengeance for their defeat by Qatar for the 2022 World Cup. If only Michel Platini had stuck with his original plan to back the US, he told me ruefully. 'Then USA would have had the World Cup and then the whole organisation of the FIFA would not have been in such a critical situation. The Americans, bad losers, attacked FIFA and so ...'

His argument is plausible but dubious. Chris Steele, the former MI6 agent hired by England's bid to collect information on rivals, had alerted an FBI agent to possible corruption in spring 2010 – months before the American defeat. On the other hand, Bill Clinton, an ambassador of the US bid, did take FIFA's vote as a personal humiliation. I'm told that Clinton's team passed information to the FBI. That may have galvanised the investigation.

Either way, the raids at the Baur au Lac exposed Blatter's FIFA as a giant kickback scheme. What could the delegates left in the hotel do after the arrests? They went right ahead with the business for which they had gathered: re-electing Blatter. 'The football family', as he called it, wasn't bothered about the FBI or the media. The 'family' was discredited in the eyes of the world, but it didn't care about the world. It cared about its kickbacks. Most family members came from countries where this was how politics and business were done.

And so, after the arrests, while FIFA officials shredded documents at headquarters, the seventy-nine-year-old Blatter won his fifth presidential term in a farcical election. He got votes from corrupt autocracies, but also from the French and Spanish federations. Some delegates photographed their secret votes as proof of their fealty to him. Others compared him to Mandela or Jesus.

But the pressure from media, the FBI and Switzerland (tired of being embarrassed by FIFA) was becoming unbearable. Blatter's daughter Corinna, his chief confidante, had been urging him for some time to retire with honour after the success of the Brazilian World Cup. Whenever he banged on about 'the football family', she'd say, 'The family is me.'

He told me in the empty Zurich restaurant: 'Would I have listened to my daughter.' His personal press officer beside him nodded: 'Should have retired in 2014.'

Blatter turned on the man: 'It's a nonsense to say what you should have done, because time is running and you haven't done it! So it's also nonsense to say it was a big mistake. It was an error. Definitely. But life is going on and I'm still there.'

Four days after his re-election, he stepped down. In December 2015 he and Platini were jointly banned from football. Their falls appeared to be in character: Blatter was found to have bribed the Frenchman with two million Swiss francs. Both men appealed.

Blatter's demise felt cathartic, like the tumbling of Saddam Hussein's statue in Iraq in 2003. But this time, just as in Iraq, it turned out that the US hadn't restored a rules-based international order. In 2016 FIFA's congress elected as president another Swiss bureaucrat, Gianni Infantino, after he drew an ovation from the 209 heads of national federations with an inspired line: 'The money of FIFA is your money!'

Much about Infantino recalls Blatter: the awkward multilingual bonhomie, his mastery of patronage, and his sense of impunity. Under Infantino, FIFA's congress did pass a few reforms, including the standard corporate practice of letting an independent committee decide the pay of top executives. But when the committee set Infantino's annual salary at 1.95 million Swiss francs, he raged (on a tape that leaked) that this was 'insulting'. In 2017, FIFA didn't renew the terms of the two chairmen of the ethics committee, which had been investigating him for multiple cases of malpractice. Infantino began reorienting FIFA towards the game's new funders, Qatar (where he set up house for a while) and Saudi Arabia. He dismissed media criticism with a familiar new phrase, 'fake news'.

A few of FIFA's crooks did get caught. Of the twenty-two men who voted on the World Cup bids in 2010, seven were charged or accused by US authorities of criminal wrongdoing. Six others were sanctioned by FIFA's ethics committee. Another, Franz Beckenbauer, came under criminal investigation in Switzerland and Germany regarding his country's 2006 bid.

The list went on. João Havelange resigned as FIFA's honorary president aged ninety-seven after new revelations about kickbacks. (He died in 2016, aged 100.) Chuck Blazer would die in 2017 before he could be sentenced. Several other ageing football officials used the same method to dodge justice, but some of Blazer's pals were jailed.

All the while, Blatter continued to pretend that he had been naive not to realise that there were bad people inside FIFA. He had thought they all wanted the best for football, just like he did. And he complained that when he stopped being president, they stopped being nice to him. He told me:

> I have realised that I have not so many friends. I have had a lot of colleagues, but no friends. And suddenly, I was alone. Swiss justice came in and started an investigation, and then I was abandoned and I was very sad, sad, sad.

Blatter spent much of his eighties defending himself against multiple accusations. But the long-anticipated emotional crescendo of FIFA's corruption saga – his arrest – never came. He and Platini were acquitted of the bribery accusations in 2022, and again in 2025. It was a bit late to revive their careers.

Blatter was sulky about Infantino. He told me, 'I am astonished and surprised that out of the 211 national associations, members of FIFA, there is not one single voice against the new leadership.' However, nobody cared any longer what he thought.

At the end of the interview, I asked him how he would be remembered. At first, he sidestepped the question: 'I don't know how long the Lord will give me life, but I try, I try again.'

> Me: Let's hope the Lord gives you a lot more life, but when it ends, what do you hope people will say about you?
> Blatter: I don't care what people will say.
> Me: You do care. You care about your reputation.

That's when Blatter, trying to explain who he was, talked about his origin story:

> When I was born, I was premature. I had not even two kilos. Can you imagine what came out there? No hospital at that time. I had to fight everywhere. At school I was always the smallest one, and I became a fighter.

As FIFA president, he was still the undersized kid who had to find his own ways to defend himself. I asked again how he wanted to be remembered. Tired by this point, he switched to his native German. He used the old-fashioned word, '*korrekt*', meaning morally right. He said that if the judgement of him was *korrekt*, 'you should say, "It's the man who brought international football into the world. Two billion followers."' Football's global conquest hadn't been driven by television. It had been orchestrated by Sepp Blatter.

When I thanked him for the interview, he was all charm. He said we should have met at his house. His press officer led him out of the restaurant. At the door, Blatter turned, waved and said, 'Bye bye.' He was so tiny that his scarf hung to his knees.

18

World Cup 2018: Putin's Policeman and Me

When FIFA awarded Russia the World Cup in 2010, the country wasn't yet an international pariah. By the time the tournament rolled around eight years later, it had got most of the way there. Russia's ruthlessness had wrong-footed the West in the bidding race. It did so again in 2014, when Putin annexed Crimea; in 2015, when he barrel-bombed Syrian cities; and in 2016, when he meddled in the US election almost as if it were a World Cup vote.

In 2018 he became the first autocrat to host the World Cup since the Argentinian military junta forty years earlier. He had spared no expense. The total cost of the new stadiums was estimated at $14 billion; a record for any football tournament, a nice little earner for his cronies and a source of rage on Russian social media.

Very few western politicians were coming to Putin's tournament. But he would have to put up with thousands of foreign journalists poking around the country for a month – probably the largest international media contingent ever to enter Russia.

Moscow, 12 June 2018

A brief history of technological progress for journalists at World Cups:

> 1950s: Spend ages queuing at the telegraph office to cable your match report home
>
> 1980s: Spend ages reading your match report over the phone to bored copytaker at your newspaper
>
> Early 2000s: Spend ages trying to send your match report through dodgy internet cable
>
> 2018: Spend ages trying to send your match report on a squidgy burner laptop provided by your newspaper, without using Wi-Fi, in a probably forlorn bid to stop the Russian regime from stealing your personal data.

The *FT* had given me an elaborate security briefing before I went. They especially didn't want me to use public Wi-Fi, whether in media centres or anywhere else. Inevitably, I sometimes did. It was the only way I could function while working 24/7. I'm guessing I joined the long list of foreigners hacked by Russia.

Moscow, 13 June 2018

Arriving fans waited in endless passport queues at Sheremetyevo airport. I finally made it to the battered apartment building in central Moscow where I had booked a studio. Airbnbs had become the norm for the tournament, with Russians renting out their homes; a Russian historian joked to me that the last time so many Muscovites fled Moscow was when Napoleon invaded.

Walking around the city centre a day before the opening game, I saw more Peruvian or Chinese fans dressed in their national colours than Russian supporters, even though China had not qualified. Hardly any Russian flags hung from apartment windows or even outside shops or restaurants. The main evidence that the tournament was about to kick off were the police officers who had flooded the city.

There were echoes here of São Paulo shunning Brazil's government-backed World Cup four years earlier. Liberal Muscovites had been allergic to national symbols since the jingoism surrounding Putin's invasion of Crimea. More prosaically, Russians were embarrassed by their national team, the Sbornaya. Connoisseurs of Russian football reckoned that it was the weakest in twenty years – which was saying something.

Naturally, the state had tried its traditional sporting fix: doping. The World Anti-Doping Agency's McLaren Report of 2016 spoke of more than 150 suspicious doping tests of Russian footballers. It suggested that there was a special 'urine bank' of clean samples, and implied that the whole Sbornaya squad at the 2014 World Cup may have benefited from manipulation. Even so, Russia had been eliminated from that tournament in the first round. Doping is of limited use in skill-based, tactical football. No wonder Putin was keeping his distance from the team, while Russian media played down the World Cup. Still, there was hope. By happy chance (or perhaps not), Russia had been drawn with Uruguay, Egypt and Saudi Arabia in a group that statisticians had identified as the weakest in the tournament's history.

Russia-Saudi Arabia, Luzhniki Stadium, Moscow, 14 June 2018

The start of a World Cup is a good time to bury bad news. The day before the opening game, the Saudi crown prince Mohammed bin Salman had launched one of the bloodiest attacks of his country's war in Yemen. And on match day, the Kremlin sneaked out a plan to hike Russian retirement age by several years – the first rise since Stalin had introduced pensions.

The noisiest fans in the stadium were Latin Americans in their various national colours. A few minutes before kick-off, the home crowd managed an approximately fifteen-second chant of 'Rossiya!'. When Putin rose to speak, people applauded, but only for about ten seconds. With a smirk on his Botoxed face, he talked about football spreading love. But the home fans' attention soon wandered, and as he droned on, he was drowned out by a hubbub of chatter. The biggest cheer came when he finished.

Putin then settled down in his VIP box, chatting and laughing with his companions, Mohammed bin Salman ('MBS') and FIFA president Gianni Infantino. It was a vision of a new non-western world order, an effect enhanced by the names on the advertising boards around the pitch: Gazprom, Qatar Airways, South Korea's Kia Motors.

The slapstick Saudi side all but clinched the *FT*'s worst team award in the first forty minutes of the tournament. The highlight might have been the moment when two defenders came sliding in simultaneously and eliminated themselves before the Russian forward Denis Cheryshev even had a chance to make a feint. The Sbornaya won the 'Petrol Derby' 5-0. After one Russian goal, MBS spread out his hands towards Putin in a gesture of embarrassment.

Viewers in Mumbai or Shanghai, raised on a weekly diet of Messi, Ronaldo and Manchester City, were probably aghast to discover that this level of football existed. On my long walk back to my Airbnb, I didn't see a single honking car or a Russian dancing in the street.

Goethe Institut, Moscow, 15 June 2018

Hundreds of Russians, mostly parents and children, swamped the football-themed summer party at the German cultural centre – the world's biggest Goethe Institut. There was beer, fun and a German soap opera, but not a single screen on the premises showing the Morocco-Iran game. Nobody seemed to miss it, or to be following the game on their phones.

This afternoon was the zenith of both German–Russian friendship and of German footballing hubris. Reinhard Grindel, president of Germany's football federation, joked with the crowd about meeting Russia in the final. A fellow official explained that the Germans had set up their team camp just outside Moscow 'because we want to get to the semi-final and final in 25 minutes by bus'.

Germany-Mexico, Luzhniki Stadium, Moscow, 17 June 2018

Germany lost their first game 1-0. At the press conference afterwards, someone asked their coach Joachim Löw whether his team was going to become the next reigning world champion to get knocked out in the first round. 'That won't happen to us,' replied Löw.

The battlefield at Stalingrad, 18 June 2018

It was a sweltering mosquito-ridden afternoon in a decaying city in southern Russia. Volgograd exists on the byroads of history – except in 1942–43, when it was named Stalingrad, and was the site of the battle that arguably decided the Second World War.

Nearly two million Russians and Germans died here. The battlefields are a holy place of Russian nationalism. But today, England and Tunisia had come to town. There had been fears of drunken English fans wrapping their flags around semi-sacred monuments, and running through their repertoire of Second World War chants.

It didn't happen. I'd never seen England fans so solemn. There wasn't a chant or a beer bottle, barely even a titter. Instead, chubby middle-aged men in football shirts trooped respectfully around the memorial hill beneath a giant sword-waving woman – the largest female statue on earth, representing Mother Russia. For once the monumental Soviet scale felt appropriate. Standing in the Motherland's shadow, you looked down over the dowdy Soviet town built to replace the destroyed city of Stalingrad – and over the glittering Volgograd Arena, built for the World Cup, a future white elephant beside the Volga river.

English, Tunisians and Russians sat at Mother Russia's feet, swapping football banter. In part I think they didn't know what else to do. Everyone felt inadequate before the enormity of what had happened here. By the tomb of Lieutenant Vladimir Petrovich, 'Hero of the Soviet Union', killed on 13 November 1942, aged twenty-four, Russian fans armed with a selfie-stick dragged a black Tunisian with dreadlocks into a group photo. I wrote in my notebook that day: 'You feel, "We haven't made such a mess of our international relations these last seventy years, not yet, anyway."'

After the battlefield, I got a snack in the café of the nearby Stalin Museum – a fanboy venture full of solemn portraits of the mass murderer. Waitresses wearing mock Second World War uniforms served beer to football supporters. A party of Tunisians photographed themselves in Soviet military greatcoats and caps. Beside them, a TV was showing the Sweden-South Korea game. Beside that was another portrait of Stalin, and beside that sat a group of Russian men doing what most Russians did when the World Cup was on TV: not watching.

That evening, outside the stadium, a Chinese couple used a language app on a smartphone to ask directions from a Russian policeman. Every World Cup offers these kinds of dream snapshots of the host country as it could be. Here, in one image, was a Russia of world-class infrastructure, international brotherhood and helpful police. I remembered these scenes long after I'd forgotten the England-Tunisia game (2-1) that brought me to Volgograd.

Poland-Senegal, Spartak Stadium, Moscow, 19 June 2018

The vast majority of the crowd were Poles, symbolically invading the city whose rulers had so often invaded Poland over the centuries. The visitors bellowed out their anthem: 'Poland has not yet perished …' Then they watched their team achieve an almost unheard-of feat for a European side at a World Cup: losing a match to an African country.

As thousands of disconsolate Poles trudged out of the stadium, a young Russian woman – one of the party animators hired by the hosts – bellowed at them, in English, through a megaphone: 'Did you enjoy the game!?' Faced with a wall of silence, she persevered, 'Come on, let's hear some noise!' This was service with a smile, Russian-style.

Airbnbs across Russia, June–July 2018

There may never have been an easier month to visit provincial Russia. Flying around the country, I glimpsed lives that I hadn't known existed, and that nonetheless felt recognisable. I couldn't have done it without Yandex (Russia's equivalent of Uber) or Airbnb. Yandex's English-language taxi app meant no more haggling with drivers in my 100 words of Russian. And Airbnb brought me inside charming, impeccably kept, affordable homes in peeling Soviet-era apartment blocks – helped by the fact that just for this month, the hosts didn't seem bothered about registering guests with the authorities.

My hostess in Volgograd was a medical student who lived in a decaying suburban apartment building for which she apologised the moment we met. She told me about her time studying in Montenegro, and her treasured biannual trips abroad. I'll never see her again, but I left feeling that she was an internationally-minded person who wanted the same sort of things from life as I did, except that her chances of getting them were a lot slimmer.

That tournament, I stayed in Airbnbs in five different cities. All my hosts were women, aged under forty, who spoke good English and had seized the opportunity to monetise homes that no foreigner would ever want to stay in again. My hostess in Nizhny Novgorod, thousands of miles and hefty visa requirements removed from Paris, was studying French. When I went out in the city, a middle-aged woman came up and chatted to me in impeccable English. She explained that she taught English at the local university. I later calculated that she must have learned it in Soviet times, when Nizhny was closed to foreigners. Only much later did it occur to me that she might have been a security operative, sent to check on visiting journalists.

England beat Panama 6-1 in Nizhny's new stadium. Exploring the town, and feasting in an excellent hipster dumpling joint called Testo, I hoped that I would visit again one day, though I realised even then that I probably never would.

In Samara, my Airbnb hostess was away but her mother wordlessly presented me with a specially made jar of her apricot jam. I wish I could have taken it with me on the flight back to Moscow.

The Russians I saw didn't seem to be consuming the World Cup in a patriotic frenzy. While staying in their tower blocks, I was reminded of an obvious truth: most people, especially in a middle-income country, are too overwhelmed by everyday life to exist in a state of political mobilisation. Paying for groceries or trying to squeeze a pram into a lift loom larger than the glory of the motherland. Only 1 or 2 per cent of Russians were politically active, I was told by Sergey Bondarenko, of the human rights group Memorial. Why bother, when they had no sense of agency?

During communism, too, most Russians had had better things to think about than politics. The notion of the fanatical totalitarian citizen didn't survive archival research into daily life. For instance, I heard from Robert Edelman, historian of Soviet sport, that many Soviet football fans had been much more invested in supporting their clubs than in supporting the party state.

Meeting these provincial Russian women who yearned for the world, I kept being reminded of *Three Sisters*. In Chekhov's play, the sisters living in a forgotten garrison town dream of Moscow. One of them laments, 'I don't think there can really be a town so dull and stupid as to have no place for a clever, cultured person. Let us suppose even that among the hundred thousand inhabitants of this backward and uneducated town, there are only three persons like yourself. It stands to reason that you won't be able to conquer that dark mob around you. Their life will suck you up in itself, but still, you won't disappear having influenced nobody: later on, others like you will come, perhaps six of them, then twelve, and so on, until at last your sort will be in the majority.'

In the summer of 2018, I thought this was starting to happen in Russia.

A metro station, Moscow, June 2018

Half of Peru seemed to have come to Russia for their team's brief, disappointing campaign. One morning I watched an endless line of Peruvians descend an escalator into the metro station, each holding a smartphone to their face, filming themselves. I know this is now a cliché about modern life, but it wasn't like that as recently as Brazil in 2014, when videos on social media weren't yet so common.

By 2018, the World Cup was becoming a virtual experience even if you were actually there. Whenever a knot of fans started behaving like fans in a Coca-Cola ad – singing their country's name while banging a drum, say – everyone else gathered round and filmed them, sending the 'passion' viral. Any spectator in fancy dress would get picked out by the TV cameras. Then people watching in Dayton, Ohio, or Ouagadougou in Burkina Faso would wish they were at the World Cup.

Stadium media centre, Moscow, 27 June 2018

A hall full of journalists watched the TV screens in stupefaction. Germany, the team that always won in the last minute, conceded twice in injury time in Kazan. South Korea's second goal was tapped into an empty German net, with goalkeeper Manuel Neuer stranded upfield looking to score the equaliser. Once again, the world champions had exited the tournament in the first round.

England-Belgium, Kaliningrad, 28 June 2018

The Russian host city that I'll always remember is Kaliningrad. Strolling through a pleasantly landscaped park in the centre of town, I suddenly realised that I was walking on top of what until 1945 had been the German city of Königsberg.

Königsberg was a rich, beautiful, German-speaking port, a kind of eastern Hamburg. After its destruction by the Red Army, it was replaced by a concrete Soviet town. By 2018, many Russian locals mourned the loss. In black-and-white photos displayed in the park and in local museums, you could admire Königsberg's swinging cafés, its art nouveau buildings, the German kids playing on the streets, and the electric trams that ran here in the 1880s.

In the final years of Königsberg, the city's central square was called Adolf Hitler Platz; after the Soviets took the city, they renamed it Ploshchad Pobedy, or 'Victory Square'. It was here, outside a McDonald's, that beer-drinking English and Belgian fans gathered before the game. As in Volgograd, there was cheery fraternisation on the site of unimaginable bloodbaths. Local families posed for selfies arm in arm with fat Englishmen. Belgians sang, 'Come on Belgium!' in English. A group of Argentinians watched benevolently from nearby. The English fans I spoke to (all men) told me that none of the Russian violence they had feared before the tournament had materialised.

The Russian–British political relationship in 2018 was literally toxic. Three months before the World Cup, Russian agents had poisoned the Russian defector Sergei Skripal and his daughter Iulia in Salisbury. That had sparked a diplomatic crisis, during which Russia expelled, among many others, the British embassy official in charge of fan security. There were worries of a rerun of events during Euro 2016, when Russian thugs had attacked English supporters in Marseille. 'BLOODBATH: Russian hooligans warn England fans "Prepare to DIE"', the *Daily Express* had reported in a traditional pre-World Cup 'all-out hooligan-war' piece.

England's first two games in Russia, against Tunisia and Panama, each drew fewer than 2,000 English fans, according to official figures. The 6-1 thumping of Panama, England's record win at a World Cup, was one of their least supported matches at a modern tournament – though still probably the largest ever influx of English speakers into Nizhny Novgorod.

In Kaliningrad I interviewed England fans. Joe Smith from Romford, who drove a black cab back home, told me that the thrill-seeking young men who followed England to more hedonistic venues had generally stayed away from Russia. Most of the fans who had dared come initially avoided wearing England shirts in public, but they soon began to embrace Russia. On flights and trains, instead of the old-fashioned anti-German singing, English fans slept, chatted with foreigners or read books. Their most aggressive chant that I heard that tournament was, 'Are you watching, Scotland?'

Nobody hurt them. Russia traditionally weeded out 'unwanted elements' before international events; the security services appeared to have visited the country's hooligan gangs and ordered them to sit out the World Cup.

Josh McStay, a student from Carlisle, who like many fans had travelled to Kaliningrad by bus from Gdansk, had gone from not wearing his England shirt to wearing it without a second thought even in Kaliningrad's decaying backstreets. Russians tended to respond well to it. Some came to England games wearing their own England shirts.

Political issues cropped up only rarely, said McStay. 'Yesterday a girl serving us in a restaurant was complaining about how British and American media portray Russians as monsters. She said, "We are not monsters, are we?" We laughed and said no.'

Howard Keyworth and Will Chatters, students from Stockport, had flown in from Tallinn in a terrifying 'tiny plane with propellers'. They were travelling with their friend Max Doyle, a Briton living in Moscow. In St Petersburg, they had encountered Zenit's feared 'ultra' fans. One had come up to them to practise his English. Chatters told me, 'He said we were the first "England" he had met in his life.' The Zenit ultras – dressed in Fred Perry gear, the traditional brand of British hooligans – had taken the visitors to a local bar and initiated them into their favourite beers. Chatters said, 'They idolised British hooligan culture of the 1980s. They saw that as the pinnacle. Now they think they are the pinnacle.' Doyle added: 'Like a weird, weird passing of the torch.'

Plane from Kaliningrad to Moscow, 29 June 2018

My flight was packed with police officers who had worked at the England-Belgium game. One of them had taken my prized window seat. I didn't dare challenge him, so I squeezed in between him and a policewoman.

The policeman smiled, shook my hand and introduced himself as Alexei, twenty-two years old, from a provincial city that I won't name for fear of getting him into trouble all these years later. I told him I was an English journalist covering the football.

Armed with a few words of each other's languages, and translation websites on our phones, we managed to chat. Alexei said he had policed four World Cup matches so far, but hadn't got to watch a minute of play. Still, he said, it had been 'very exciting'. This was only the second flight he'd ever been on.

He was also very excited to speak to a foreigner. How many, I asked, had he met in his life? He held finger and thumb an inch apart: almost none. But his unit had taken a language course before the World Cup. He'd been impressed by the foreign fans, and their multilingualism. Now he was determined to improve his languages. I asked if he had ever been abroad. Alexei typed a sentence into the translation website: 'Police are not allowed to go outside Russia.'

When the plane took off, the policewoman next to me fell asleep with her head on my shoulder, her knock-off Louis Vuitton bag at her feet. It had been a long World Cup for both our professions.

Alexei showed me pictures of his parents and his policewoman girlfriend. I showed him my wife and kids, and told him about my year at university learning intensive Russian, almost all of which I'd since forgotten. I began reciting the one Russian poem I ever memorised, by Pushkin:

Я вас любил: любовь ещё, быть может,
(I loved you: love, still, perhaps,)

Alexei interrupted me with the next line:

В душе моей угасла не совсем;
(Has not been extinguished in my soul)

'Love has not been extinguished' is the way I felt about Russia. Travelling around the country reminded me of what had first drawn me to it: the awesome heritage of war and peace and life and fate, the intense conversations – and the sense I had absorbed on my first visit here in 1992, just after the fall of communism, that our former enemies behind the Iron Curtain were quite like us.

When the plane landed, the police officers applauded, and Alexei took photographs through the window. I typed into my translation engine, 'I wish you good luck in life,' and we said goodbye.

Berlin Olympics, 1936

While I was enjoying Russia, I'd sometimes wonder: was I being seduced by Putin? Was the World Cup his propaganda master stroke? Was I, essentially, covering the 1936 Berlin Olympics?

Raves by foreigners about Russia's friendly, efficient, high-spec World Cup carried troubling echoes. Willy Brandt, the future chancellor of West Germany, who visited the friendly, efficient, high-spec 1936 Games incognito from exile in Norway, wrote: 'Why can't we admit that even people who used to vote left are impressed?'

Even the British diplomat Robert Vansittart, who had been warning against Hitler for years, predicting that he would annex Austria and invade Poland, wondered, while at the Games, whether he had misjudged the Nazis. He met Hitler and several henchmen, including Goebbels, whom he called, 'a limping, eloquent, slip of a Jacobin … My wife and I liked him and his wife at once'. That fortnight, the Nazis seduced important people.

I eventually decided that the Russian World Cup probably wasn't the Berlin Olympics. That was largely because Putin by 2018 was a better-understood entity than Hitler in 1936. Hitler at that point had said and done disturbing things, but few foreigners took him either literally or seriously. Putin's damage after eighteen years in power was harder to miss. And our generation is surely better trained at seeing through propaganda – including sportswashing – than people were in the 1930s.

I hope that I wouldn't have covered the Berlin Games. Yet I mostly felt comfortable covering this World Cup, which – like Russia itself – was bigger than Putin. I was able to write about the genius of Paul Pogba, which uplifted all of humanity, safe in the knowledge that my newspaper was also covering Russian elite corruption and Putin's cruelty to LGBT+ people. But of course it suited me to believe this.

France-Argentina, our living room in Paris, 30 June 2018

My children, Parisians born and raised, were twelve, nine and nine, and this was their first unforgettable World Cup game: a 4-3 win for their country against Messi's Argentina. The nineteen-year-old revelation Kylian Mbappé got two goals in four minutes. My son Leo told my wife years later that the second of these had been the best moment of his life. Then he paused and apologised: 'I mean, it's not like I had a baby or got married. Or got a scholarship.' Almost as good was the cracking half-volley by the out-of-nowhere French full-back Benjamin Pavard, which inspired a fans' song that my sons still know by heart.

My kids watched the game with their school friends and their friends' parents in our flat over pizzas. Afterwards, the living-room walls were smeared with red, white and blue face paint from the children's celebrations. The kids will always remember their golden summer of 2018 and the people with whom they watched, just as I can visualise entire evenings from the World Cups of 1978 and 1982. Perhaps the point of World Cups is the construction of memories.

I won't feature in my children's World Cup memories, because I was always away at the World Cup. I watched France-Argentina with British friends on TV in a hotel bar in Moscow. It was pleasant, but the emotional locus of any World Cup is more in the world's living rooms than in the host country. For the peak World Cup experience, stay home. The atmosphere in most Russian stadiums was tamer than in my own flat.

I watched matches squeezed in among other British journalists, while eating my dinner of peanuts bought from a stadium vending machine. I rarely cared who won. Nor, usually, did the Russian majority in the stands, who filled the duller stretches of games with chants of 'Rossiya' (the full extent of their repertoire).

That's the norm for a modern World Cup. The venue is what the French anthropologist Marc Augé calls a 'non-place' – broadly, a 'supermodern' site of transience, like an airport or hotel lobby, where humans barely leave their idiosyncratic marks. Most of the stadiums are new, without handed-down history. They serve as film sets, or Instagram backdrops. You're in Nizhny Novgorod but it could have been Johannesburg. There is no 'there' here.

Argentinian postscript

According to one popular Argentinian conspiracy theory, the national team's World Cup went off track when they pulled out of a warm-up match in Israel, apparently in protest against Israeli treatment of Palestinians. The theory was that the Israeli secret service Mossad took revenge by sabotaging Messi.

After Argentina's 3-0 thrashing by Croatia in a group match, pundits in an Argentinian TV studio observed a minute's silence. Osvaldo Ardiles, an Argentinian world champion of 1978, called the 2018 side the country's 'worst team in history'. I wrote in the *FT*, with my usual prescience:

> The country's domestic league has already been bought dry, and going to a game in certain [Argentinian] hooligan-infested stadiums is considered rather like going to the Apocalypse. One of football's great national traditions may soon need that moment of silence. If anyone believes it can't happen, remember, Hungarian football used to be great, too.

Russia-Spain, Luzhniki Stadium, Moscow, 1 July 2018

When the last-sixteen knockout match went to a shoot-out, the Spaniards seemed surprised, as if the possibility had never occurred to them. They gathered in a huddle, apparently debating who should take their penalties. The forward Diego Costa was caught by a TV camera advising against choosing Koke, his teammate at Atlético Madrid. Fernando Hierro, Spain's coach, insisted, 'Koke is good.' After Koke missed the decisive penalty, Diego Costa growled, 'I told you.'

Russia had reached their first World Cup quarter-final since 1970. It was probably the emotional peak of the country's football history, but Putin hadn't been in the stadium, presumably because he expected the Sbornaya to lose. He wasn't good at showing joy anyway.

After the game, the players held up a banner to the crowd that said, 'We played for you' – not a message that Russian supporters had seen before. That night, crowds drank and danced in front of the Kremlin. Red Square belonged to them. In most countries, this would have been a normal scene after a big football victory. In Moscow, it was extraordinary – probably the city's largest spontaneous street party since Germany surrendered in 1945.

The Russians had been inspired by Peruvians, Poles and Senegalese, who danced on the streets earlier in the tournament. The foreign visitors took it for granted that the streets were theirs, that they could drink all night on Nikolskaya in downtown Moscow. Russians had never felt that freedom to use public spaces. But gradually they began joining in, while police officers looked on benevolently and posed for selfies. Russian and Ukrainian fans in central Moscow had sung Ukrainian songs together, something that could have got them arrested before the World Cup – while at the same time, the Ukrainian film director Oleg Sentsov, serving twenty years in a Russian jail, was critically ill on hunger strike.

A World Cup is a carnival, and carnivals reverse the usual order of things. In medieval folk carnivals, men dressed up as women and women as men. At the World Cup, Russian civilians reclaimed their streets from the security forces.

But when a carnival ends, the world returns to normal. Putin's deepest fear was a popular revolution of the kind he had witnessed as a junior KGB agent in Dresden, East Germany in 1989.

He didn't want Russians to feel that they owned the public spaces. A video was going around of a Russian asking two policemen whether drinking in the street would be allowed after the World Cup. 'Are you Russian?' was the reply. 'Then no.' This tournament was going to fade like a dream.

Belgium-Japan, Rostov-on-Don, 2 July 2018

My on-field moment of the tournament was Romelu Lukaku's stepover that allowed Nacer Chadli to score Belgium's last-minute 3-2 winner against Japan. Lukaku left the ball because he sensed, after years of playing together, that Chadli was steaming up behind him. That's what differentiated Belgium from other national teams: the players knew each other so well that they were able to combine like the smoothest club side.

Weirdly, the superiority of club football over national teams had been explained to me before the tournament by Belgium's Spanish manager, Roberto Martínez. He said that everyone, including him, just had to accept the quality gap. 'It's normal,' he shrugged. 'At club level, you have between fifty and sixty training sessions in pre-season. Then you play thirty-eight games and become good by practising and understanding and anticipating things.' By contrast, he said, a national team knew each other less well while playing under more pressure. Martínez was stating a general truth about World Cups, but he must have known that it didn't apply to his own team.

Most of the Belgian innocents whom I'd watched lose to Turkey in Istanbul in 2010 were still in the side eight years on, but they were now able to find each other blindfolded. Kevin De Bruyne and Eden Hazard ran midfield, every key player was in the prime age range of twenty-four to thirty-one, and the vast majority had played more than sixty internationals. They played without much pressure, because a nation of eleven million people could hardly demand a world title.

Almost every player had been globalised since their teens,

when they had left the tinpot Belgian league to acquire football know-how in England, France or the Netherlands. When they returned to play for Belgium with their companions since adolescence, the camp felt like a school reunion. Martínez said: 'I've been incredibly satisfied by how much they enjoy to be with each other.' The squad were amusing themselves in Russia by endlessly rewatching the video of their striker Michy Batshuayi celebrating a goal by accidentally kicking a ball off the post into his own face.

Khachapuri restaurant, Prospekt Mira, Moscow, 4 July 2018

In a Georgian restaurant overlooking the university gardens, I had a lovely dinner with the Russian historian Yuri Slezkine, who taught at Berkeley in California. Slezkine had grown up in Moscow, loving football ('Everyone I know in 1966 was rooting for England') to the dismay of his intelligentsia parents.

He said that his generation of educated Muscovites had worshipped western culture. 'In my day every western record, or even record sleeve, was treasured – a highly valued object.'

Now he was spending the World Cup in Moscow, watching western culture invade his home town. Seeing the foreign fans without visas going around was 'a sort of map of the world incarnate', he marvelled.

In cities like Nizhny or Samara that had hardly seen a foreigner before, it was almost as if UFOs had landed and disgorged unexpectedly friendly aliens. The Russians' delight in foreign contact may have surprised Putin. It clashed with his core message that the West wanted to destroy Russia.

Slezkine compared the World Cup with the International Youth Festival in Moscow in 1957, when Nikita Khrushchev briefly parted the Iron Curtain and 34,000 visitors from about 130 countries came to town. Sixty years later, people still talked of the 'deti festivalya' – the biracial children who were supposedly born to Soviet women nine months later. There were few moments in Russian history when Russians got a chance to feel connected to foreigners. Some of the people experiencing this during the World Cup might remember it for a long time.

Belgium-Brazil, quarter-final, Kazan, 6 July 2018

Brazil were probably the best team in the tournament – much better than their 2014 selves – but there's no rule saying that the best team has to win the World Cup. Belgium knocked them out 2-1, thanks to a freakish own goal off the shoulder of Brazil's Fernandinho, equally freakish goalkeeping by Belgium's Thibaut Courtois, and oodles of good luck.

That teed up the hilarious prospect of the world's least nationalistic nation winning the World Cup. Belgians – riven between Dutch and French speakers, natives and immigrants – were now mostly supporting Belgium. Yet they were so casual about their national symbols that none of them made a fuss about the team's working language being English, or a beer sponsor plastering its logo across the middle of the country's flag.

No Belgian pretended that victory in the World Cup would durably unite the country. The largest Belgian political party, the Dutch-speaking Flemish nationalist N-VA, wasn't even very keen on the national side. When Belgium's parliament applauded the team for topping FIFA's world rankings in 2015, N-VA MPs hadn't joined in.

But nationalism didn't seem to correlate with winning World Cups. In fact, the Red Devils (*Rode Duivels* to Dutch speakers, *Diables Rouges* to Francophones) had got good in part precisely because Belgium was so globalised. The country benefited from its open borders in the middle of football's leading region, western Europe. The outward-looking Belgians had absorbed the region's knowledge.

I'd first realised this in 2006, when I appeared in a Dutch-speaking Belgian TV debate on the topic: why was Belgium terrible at football? My fellow panellists, Flemish football dignitaries, spoke enviously about their neighbours: the French were doing that right, the Dutch this, the Germans that. I thought: these Belgians knew so much about international best practice that they were going to catch up.

The Flemish nationalist philosopher Johan Sanctorum scoffed that Belgium was 'a fake nation without citizens, regarded by the international community as a bad piece of asphalt between the Netherlands, Germany and France'. But the Devils had traversed that asphalt to acquire football know-how.

Meanwhile, Holland hadn't even qualified for Russia. I began getting anxious emails from Dutch people, whose soft support for Belgium was giving way to fear that the Devils might win a World Cup before *Oranje*. One friend wrote, 'You're there, you have to stop it.'

Samara, 7 July 2018

A passing Russian army truck leaked oil onto the empty road outside Samara's white-elephant stadium. As a metaphor, it felt overdone.

Belgium-France, semi-final, St Petersburg, 10 July 2018

The venue was the world's most expensive stadium, which had been delivered years behind schedule at a cost of $1 billion, despite being partly built by coerced North Korean labour. Belgium-France was the last top-level game that would be played here. After the tournament, the Zenit St Petersburg club were going to rent the stadium for fifty years, for less than £1.

In Russia, I'd usually take my seat in the empty media stand hours before the game, armed with my bag of peanuts, and work there rather than in the overcrowded media centre. I was almost alone in the stadium an hour and a half before kick-off, when players from both teams came out simultaneously for the pitch inspection. Several players, including France's Blaise Matuidi and Samuel Umtiti and Belgium's Kevin De Bruyne and Vincent Kompany, gathered on the field and had a long chat and a laugh with their opponents. Most players on both sides had grown up in the immigrant quarters of Francophone cities – Paris, Lyon, Marseille and Brussels. This game was practically a neighbourhood kickaround.

So little separated the sides that one goal was always likely to decide the outcome. It came on fifty-one minutes. Antoine Griezmann lifted a French corner into the penalty area, Umtiti got his head to it a fraction before Marouane Fellaini, and the ball flew in at the near post. 'It's the difference of a centimetre,' said Roberto Martínez afterwards.

France spent the rest of the game defending, as they had most of the tournament. They were a world-class side aiming to win the World Cup on the counter-attack. The French public didn't mind. France had an advantage over countries like Brazil and Holland in not having a traditional style that its fans demanded to see; *les Bleus* were free to do whatever worked. And so Belgium's greatest generation never won a World Cup.

England-Croatia, semi-final, Luzhniki Stadium, Moscow, 11 July 2018

Almost everything in England's World Cup history discourages optimism. Cheeringly, though, they had reached their first World Cup semi since 1990 playing European passing football. It wasn't done brilliantly, but, like a dog playing chess, it was remarkable to see it done at all. England's laborious combinations did not have to create chances from open play. They merely had to accomplish the simpler task of winning corners and free kicks. That's when England would unveil their great ancestral weapon: headers.

In past tournaments, that strength had been negated by opponents who wrestled England's big men on set pieces. In 2018 FIFA had cracked down on that by introducing the video assistant referee. Any opponent who grabbed an Englishman in the box now risked giving away a penalty. Suddenly international foot-ball's best heading team was getting its just deserts. On set pieces, England's chief headers of the ball would assemble in a kind of conga line, split, drag their markers around, and hope that the ball ended up on the forehead of Harry 'Slabhead' Maguire, who had won more aerial duels than any other player in the tournament.

The header is as British as the pass is European or the dribble Brazilian. It requires its own exacting technique, as well as bravery – which, in the martial tradition that the British brought to the game, was always considered a core footballing virtue.

Going into this semi-final, England had scored five headers in the tournament, and eight goals from set pieces – the latter the highest total at a World Cup since Portugal in 1966. Five minutes into the semi, they added a ninth, when Kieran Trippier curled a free kick into Croatia's net. Now they just needed to hold off a side that had few ball winners and a weak defence.

England couldn't. Their coach Gareth Southgate had spent years instilling European football into his players, but the moment the great prize loomed into view, they reverted to Englishness. That's when you saw the atavistic reflex that underlies almost any national team, whether English or Brazilian – the instinct to regress to the national style that the players absorbed as children.

The way to defend a lead for eighty-five minutes is to keep the ball by passing it around far from your own goal. But the players, like the TV audience back in England, had grown up watching their national team's eliminations from big tournaments. Every World Cup is a repetition of past World Cups, especially for a backward-looking nation like England. The players had memo-rised the negative national script: they knew what an elimination looked like.

Against Croatia, they lapsed into the traditional method of England teams defending a lead in big games: they retreated into their own penalty area, and hoofed every ball long. It was the footballing version of the British army's backs-to-the-wall Battle of Dunkirk in 1940, lathered in blood, sweat and tears.

That gave Croatia – an intelligent passing side, with a

playmaker, Luka Modric, who always saw the free man – as much of the ball as they wanted. Without passing moves, England also stopped winning the corners and free kicks near goal that were almost their only scoring weapons. Croatia won 2-1 in extra time.

England went on to lose the third-place play-off to Belgium. This meant that their achievements in Russia amounted to three wins (against Tunisia, Panama and Sweden), three defeats (against Croatia, Belgium reserves in the dead-rubber group game, and Belgium's first team) and a draw against Columbia, followed by their first win in a penalty shoot-out since 1996. Southgate's England hadn't been better than past Englands, just luckier, younger and more cheerful. Still, they had created a flickering vision of a new England: a merger of European passing with English heading.

France-Croatia, World Cup final, Luzhniki Stadium, Moscow, 15 July 2018

Years later, Kylian Mbappé told me his memories of winning the World Cup aged nineteen. The night before the final, he said, 'I was a bit stressed. I didn't manage to sleep much. But the nearer the match came, the less stressed I was. When you're in the World Cup final, you're convinced that you're going to win. Even the Croats were convinced they were going to win. You walk onto the field and the trophy is there, between the two teams, and you tell yourself it's impossible that the other team will take it. That's why there's such disappointment afterwards if you don't win.'

On sixty-five minutes, from just outside the Croatian penalty area, he curved a right-footed shot into the net, becoming the youngest player to score in a World Cup final since seventeen-year-old Pelé in 1958. France won 4-2. Interviewed on the field afterwards, he said, 'World champion, that's already good.' He meant that it was only a start.

He later admitted that he'd been too young to take it all in. But he also needed to put the triumph behind him if he was to build a great career. He told me: 'For me it wasn't an outcome, a finality. I don't think of that trophy now at all.'

Straight after the final whistle, the French players literally wrapped themselves in tricolours, in what was clearly a pre-planned patriotic offensive. 'We love the French, we are proud to be French, to be *Bleus*. *Vive la République*,' their coach, Didier Deschamps, said on French TV.

This was a campaign of outreach to mostly white fans who still hadn't forgiven the mostly non-white *Bleus* for going on strike in 2010. Yet the players' patriotism was also heartfelt. They felt deeply French, among various other identities. Paul Pogba, France's man of the tournament, was black, Muslim, a Parisian product of the suburb Roissy-en-Brie, African by origin, and a quadrilingual cosmopolitan. He yearned to be accepted by France as himself. He told French radio after the final, 'Now there is no colour, black, yellow, everything, we are all united. Now you are all proud of us. Forever.'

For this generation of *Bleus*, multiple identities were natural. Antoine Griezmann, born in the Burgundian wine region of Mâcon, son of a German father and a French-Portuguese mother, had spent his whole playing career in Spain, but also loved Uruguay. He did the press conference after the final wrapped in a Uruguayan flag, given him by a Uruguayan journalist. He was still French, though.

So were the multiracial crowds watching the game on big screens in Bondy, Mbappé's home suburb – even if on another day they might cheer for other national teams. Mbappé, with his Cameroonian-born dad and Algerian-origin mum, was a typical mixed product of the Parisian suburbs.

I knew these multiple identities from my own home. I'd already learned from my post-match call home on FaceTime that there is no greater joy on this earth than being a nine-year-old whose team has just won the World Cup. My children, like Pogba, had been raised by foreigners yet identified uncomplicatedly as French.

The announcer in the Luzhniki told us that Germany's former captain Philipp Lahm and a supermodel would present the French with 'the legendary FIFA World Cup trophy' in its 'Louis Vuitton fully designed travel case'. I wondered what Lenin, whose statue stood outside the stadium, would have made of this.

Putin and Gianni Infantino took the field to hand out the medals. The duo had had a good tournament, bar the four-person pitch invasion by the Russian feminist punk group Pussy Riot during the final. (The quartet had snuck into the ground dressed as police officers, knowing that no Russian would dare challenge the police. They got off relatively lightly with fifteen-day prison sentences.)

A rainstorm burst during the medals ceremony, and Putin was briefly the only dignitary equipped with an umbrella. French president Emmanuel Macron stood beside him, soaked in his suit, the happiest man in the Luzhniki. He hugged the Croatian players as they passed, but truly got going when *les Bleus* arrived, embracing each one like a brother and planting a kiss on Mbappé's forehead. Like so many politicians before him, Macron was overestimating the World Cup's potential to rub off on him. The uprising of the *gilet jaunes*, the 'yellow vests' – the most widespread French revolt since 1789 – would break out four months later.

African postscript

The day after France's victory, the South African comedian Trevor Noah crowed, half-jokingly, on his American TV show: 'Africa won the World Cup.'

It was an assertion made all the time – sometimes by Africans, eager to claim these heroes for their continent, and sometimes by French or foreign racists or ignoramuses who accused France of cynically importing talented African footballers. Once, when the French far-right leader Jean-Marie Le Pen reran his favourite rant about 'black' players, Lilian Thuram, a black French world champion of 1998, had retorted: 'Personally, I don't know what he's talking about. I'm not black, I'm French.'

So were all the other *Bleus*. Of the fourteen Frenchmen who appeared in the 2018 final, all were born in France except Samuel Umtiti, who immigrated with his family from Cameroon at the age of two. It had been the same story for the world champions of 1998. Thuram was born in the Caribbean territory of Guadeloupe, which is part of France, and moved to the mainland aged nine. Marcel Desailly arrived from Ghana as a toddler, and Patrick Vieira from Senegal aged eight. This was regular immigration, not a national football strategy.

These players were products of the French sporting system. They had grown up playing in state-subsidised French amateur clubs, trained by credentialled coaches (such as Mbappé's dad and uncle), in the only field of French life that was an almost colour-blind meritocracy. France's system was the reason why it won the World Cup and 'Africa' couldn't.

French postscript

Back home from Russia, I gave my twin sons a fatherly lecture. 'Listen,' I said, 'You're nine years old and you're world champions. This is as good as it's going to get. Enjoy it. Everything after this in your fan careers is going to be an anticlimax.'

They just felt sorry for me. Poor Daddy's team hadn't even qualified for the tournament.

Russian postscript

I'm writing this in 2025, after three years of full-scale war in Ukraine, when the notion of visiting Russia again feels unimaginable. What happened to the Russians who hosted me in their Airbnbs, and who danced on the streets with Peruvians? Do they miss us? Or do they still consider themselves the luckiest generation in Russian history, doing OK despite it all?

*

Our living room, Paris, 14 April 2020

France was in full lockdown for the pandemic. Football had ceased, so French TV was screening great games of the past. Tonight my kids and I watched the France-Holland qualifier of 1981, when Michel Platini's team reached the 1982 World Cup at Dutch expense. I had been twelve years old then, and I'd cried afterwards. The match still lived on in my mind as an epic clash.

Watching it nearly forty years later, my children found it hilarious: 'So much space!' 'No pressing!' 'Such bad hair!' 'Our coach would shout at us if we defended like that.'

Zurich, 24 February 2022

The moment Sepp Blatter heard that the Russian army had invaded Ukraine, he rang Putin's press secretary, Dmitry Peskov. There was no reply. 'But,' Blatter told me, 'he received my message, because it was not refused.'

I asked Blatter why he'd made the call. He said, 'I wanted to speak with the boss,' referring to his old chum Putin.

Did he think he could talk him out of the invasion? 'Yeah. I would ask him, "Hey, hey, what's the matter?"'

Blatter never heard back from Peskov.

La Finca outside Madrid, 29 May 2022

Where do footballers spend their days between World Cups? In 2021 my family moved to Madrid for a year. One Sunday we visited friends in La Finca, a wealthy gated community west of the city that looks more like suburban Florida. Many Madrilene footballers past and present – Cristiano Ronaldo, Antoine Griezmann, Gareth Bale – had inhabited La Finca's flat grey modernist mansions, with gardens and swimming pools hidden behind high fences. Hardly anything moved on the lanes except the Vigilancia security cars puttering to and fro. La Finca couldn't be further in spirit from bustling Madrid.

When we said goodbye to our friends, we called an Uber. We came out to find it, only to see that it had stopped eighty yards away, in front of the only other person out in the lane: a man wearing a suit so expensive that we could see it shimmering from where we stood. He was Eden Hazard, Real Madrid's great but injured Belgian. He must have been about to go to town for the club's celebrations after winning the Champions League final – a game in which he hadn't featured. Hazard pointed the driver towards us, the only people in La Finca without their own car.

Just then, a toddler, wearing a national team shirt with his famous father's name on the back (not Hazard), rolled across the empty lane in an unfeasibly large toy truck, trailed by his nanny. Back home, we verified from online photographs that he was indeed his father's son. A few months later, the kid's daddy and Hazard would exchange their habitual seclusion at home in La Finca for the seclusion of their team camps at the World Cup in Qatar. We all obsessed over these men, but they didn't quite live in our world.

19

World Cup 2022: This Way, Metro

I had never seen so much outrage ahead of a World Cup, almost all of it from western countries. A Scottish craft brewer caught the mood with a pre-tournament billboard ad: 'FIRST RUSSIA, THEN QATAR. CAN'T WAIT FOR NORTH KOREA.' Qatar pushed almost every western button because it flouted so many of our norms (or, at least, the norms that we claimed were western): it was a male-ruled fossil-fuelled autocracy with a hierarchy of ethnic groups.

The microscopic emirate treated – and still treats – LGBT+ people and women as second-class citizens. Lowest of all ranked the migrants who did Qatar's poorly paid work. By 2022 there were about 2.35 million foreigners in the country, or around seven for every Qatari citizen. Under Qatar's traditional 'kafala' system, migrant workers were practically the property of their employers. A boss could deport an employee for no reason, or hold their passport and keep them in Qatar against their will. An unknown number of mostly South Asian migrants had died building the tournament's infrastructure.

Yet for all the outrage, no country, player or sponsor was boycotting the World Cup. The Dutch coach Louis van Gaal called FIFA's choice of Qatar 'ridiculous', and said that the supporters boycotting the tournament 'are right', but he went anyway. Nonetheless, FIFA officials headed for Qatar quietly fearful: an ugly World Cup could damage the tournament's long-term standing. My question was: should we all be going?

Before the tournament, I spoke to players, human rights organisations and trade unions who made the case for participating in the World Cup rather than boycotting it. One renowned ex-footballer who had played in World Cups told me that if he were still playing, he would go to Qatar. A World Cup brought joy to people around the world, many of whom had difficult lives, he argued. Another tournament veteran told me: you dream your whole life of playing in a World Cup. Perhaps you'll only play one. Should you forgo it just to protest against the host?

Some activists argued that going to Qatar might do some good. Their precedent was 1978, when the World Cup was hosted by an Argentinian military junta that had 'disappeared' thousands of dissidents. Back then, too, every team went. Not even Amnesty International had called for a boycott. Steve Cockburn, head of economic and social justice for the NGO, sifted through Amnesty's 1970s archives and found arguments much like those made about Qatar. His predecessors had decided to use the spotlight of the Argentinian World Cup to pressure the junta into reforms. With hindsight, they felt that the strategy had worked.

Authoritarian regimes often imagine that hosting sporting events will burnish their reputations. But in 1978, Argentina's attempted 'sportswashing' backfired internationally. Foreign journalists picked up the critiques of organisations like Amnesty. A popular bumper sticker depicted a football covered with barbed wire. A member of the Madres de la Plaza de Mayo, the organisation of mothers of Argentina's disappeared, told me in 1993: 'It's thanks to the World Cup that we became known around the world.'

When Amnesty staff reviewed the tournament internally, they argued that it had ratcheted up scrutiny of a previously overlooked regime. Some countries, jolted by the publicity around the World Cup, agreed to take more Argentinian refugees. On the other hand, Amnesty concluded that the tournament bolstered the junta's reputation inside Argentina.

Engagement achieved something in 1978 because the anti-communist Argentinian regime cared what its western allies thought. Qatar in 2022 cared too. Sandwiched between Saudi Arabia and Iran, the mini-state needed western military protection. Indeed,

Qatar had bid for the World Cup partly because its long-term policy was to buy influence in the West.

That gave NGOs and trade unions leverage to pressure Qatar into reforms. There were countless issues to target, but the one that gained traction ahead of the World Cup was Qatar's treatment of migrant workers. As in 1978, media amplified the NGOs' critiques.

This pressure took years to work. From 2010 until about 2017, FIFA, sponsors and Qatar tried to ignore the critics. In this period, migrant workers had almost no rights. Still, something had already changed: for the first time, there was an ongoing discussion about what kind of country Qatar should be. Even Qataris had barely asked that question before.

And the foreign attacks upset the monarchy. A tournament meant to 'sportswash' the country's reputation had damaged it instead. Then, after Saudi Arabia led a neighbours' blockade of Qatar in 2017, the emirate's need for western friends grew acute.

That was when Qatar pledged to soften its 'kafala' system. This was a big concession, because most Qataris probably wanted *more* kafala – more control over the migrants who outnumbered them in their own country, and even, in the form of domestic servants, inside their own homes. The emirate signed an agreement with the International Labour Organization and entered dialogue with human rights groups. Just before the tournament, Amnesty summed up the gains:

> Reforms enacted by Qatar since 2017 include a law regulating working conditions for live-in domestic workers, labour tribunals to facilitate access to justice, a fund to support payment of unpaid wages, and a minimum wage. Qatar has also ratified two key international human rights treaties, albeit without recognising the right of migrant workers to join a trade union.

It wasn't nearly enough, but it was something.

True, some of the promised reforms were barely implemented.

Think of the Bangladeshi security guard in Qatar who told Amnesty that he hadn't had a day off in three years. Still, the critics of Qatar that I spoke to offered qualified praise. Tim Noonan of the International Trade Union Confederation said Qataris had brought 'their industrial relations system into this century'. Lise Klaveness, president of Norway's football federation, remarked that 'everyone should applaud' the amount of labour reform made in such a conservative country. (Norway, whose team finally didn't qualify for the World Cup, was the federation that came closest to a boycott.)

Steve Cockburn said that Amnesty felt 'slightly validated' in having chosen to engage with Qatar. The NGO's aim during the tournament itself would be to get Qatar and FIFA to agree to create a compensation fund worth at least $440 million – the total prize money on offer at the World Cup – for workers exploited in the building of the infrastructure.

NGOs and trade unions also hoped that Qatar's reforms would have a 'demonstrative impact' on its neighbours, the United Arab Emirates and, especially, the big one, Saudi Arabia – a country with by far the Gulf's largest contingent of migrant workers, who continued to be shamelessly exploited.

The upshot was that by 2022, the world knew infinitely more about Qatar's abuses than it had in the era when the abuses were worse. The spotlight was working – but once it was switched off after the World Cup, the monarchy was likely to backslide. And Qatar had barely conceded anything on LGBT+ rights, women's rights or the freedom of visiting journalists to report on matters beyond football.

I had originally expected that some players would use the platform of the World Cup to speak out. After all, this was an unprecedentedly educated and activist generation of football-ers. Countless teams had 'taken the knee' to support Black Lives Matter; Kylian Mbappé had spoken out against French police violence; and eight team captains going to Qatar, including England's Harry Kane, had said they would wear rainbow armbands in solidarity with LGBT+ people.

But when I asked players and agents about potential activism, I realised that it wasn't going to happen. A footballer like England's Marcus Rashford could campaign against racism and for free meals for impoverished British children during school holidays because he understood these issues from personal experience. By contrast, few players felt confident discussing kafala.

There was another obstacle: Gulf monarchies had co-opted much of the football industry by buying or sponsoring clubs. Speaking out was tricky for players like Messi, Neymar and Mbappé, who worked for Qatari-owned Paris Saint-Germain. Their co-option was part of the broader Qatarisation of the West. Especially in France and Britain, the mini-state had bought prestige properties such as Harrods and London's Shard skyscraper, and provided well-paid gigs to members of the British and French elites who would always pick up the phone when Doha rang. Many countries relied on Qatari natural gas, especially after Russia invaded Ukraine nine months before the World Cup. Europeans were in hock to Qatar.

What about footballers at the World Cup who weren't working for the emirate? Well, any of them who made political statements would be running another kind of risk, ex-players explained to me. If someone spoke out and then played badly, he'd become a global target on social media. Look at the abuse that Rashford had taken after missing a penalty in the Euro 2020 final.

In any case, western criticisms of Qatar generally weren't echoed in other parts of the world. Much of the Global South dismissed the attacks as hypocrisy from sore losers who couldn't handle the first Islamic World Cup. The tournament was going ahead in Qatar whether westerners liked it or not.

Most Qataris probably wished that it wasn't. Over the twelve years since a few venal Exco members had given the ministate the nod, Qatar had acquired both a global image and an image problem. Now, a conversative, teetotal society, with no experience of free media, would have to host the world's biggest party.

I know that this sounds like a cop-out, but I flew to Doha eager to report on the football while my *Financial Times* colleagues in

Qatar covered the serious stuff. The idea was to hold two thoughts in our heads simultaneously: to fight sportswashing while enjoying the sport.

Al-Mansoura neighbourhood, Doha, 17 November 2022

New streets sprouted so quickly in Doha that Google Maps barely worked here. Add in the fact that most inhabitants were recently arrived migrants, and hardly anybody knew where anything was. My taxi driver from the airport searched for half an hour before locating the building in the Al-Mansoura neighbourhood where the *Financial Times* had rented an apartment for me and my colleague Josh. Our suite, with its brown armchairs, looked like a Soviet showroom apartment circa 1983. The building's friendly receptionists, cleaners and odd-job men were mostly Indians, Ugandans, Filipinos and black South African women.

That first evening, Josh and I wandered out for dinner and found ourselves in streets populated by South Indian men. There was hardly a woman or a Qatari to be seen. Here we were, in one of the richest cities on earth, and it felt like a mid-market neighbourhood of Chennai. The single men of Al-Mansoura were known in Doha English as 'executive bachelors'. They were the city's lower middle class: hotel receptionists, shopworkers and the like, a cut above the construction workers who lived in barracks outside town.

Our meal for two in a South Indian restaurant cost twenty-two riyals, less than £5, though admittedly we didn't know exactly what we were eating. A shop a couple of doors down was selling live chickens, kept in cages. We stocked up on supplies in the Loyal City supermarket, where all the soaps promised 'whitening'. Doha apparently also had Filipino, Ghanaian and other largely monoethnic neighbourhoods.

The multinational city felt safe. The back entrance of our building was open and unguarded; I'd go in and out that way. But a printed note on the door affirmed the local caste system:

'DELIVERY GUYS AND COURIER GUYS NOT ALLOWED –
USE MAIN ENTRANCE.'

During the tournament, I hardly ever noticed the neighbourhood Indians talking football or watching games on screens in
restaurants. You certainly didn't see them in the stadiums. Every
night after the last match, I'd travel from the World Cup to another
country, grabbing a 2 a.m. samosa before bedtime.

Doha, 18 November 2022

Two days before the tournament kicked off, Qatar banned the
sale of beer at stadiums. Only the luxury suites for VIP spectators
would be allowed to serve alcohol.

The word was that the ban had been ordered spontaneously
by the emir's brother. In one stroke, it had wiped out the marketing plans of FIFA's sponsor Budweiser. The emirate was divided
between conservatives and liberals just like any western country,
and the local conservative Muslims were pleased.

The ban was the biggest media story out of Qatar until the
football kicked off. Some Muslims observing the fuss might have
concluded that western societies really were addicted.

Doha, November–December 2022

Travelling around during the tournament, I realised that the Qataris had spent the twenty-first century literally building a country. Doha's population had approximately quadrupled since 2000, to 2.7 million people, and the World Cup had supercharged the growth. Most constructions – the metro, stadiums, skyscrapers, malls, apartment blocks for 'executive bachelors' and so on – had gone up since 2010. Going around town felt like being in *The Truman Show*: Qatar had built an entire decor just for us. The World Cup is almost always its own country, but usually it is dropped into an existing country. Not in Doha.

The new city was all motorways and office towers, a 1960s vision of modernity built in the 2010s. Qatar hadn't spent any of its fossil-fuel fortune on aesthetics. Most of the buildings were cheaply built Arabian kitsch. Outdoors, you felt the constant roar of passing cars. Official billboards tried valiantly to inject some cheer: 'Visit the public parks with their various attractions.'

Qatar had imported migrants to build it all. It had then built more houses to house the migrants, and imported other migrants to sell them samosas and soap. One of the very few Qataris I met in Doha told me, 'I grew up in a small town. Now it's a big city. You don't often see that change in one generation.'

Qataris seemed mostly to seal themselves off in their big houses, or gather with other Qataris in luxury shopping malls, or in expensive restaurants hidden away along a lagoon. They had ceded their city to foreigners, and kept only the money.

There is an alternate universe in which Platini and his associates stuck to their original plan for 2022 and gave the US the World Cup. Then Doha could have remained a cosy small town. Qataris might have preferred that.

Porto Arabia, The Pearl, Doha, 19 November 2022

Meteorologically at least, the Qataris had timed the tournament right. On a balmy November evening the night before the opening game, wealthy white and Qatari families strolled along the promenade of the yacht harbour by the Rolls-Royce showroom. Street cleaners swept up invisible grains of dirt. I saw my first Qatari fans: a veiled mother leading three small boys, one in full Argentina kit complete with football boots, another dressed as Brazil's Neymar, and a toddler in civilian clothing guarded by a migrant nanny. Let the games begin.

A hostel at Qatar University, Doha, 20 November 2022

The morning of the opening match, I visited an underpaid assistant coach I knew in the Argentinian camp. For some reason, while other teams were in five-star hotels, the Argentinians were staying in a repurposed hostel for female students at Qatar University. Migrant security guards stood wilting in the sun, guarding the barrack-style edifice like a presidential palace. They treated me as a probable terrorist. After an endless exchange of WhatsApp messages with my friend, he came out and we grabbed a fifteen-minute chat about the team in the shade beside their training ground.

He spent the entire World Cup locked up in camp, working nonstop and seeing almost nothing of Qatar except the roads to the stadiums. That's how strong the Argentinians were: they had the willpower to keep winning and stay in their hostel.

Qatar-Ecuador, opening match, Al Bayt Stadium in the desert outside Doha, 20 November 2022

After the hostel, I took the media shuttle to the opening game. We glided along a gleaming motorway empty except for other FIFA and VIP vehicles, as if the road had been built only to take us to Al Bayt during the tournament. Like the other stadiums, Al Bayt had no reason for existing after the World Cup, in a country where almost nobody watched club football. Beside the motorway, a new bike path ran through the desert, shadowed by freshly planted little trees. There wasn't a bicycle on it.

I'm aware that I'm overusing superlatives, but the home crowd at the stadium was possibly the wealthiest in football history: rows of Qatari men in their traditional white robes, and Qatari women dressed in black. At the end of an overproduced opening ceremony, the announcer started a loud countdown of ten seconds till kick-off. When he got to four, the game began, but he gamely kept counting.

After twelve years of build-up to the national coming-out party, it took just fifteen minutes for Qatar to reveal themselves as the worst side I have seen at a World Cup. Their keeper and defenders didn't seem to have seen a ball in the air before, and had no idea how to conceal fouls. The Saudi crown prince Mohammed bin Salman, or 'MBS', watching the game in a Qatari scarf as part of his peace offensive, but jealous of Qatar's new fame, must have been silently laughing his head off. When half-time came with the village team 2-0 down, there was an exodus of men in white robes to their SUVs. In a second half played to thousands of empty seats, Ecuador didn't bother scoring again. For the rest of the tournament, the emptiest stand in most stadiums was the VIP section.

England-Iran, Doha, 21 November 2022

This was the sequence of events in the minutes before kick-off: England's captain Harry Kane took the field without the pro-LBTQ+ rainbow armband, after FIFA had promised an instant yellow card to any captain who wore one. Then Iran's team stood in silence for their national anthem, to show solidarity with the demonstrators against the mullahs' regime at home. Just before kick-off, England's players kneeled in protest against racism.

England won the match 6-2, while pro- and anti-regime Iranians (and reportedly some Iranian secret policemen) scuffled in the stands. A Qatari official told me weeks later that Turkish riot police (another consignment of migrant labour) had had to separate the Iranians, and confiscate Iranian flags bearing portraits of the Shah. The official said it was the worst incident of fan trouble all tournament. And people say that football has nothing to do with politics.

Argentina-Saudi Arabia, Doha, 22 November 2022

Teams tend to start a World Cup with a line-up full of big names. Often, it's because the coach doesn't want to upset the stars, the national media or the fans. Then, once everyone has seen that the old boys aren't up to it, the coach has permission to bring in youngsters.

In the case of Argentina, undefeated since 2019, their coach Lionel Scaloni genuinely believed he was entering the tournament with the right line-up. His team performed respectably against Saudi Arabia, but lost 2-1 due to bad luck, goals ruled fractionally offside, and two Saudi strikes netted from improbable positions. The Saudi fans who had driven across the border – thousands of men, and by my count, one woman in a burkha – went wild. Finally, they weren't the joke of World Cups.

Argentina's team wasn't bad, but it was more Argentinian than global: skilful, hard, undynamic, frighteningly uncreative, and a gear slower than the leading European teams. Messi seemed headed for one last failed World Cup.

Brasilia, 24 November 2022

A great competitor forges his reputation in the greatest contests. The greatest of all comes along once every four years, and Neymar had just lost it. In the Brazilian elections shortly before the World Cup, he had endorsed the far-right candidate Jair Bolsonaro, and even danced to a campaign jingle – breaking a pact in Brazil's squad to stay neutral. Bolsonaro's left-wing opponent, Lula, had explained: 'I think he is afraid that if I win, I will find out what Bolsonaro pardoned from his income tax debt.' Lula did win.

The elections had been football-themed. Bolsonaro and his supporters hijacked Brazil's traditional yellow *canarinho* team shirt, wearing it as their uniform during the campaign. But as Brazil prepared for their first match of the World Cup against Serbia, Lula announced that he would be watching in a *canarinho*. He said, 'We can't be ashamed of wearing our green and yellow shirt.' Still, it would take years of work to convert a partisan symbol back into a national one.

Brazil-Serbia, Doha, 24 November 2022

I love globalisation. The hordes of fans in Brazilian *canarinho* shirts tonight almost all turned out on closer inspection to be Indians or Arabs. Brazil remained the standard-bearer of the Global South, supported by Israelis, Palestinians and everyone else in between. No matter where in the world you came from, you could find a Brazilian player with your skin shade. A fan who lived in a shack without air conditioning in Bangkok or Nairobi, who would never earn $5,000 a year, let alone attend a World Cup, had just one indisputably world-class attachment: the Seleçâo.

And Brazil had rediscovered their power to humiliate Europeans. As they had at the 2018 World Cup, they played with a Brazilian touch but at the pace of Bayern Munich. Almost every starting player was good enough for the knockout stages of the Champions League. With a forward line of Raphinha, Vinícius Junior and Richarlison, backed up by Neymar, they coasted past Serbia 2-0.

China, late November 2022

At this point, the Chinese were still living under stringent 'zero-Covid' lockdowns that had lasted nearly three years. Many of them imagined that similar conditions prevailed worldwide – until, that is, they saw the World Cup on TV. The sight of maskless fans in Qatar singing and hugging helped fuel a rare wave of Chinese protests against their own captivity. Chinese state TV responded by cutting out crowd shots from its coverage. But within a week of the tournament starting, the government began to free its people from lockdown.

Doha, November–December 2022

With all the stadiums in one city, it was the first World Cup where fans and journalists were routinely able to attend two matches a day. I'd typically wake up at about 10 a.m., walk to the coffee shop in the Xclusive Fitness franchise overlooking the highway, start work on my burner laptop over breakfast, and write nonstop till about four o'clock. Then I'd go to my first game, from where I would take a media shuttle to the second one, which usually kicked off at 10 p.m.

In the first one hundred hours of the World Cup, I attended nine matches. The only people to have ever notched up those kinds of numbers before were the likes of Blatter and Beckenbauer, who flitted around tournaments in helicopters.

Life was a pleasant blur, like being dropped into a foot-ball-themed video ad. On almost every trip in Doha you'd pass a couple of stupendous pop-up World Cup stadiums, like magical creatures glimpsed on the Galapagos Islands.

I'd eat in a stadium's media canteen, where the staff was international but the contempt for the environment was Qatari. Every apple came wrapped in plastic, and every so-called 'pain au chocolat' arrived in its own cardboard box. At mealtimes, the journalists stood in line for the miraculous chicken biryani with a cold, yoghurty sauce. Who made it? Why was it so good?

After my second match ended at midnight, I'd queue with thousands of people at the metro station, usually listening to a football podcast on my AirPods for research purposes. I'd be in bed by 2 a.m., and then repeat the next day, and every day after that. I was living in the World Cup.

Doha metro, November–December 2022

The first stations of Qatar's metro rail system opened in 2019. Would any of it, let alone the seven stops at the pop-up stadiums, have been built without the World Cup?

The metro system operated on the assumption that passengers had never used a metro before. All day long, every time a train pulled up at the platform, Filipina 'event team' members would point at it and recite, 'Sir, you can get into the train.'

They exemplified the broader Qatari tendency to de-automate everything, and just use underpaid migrant labour. Instead of a sign to the stadium, there'd be a young African baking in the sun, pointing the way.

The supposition that nobody knew how to use the metro may have been correct. Doha didn't have a century-old metro etiquette guiding passenger behaviour. Instead, when the train doors opened, hordes of people would storm in while simultaneously hordes of others tried to storm off. Perhaps it had been like this in London in 1863, when the first Underground line opened. I imagined that over time, the locals would work out an etiquette. But when I mentioned this to a colleague who had lived in China, he said that decades after Chinese metro systems opened, the passengers still stormed the trains.

Doha had few public spaces where people could hang out, so the metro was the place where the world mixed. Going into the World Cup, the story had been the clash of civilisations: westerners were bashing Qatar, while Arabs called us hypocritical racists. Westerners wanted to wear OneLove armbands, while Arab fans wore 'Free Palestine' armbands. In short: nationalism, hatred and incomprehension seemed to reign.

That backdrop made riding the metro confusing. On the trains, the civilisations seemed to be getting along just fine. To quote FIFA's cheesy but possibly accurate slogan: 'Football unites the world.'

In a typical metro carriage during the first round, you might see male Saudis packed together with Iranian men and women, watched benignly by fat shaven-headed Englishmen, everyone filming everyone else, and bantering in basic English, while a group of Americans chanted, 'I believe that we will win!' Women in full hijab mingled with women in shorts. Brazilians even mingled with Argentinians. People weren't just tolerant of religious difference; they were tolerant of breathing in somebody's body odour and listening to their terrible music on speaker at 1 a.m. in a crammed carriage after their team had lost. Maybe there was something to the old canard that if you just brought ordinary people from different countries together without politicians getting in the way they'd get along.

The most visible civilisational divide in the trains was by height: fans from rich countries were on average a head taller than those from the Global South.* Almost all the visiting supporters were, by definition, well-off. They tended to come from the upper middle class of rich countries, from the English and Welsh skilled working class, and from the upper class of poorer countries. Ecuador's fanbase, for instance, was much whiter than Ecuador's team. Many spectators were non-partisan football tourists, who came from everywhere from Dubai to Durban. These people tended to fly in with tickets for two games in a day, watch teams they didn't particularly support, and leave the same night. The ambient mood was pretty sedate, partly because this was the first almost alcohol-free World Cup. (I enjoyed drying out for a month, treating myself to the odd £13 beer in a hotel lounge only on special occasions.) Nobody worried about hooligans. The number of police incidents involving English and Welsh fans in Qatar during the tournament was zero; on the other hand, there was some World Cup-related violence in England and Wales.

The only poor people at the tournament were the workers, who, as we fought our way out of the train, would chant, pointlessly, through their megaphones: 'THIS WAY, STADIUM!'

Postscript, 2025

I'm told that in quiet post-World Cup Doha, the metro is mostly deserted.

Argentina-Mexico, Doha, 24 November 2022

Argentina's opening defeat to Saudi Arabia had set up a satisfying

---

* I was somewhere between the two.

cliffhanger scenario for the rest of their tournament. From now on, they would have to win every match. And for thirty-five-year-old Messi, each game risked being his last at a World Cup.

Their coach Lionel Scaloni had rectified his line-up with unusual speed. The striker Julián Álvarez (twenty-two years old and still pimpled, a reserve at Manchester City just four months after moving to Europe), and midfielder Enzo Fernández (twenty-one, as much a Messi fan as an international footballer) had come on as subs during the Saudi defeat. Alexis Mac Allister (twenty-three) started against Mexico. That trio transformed the team.

A video from inside Argentina's changing room after their 2-0 win over the Mexicans showed the players bouncing up and down together, thumping their lockers and shouting, tunelessly, the song of their own fans:

I was born in Argentina
Land of Diego and Lionel
Of the boys of the Malvinas, whom I'll never forget…

Messi, an émigré long distrusted at home, had finally been given a place of honour in the national narrative, alongside the conscripts killed in the Falklands (or Malvinas) war of 1982.

And the revised Argentinian team was playing the football he had always favoured. I had a sense of what that was from watching clips of his pre-match team talks at Barcelona. In the changing room, after the coach's tactical talk, Messi would generally deliver a brief speech, calling for calm thinking. Before a game against Atlético Madrid, for instance, he told his teammates, in his characteristic monotone, '*Tranquilo*, like always, without losing our heads. Not too quickly.' At half-time in the home leg of the 2019 Champions League semi-final against Liverpool, he urged: 'Try to calm the match …If we play one against one, they're stronger. We're not used to it; they're quick. Then we're going up and down; it's a lottery. If we have control, it's another story.' Controlled possession, rather than helter-skelter pelts back and forth, had always been his ideal for Argentina. The revised 2022 eleven could play it. After beating Mexico, he said, 'We realised we had to play with more tranquillity.'

It was the first time in several World Cups that I'd seen Argentina control the ball. This was the slow, traditional Latin American game that Argentinians called '*la nuestra*' – 'ours'. They couldn't match European tempo, and they covered fewer kilometres than any other team in the group phase, but it seemed to work. When they advanced as a bloc on the ball, it was easier for players to find Messi, who would generally be hanging around near the centre circle. He would orchestrate the attack, and then materialise near the penalty area to finish it off or provide the assist. For Argentina's two goals against Mexico, he did both.

Morocco-Belgium, Doha, 27 November 2022

Morocco won 2-0, and introduced a new religious gesture into the hitherto largely Catholic iconography of World Cups: their players celebrated goals by prostrating themselves on the field as if in prayer. Morocco were emerging as the tournament's most multi-faceted team: Islamic, Arabic, African and European all in one.

The team relied more on the 4.2 million or so Moroccans in the European diaspora than on the country's population of thirty-seven million. Their first goal against Belgium was scored by Romain Saïss, son of a Moroccan father and French mother, who used to wash dishes in his dad's restaurant in the south of France; the second goal, in extra time, came from Rotterdam-born Zakaria Aboukhlal. Fourteen of Morocco's twenty-six-man squad were born outside the country – the highest ratio in the tournament – including four each from the Netherlands and Belgium. Many players spoke shaky Arabic, but there were multiple dressing-room languages.

The triumph of an 'African' side therefore served chiefly to confirm the superiority of western European football. Italy, Spain, Germany and France had won the previous four World Cups, the longest reign of any region in the tournament's history. Mark Wotte, a Dutchman who had coached Morocco's under-twenty-three team, told me: 'On average, the Moroccan trained in Europe is better in every respect than the Moroccan trained in Morocco. Moroccan players always had skill, but the problem was ball-winning and the defensive aspect. With the local boys, I'm always working on decision-making.'

But there was another factor behind Morocco's success: European racism. Watching as a Dutch fan, I felt sadness that their skinny Dutch-born playmaker, Hakim Ziyech, wasn't playing for Holland, who didn't have a playmaker. At twenty-nine and in his prime, Ziyech played the World Cup in a state of what psychologists call 'flow'. You'd see him waving both arms above his head, begging for a pass. Morocco had made him their designated risk-taker, letting him play his natural game: he attempted a decisive action almost every time he got the ball.

I understood his choice of nation. Morocco's football federation had spent years wooing diaspora players with a campaign called 'Bring back talents belonging to the soil'. Meanwhile, for most of Ziyech's life, the Netherlands had rejected him.

He was born in the small town of Dronten, a place so Dutch that it had been founded only twenty years before on land reclaimed from the sea. Like most European Moroccans, he grew up with a mixed identity: Dutch, Muslim and Moroccan. But when he was eight years old, the terrorist attacks of 11 September 2001 fuelled European fear and loathing of Muslims. Tellingly, Dutch-Moroccans were usually referred to in Dutch discourse as 'Marokkanen' – meaning 'Moroccans', as if they had no Dutch identity at all. The Dutch far-right politician Geert Wilders incited a crowd to chant for 'fewer' of them. Kids like Ziyech were pushed into embracing the identity of their parents' homeland where they'd never lived.

In 2015 *Oranje* called up the youngster for a training camp, only for him to pull out after a couple of days, pleading injury. Holland's then coach, Guus Hiddink, recalled thinking: 'A shame, but I had the feeling his future with *Oranje* would come.' It didn't:

Ziyech chose Morocco. Holland's assistant coach Marco van Basten called him a 'dumb boy'.

Now the '*Marokkaan*' was starring for the best Morocco he would ever play for, practically the home team of the first Arab World Cup, cheered on by Arabs from three continents, who whistled whenever the opponents had the temerity to attack. Many of the fans waved Palestinian flags and 'Free Palestine' signs. Qatar officially confiscated the latter as political, but in practice, given that much of the World Cup's police force was borrowed from Morocco and other poorer Arab countries, the signs were usually waved through. A group of footballers who had grown up being humiliated had become the team of a region that knew what that felt like.

Germany, November 2022

Sweden and Norway hadn't qualified for the World Cup, so Germany was the participating nation that led the informal boycott movement. The tournament's opening game had drawn fewer German TV viewers than some detective series, and although seventeen million Germans watched their team's 1-1 tie with Spain, that was still nine million down on the Germany-Mexico group match at the previous World Cup. Socially committed Werder Bremen, club of the new national hero, centre-forward Niclas Füllkrug, stated that 'the World Cup should never have been given to Qatar'. Werder promised to 'refrain in communications from being passionate about this tournament'. That vow would prove easy to keep: Germany went out in the first round.

Souq Waqif, Doha, late November 2022

Hundreds of poor Asian and African workers spent the tournament standing in the sun outside stadiums, shouting, 'This way, metro!' The chant became world-famous. The hero of the story was a charming young Kenyan, Abubakr Abbass, working in Qatar on a three-month contract, who sat outside Doha's fake-ancient souk on a kind of tennis umpire's chair, chanting 'Metro! Metro? *Metro!*', in ever-changing intonations, and pointing the way with a large foam finger. Passing fans would sing back at him, 'This way!' After a video went viral, Abbass became known worldwide as 'Metro Guy'.

The Qatari authorities approved: for once, a happy migrant story. In a special ceremony, they presented Abbass with what looked like World Cup merchandise. From then on, presumably with official encouragement, workers at other venues improvised their own, 'This way, metro!' dances. Fans loved it, and Abbass's mother issued a public appeal to Qatar to give her son another job after the tournament.

Postscript, January 2024

Her appeal seemed to work. As Qatar prepared to host the Asian Cup, Abbass starred in a promotional video for 'Doha Metro's Event Team'.

Lift in the Al Mansoura building, 2 a.m., 28 November

Returning 'home' (as we now called our 'executive apartment') after Spain-Germany, Josh and I shared a lift with three teenaged Arab brothers from Dubai. One wore a Germany shirt; another wore a Spain one while also holding a bag of Portuguese flags, ready for the next day's match. We asked if they were confused about who they supported. The oldest brother, not wearing any team shirt, explained: 'Sibling rivalry.'

Uruguay-Ghana, Doha, 2 December 2022

Going into this group game, every fan carried the memory of the Uruguay-Ghana game from 2010: Luis Suárez's last-minute handball to prevent a Ghananian goal, his sending-off, Ghana's penalty pinging off the crossbar, Suárez's explosion of joy on the touchline, and Uruguay's victory in the penalty shoot-out. It was one of the quintessential World Cup victories of Evil over Good.

Beautifully, the ageing Uruguayan team of 2022 served as a tribute act to 2010, complete with the thirty-five-year-old Suárez. He had aged beyond the prime years of male delinquency, and creditably, didn't bite a single person all tournament, but Ghanaians hadn't forgiven him. Their fans wanted revenge. As Ghana's president, Nana Akufo-Addo, warned Uruguay: 'This time the hand of Suárez will not save them.'

'But,' I wrote in the *FT* before the game, 'footballers do not think like fans. Players are obsessed with today's performance. Far from wanting to avenge the past, they often have an uneasy relationship with their predecessors' – who envied their pay and were always criticising them in the media. I said Ghana's players in Doha wouldn't have 2010 on their minds.

Sitting in the stadium as the game ticked towards its end, I realised how wrong I had been about how footballers felt. Uruguay were winning 2-0, with Suárez involved in both goals, but with that score they would go out of the tournament on goal difference. They needed one more goal to reach the second round.

The Ghanaians were already eliminated. On paper, they had nothing left to play for. But their World Cup was now about taking Uruguay out with them. They put ten men in front of goal, tackled like demons, and wasted every second they could to stop Uruguay scoring a third. They succeeded. When the big screen showed the recently substituted Suárez on the bench with his head in his hands, the Ghanaian fans in the stadium gave the cheer of the night. Emotionally, they had beaten Uruguay.

I realised then: the World Cup is the one competition where most players are also fans. Unlike in club football, they are playing for the team they have supported all their lives. They share commonalities with their teammates that they don't feel with their opponents. Most care like the fans do, and that's part of the joy of the tournament.

Brazil-Cameroon, Doha, 2 December 2022

World Cups were getting kinder. Gen Zers tended to treat opponents as colleagues. After the US eliminated Iran, American players (including Timothy Weah, the son of Liberia's president) consoled weeping Iranians. The angry exception was Serbia-Switzerland, which briefly erupted into a classic World Cup brawl after Granit Xhaka, the Swiss player of Kosovar origin, provoked Serbian opponents. (Serbians and Kosovars had been at war as recently as 1999.) But when the game ended with Serbia's elimination, another Swiss-Kosovar, the brilliant Xherdan Shaqiri, waddled around the field hugging Serbs. Other than the ritual enraged Uruguayan exit blaming the referee, the worst aggro here was between Belgian players.

There were only four red cards at this World Cup, down from twenty-eight in 2006, and the best of them was for Cameroon's chubby Vincent Aboubakar. He already had a yellow card when he scored the last-minute winner against Brazil (OK, Brazil's second eleven) and took off his shirt, an offence that meant an automatic yellow. The referee smiled, patted him fondly on the head, then apologetically sent him off. Aboubakar saluted him amicably, and happily jogged out of the tournament.

A villa in Doha, November–December 2022

Chinese journalists had progressed from trying to storm the media stand in South Africa in 2010. They still couldn't get tickets to most games: once again, China hadn't qualified, and there was a surplus of Chinese reporters in Qatar, so they remained bottom of FIFA's list.

But this time, Chinese media had paid a succession of great ex-players to drop by a local villa and talk to them about the tournament. One day their guest might be Roberto Carlos, and the next Michael Owen. The journalists would interview the star and post the videos on Chinese social media. The games themselves were sideshows.

The Chinese journalist who passed on this story was feeling down about our profession. There was no point practising journalism in Xi Jingping's dictatorial China, he complained, but what else could he do with his life?

England-Senegal, Al Bayt Stadium in the desert, 4 December 2022

One oddity of World Cups is that a journeyman footballer who isn't good enough for top-division football might find himself playing in the same national team as a superstar. That never happens in club football. The trick, for the opposing side, is to exploit the journeyman's weakness. As Johan Cruyff said, you have to make a bad player play badly.

That's what England did in this match. The journeyman was Senegal's right-back, Youssouf Sabaly, a reserve at Real Betis in Seville. England's coach Gareth Southgate stationed Jude Bellingham and Phil Foden on Sabaly's flank, where they constantly attacked him, with other English players flooding his zone. The final score of 3-0 was reached in fifty-seven minutes. Nobody in the England camp was so rude as to explain the strategy in post-match interviews.

Morocco-Spain, Doha, 6 December 2022

Tonight the Dutch-Moroccan midfielder Sofyan Amrabat was man of the match. Almost faultless and impossibly fit, he was still doing one-man presses in extra time. Several of his tackles would

have earned instant yellow cards in club football, but at World
Cups players try harder, and referees tend to allow more. Thanks
largely to Amrabat, Morocco held Spain to 0-0, before winning
3-0 on penalties. On this form, he was a world-beater.

But usually he wasn't. I remembered him as a journeyman
even in the Dutch league; by 2022 he was playing for Italian also-
rans Fiorentina. In short, aged twenty-six, he had nothing in his
long-term record to indicate anything special.

It used to be common to discover great players from faraway
lands at a World Cup, but that no longer happens. All the best
footballers today are known quantities. The scouting system is
global and nearly infallible. If an unregarded figure like Asamoah
Gyan in 2010 or Amrabat in 2022 has an amazing tournament, it's
almost certainly an unrepeatable one-off.

Amrabat exemplified the kind of player who can bring himself
to a peak for the month of a World Cup, before relapsing into
mediocrity. The king of tournament players had been Jürgen
Klinsmann. He was rarely top-class in club football, but would
tailor his individual training to enter tournaments in top form,
much as Olympic athletes do. Klinsmann won the 1990 World
Cup with Germany, yet at Bayern Munich his teammates were
so sniffy about his technique that they nicknamed him 'Flipper',
after the dolphin star of a popular German TV show.

Postscript

It was probably physically and mentally impossible for Amrabat
to sustain the intensity that he displayed in Qatar. Yet after the
tournament, several big clubs fought for his signature. Manchester United were the unlucky winners. As I write, he is on loan at
Fenerbahçe in Turkey.

Profiles by Roastado, Doha, 8 December 2022

Three of us from the *Financial Times* had coffee with a senior Qatari official in a swish café opposite the local branch of Harrods. It was a rest day at the World Cup, there was hardly a soul on the street, and at 10 a.m. on a Gulf winter's morning, the South Asian waiter was already switching on the terrace air conditioning.

The official wore the traditional Qatari white robe, but spoke perfect English, and had been around. He was bothered by the foreign criticisms of Qatar, but said they were exaggerated. Qatar was treating migrants much better than it used to, and western countries weren't saints themselves in that regard. Happily, he added, the negative publicity had been geographically limited. It mostly came from the UK, Germany, and Scandinavia. The emirate didn't worry much about Scandinavia, and for all the British and German attacks, Qatar was quietly supplying these countries with natural gas. Western politicians bashed Qatar while they were in opposition, but once they got into government, they found out that they needed the world's biggest gas exporter.

The dependency was mutual, admitted the official. Qatar needed western military help. Look at the gas fields that the mini-state shared with giant Iran. 'There is nothing to stop Iran from taking two-thirds of them or more.' Then there was Qatar's Saudi problem. There had been a time during the Saudi blockade when the Qataris worried that young MBS might actually be stoked enough to invade them. What had stopped him? The French, the Germans and the US military, which finally got on the phone to President Trump and asked him to cool MBS down.

Now, with the World Cup nearing its end, the official was feeling relieved. Most of the world had praised Qatar's hosting. The mini-state had survived its ordeal.

Brazil-Croatia, quarter-final, Doha, 9 December 2022

As in 2018, Brazil had looked the team of the tournament. They outplayed the Croats, hitting twelve shots on target to Croatia's one. But the Croatian keeper Dominik Livaković made eleven saves, a record for any World Cup game since 2014. Neymar finally scored the opening goal in extra time, but with three minutes left, a shot by Bruno Petkovic took a flukish deflection and flew past Brazil's unbeatable keeper Alysson. Inevitably, Croatia won the penalty shoot-out.

Brazil flew home to mockery. In truth, they had simply been unlucky again. If quality guaranteed victory, they would probably have been world champions in both 2018 and 2022. Yet a convention of football reporting is to tailor the analysis to the result. The technical term for this is 'scoreboard journalism'.

Netherlands-Argentina, quarter-final, Doha, 9 December 2022

I was sitting in the media stand, three journalists to a desk, everyone's eyes glued to the game, when forty yards to my left, a few colleagues stood up and began shouting for help. There was fright on their faces. Eventually the stewards understood, and rushed over. Word spread through the stand that a journalist had had a suspected heart attack. Somebody was lying on the ground. Paramedics arrived and began working away on him. A defibrillator was brought out. Then another journalist told me: the man down was our American colleague, Grant Wahl.

We all liked Grant. I'd been on his podcast the year before. Here in Doha, while most journalists focused only on the football, he had continued campaigning against Qatar's wrongdoings. He'd been briefly detained for showing up to a game in a rainbow T-shirt to support LGBT+ rights.

So, there to my left was someone I knew and admired, possibly dying. But in front of me was *Oranje*, my team, playing a thriller. I'm not proud to say this, but I spent half an hour swivelling my head between Grant and the match. So did a lot of the journalists around me. When the game went to a penalty shoot-out, the entire stand stared at the field for each kick, then stared at Grant until the next kick. After the Dutch defeat in the shoot-out,

I fled home. Waking up the next morning, I checked my phone and saw that Grant had died. An undetected aortic aneurysm had ruptured during the game. He had just turned forty-nine.

Grant's death scene was a personal tragedy, but it also summed up the quandary of this World Cup: should we have kept our eyes on the field, or on the horrors happening off it?

I heard one view from the American writer Benjamin Moser. People shouldn't be watching the football, he told me in a stream of WhatsApp messages. Ben, who is gay, felt Qatar's criminalisation of homosexuality more viscerally than most heterosexuals do. Here (with Ben's permission) are bits from our exchange:

Ben: How horrible that people go to this thing, pretend like it's about sports, etc., but who cares about a hated and persecuted minority, it's all good fun anyway.

Me: I don't believe whataboutism is a proper argument, but what would you say to the response: well, you grew up in Texas where gay sex was illegal until 2003? I've been repeatedly told that homosexuality here in Qatar is de facto tolerated as long as it's private. Is what I'm saying absurd? If so, please tell me.

Ben: Your point re Texas is well taken. But if it was any other group this wouldn't be a question. It sends a clear message that gay people are dispensable.

Me: FIFA chose Qatar as host. That forced billions of people to choose between watching games played in Q. or missing the joy of a World Cup.

Ben: I just am not sure what there is to enjoy in those circumstances. If you went to a shop and tried on a shirt and the saleswoman was like 'this was made by a seven-year-old in Bangladesh who is kept in a cage,' would you say 'yeah but this colour looks good on me'?

Me: When Holland score in the last minute I feel joy – I can't help it.

Ben: It's similar to the line vegetarians get: 'You're right of course but I just LOVE CHEESEBURGERS!' Because people think that the right to consume overrides everyone else's rights.

Grant shared Ben's outrage. His last blog, about Qatar's response to deaths of migrant workers, began, 'They just don't care'. Grant did care about poor people's suffering, and he spent countless hours documenting it. Before the World Cup he went around hotels trying to interview staff about their working conditions, while evading the Qatari authorities. Not many journalists write from the viewpoint of the downtrodden.

But Grant also loved soccer. His last tweet, after the trick free kick that created Holland's last-minute equaliser was: 'Just an incredible designed set-piece goal by the Netherlands.' In fact, his love of the game may have helped kill him. As noted earlier in this book, watching a big football match raises the risk of heart failure. Imagine the effect on middle-aged journalists working 100 hours a week in Doha, living on stadium food, and soldiering on after their bodies break down, as Grant had, in fact, written that his had. He explained, wrongly as it turns out: 'Three weeks of little sleep, high stress, and lots of work can do that to you.' The weekend he dropped dead, so did the Qatari photojournalist Khalid al-Misslam.

I reckon Grant got it right: he kept his eyes both on the field and off it. If people aren't entitled to earthly pleasures like football while others suffer, then nobody who ever lived was entitled to earthly pleasures. But then I would say that, wouldn't I? Maybe Ben was right.

Morocco-Portugal, quarter-final, 10 December 2022

At thirty-seven, Cristiano Ronaldo had had a terrible World Cup. It started with being dumped by Manchester United after he insulted the club in a TV interview with Piers Morgan, and it got worse with each Portuguese match. Ronaldo displayed his late style: hanging around the edge of the penalty box, waving an arm, demanding that every attack finish with him, and looking devastated when teammates didn't deliver.

Portugal finally dared drop him for the knockout match against Switzerland – and, disastrously for him, his young replacement Gonçalo Ramos scored a hat-trick as Portugal won 6-1. Ronaldo spent the next game against Morocco on the bench. After Portugal's 1-0 defeat, he burst into tears – his characteristic reaction to any event, happy or sad. Assuming that he wouldn't redeem himself in 2026, aged forty-one, his record at World Cups had been a failure. He hadn't scored once in eight knockout matches at the tournament, and his teams never finished higher than fourth place (at his first attempt, in 2006).

You could say: well, a small country like Portugal can't expect to win World Cups. But that wasn't how Ronaldo saw it. In his mind, if he was playing, his team should win.

England-France, quarter-final, Al Bayt Stadium, 11 December 2022

Harry Kane went into every match knowing which side of the goal he would shoot to if he got a penalty. In the days before the game, he'd practise exactly that kick. Any keeper facing him on a penalty had to pick a side randomly, and dive instantly. Good luck: a well-struck Kane kick was practically unstoppable.

So when England won a penalty against France on fifty-four minutes, he smashed it routinely into the right-hand side of the net. No matter that it was against the keeper who knew him best, France's Hugo Lloris, his teammate at Spurs for the previous nine years. They must have faced each other over countless meaningless penalties at the club's training ground in Enfield, North London.

But then, with about ten minutes left to play and France winning 2-1, England were awarded a second penalty. This was Kane's moment of truth. His English generation were at the peak of their cycle. For him and several other players, it was their third consecutive long run in a major tournament. Few teams get three tournaments together, and England had only one objective in Qatar. If they beat France, they faced an eminently winnable semi-final against Morocco. A second converted penalty in the Al-Bayt could give them a clear run to lifting the World Cup. For Kane, aged twenty-nine, it would be the first trophy of any kind in his career.

Now he faced a dilemma. In fact, a statistical study conducted by an expert suggests that his situation was without precedent in football history: taking a second penalty in an extremely high-stakes match against a long-standing teammate. Kane had already shown Lloris his penalty strategy for the night: shoot to the keeper's right. Should he do it again?

He decided instead to hit the least stoppable penalty in the book: high and hard. If it's on target, it's almost guaranteed to go in, even if the keeper guesses correctly.

Kane's shot flew over the bar, Kylian Mbappé laughed, and England were out. In their changing rooms afterwards, Kane and Lloris exchanged text messages. Lloris remarked later: 'It was not easy to find the words.'[*]

France-Morocco semi-final, Al-Bayt stadium, 14 December 2022

After France's 2-0 win, the Moroccans lodged an official complaint with FIFA about the referee. Their federation wrote that 'arbitration situations [had] deprived the Moroccan selection of two indisputable penalties in the opinion of several arbitration specialists'.

Most teams eliminated in the latter stages of this World Cup went home raging at a referee. The method was to latch onto a particular call, and blame it for their defeat. Often, the team had a superficial point. That call might have gone the other way. In

---

[*] To indicate what an outlier Kane's miss was: he netted his next thirty penalties.

most player-versus-player duels at a World Cup, a foul could reasonably be called. Usually the defender is pulling the attacker's shirt, pushing him off balance, or kicking him, intentionally or not. Whether the referee calls the foul is to some degree a matter of discretion. If he blew his whistle every time, there would be no football played.

Yet the teams' laments were unconvincing. That's because they never complained about calls that went their way: for instance, an offside wrongly flagged against an opponent. A refereeing trio makes about seventy calls a match. Let's say that five of these directly affect the game's outcome. Add on another five calls that a referee *doesn't* make, when he dismisses appeals for a foul and allows play to continue, and that's ten big calls a game. Any team can identify one or two of these that went against them. Doing this is emotionally satisfying, and serves as an excuse back home, but cherry-picking isn't analysis. It's also the most boring argument in football.

Ubers in Doha, November–December 2022

Sometimes I travelled to games by Uber rather than the metro. Whenever I did, I'd use the opportunity to conduct a survey: I'd ask the driver, always a South Asian man, whether he liked living in Qatar. I tried to phrase the question as neutrally as possibly, and then prompt the driver to keep talking, admittedly in what was usually limited English.

I must have taken about thirty or forty Ubers during the tournament, and I learned to predict most of the answers. The driver would always say that he missed home. He didn't like living in Qatar but he appreciated the money he was making, which he sent to his family back home. Many drivers described Qatar as 'safe'. A number praised the healthcare system: for about £20, a migrant worker could buy a health card that gave him a right to most treatments. No such thing existed in their home countries.

I'm not trying to whitewash Qatar, only reporting what these men said. The country denies migrants many rights. The Uber drivers were born near the bottom of the global ladder, and had few choices in life. But given where they came from, they were pleased to be in Qatar.

Xclusive Fitness coffee shop, Doha, 15 December 2022

An editor friend sent me an extract from a book he had just published, *Maradona: The Last Interview.* I read it in what was now my local coffee shop, where I was usually alone with the Filipina barista. As Messi prepared in the university hostel for the World Cup final, his last chance to emulate his predecessor, Maradona was blessing him from beyond the grave.

Maradona's journalistic confidant, Daniel Arcucci, had asked him at his kitchen table in Dubai in 2014 whether Messi needed to win a World Cup to prove his greatness. 'What?' Maradona had exclaimed. 'No! Messi doesn't need to win the World Cup to be the best footballer in the world. It has nothing to do with it. Don't confuse the two. Winning the World Cup would be fantastic for Argentina, fantastic for the fans, and fantastic for Lío. But a World Cup will not take away anything he has done to get where he is.'

Two components go into the making of a sporting legend: brilliance and persona. Maradona had both. Raised in a slum outside Buenos Aires, he was drenched in Argentinian lore. In 1986 he understood that his defeat of England avenged the Falklands War.

Messi, by contrast, didn't even aspire to have a persona. It was as if he played like The Beatles with the charisma of an accountant. Whereas Maradona expressed his personality on the field, Messi aimed solely for efficiency. He offered no unnecessary flourishes, never a hint of art for art's sake.

Having moved to Barcelona aged thirteen, he embodied the émigré generation that fled Argentina's economic collapse. He was raised almost outside society, the joint product of a family and FC Barcelona's academy. He may never live in Argentina again.

And Maradona came first. World Cups are a sequence of repetitions, and Argentinians judged Messi's career as a would-be repeat of Maradona's. But even if Sunday's final against France ended in anticlimactic defeat, Messi would be the greatest – probably of all time. Maradona understood.

Times Literary Supplement, London, 16 December 2022

The standard retort to western criticisms of Qatar went more or less like this: 'Who are you to criticise? You westerners colonised the world and committed terrible crimes. You have no right to complain about Qatar's customs on homosexuality, gender roles or migrants. Outsiders can't judge Qatari culture.'

The argument was often made by Muslims, but also by some westerners. The Argentinian Jorge Valdano accused the West of playing the 'cultural police'. For a while I wasn't sure how to respond to this reasoning. It seemed to make a certain sense. But late in the tournament, I read an article in the *Times Literary Supplement* by Regina Rini, a philosopher at York University in Toronto, who demolished it. A good essay turns on the light and helps you see things you had been dimly grasping for. I'm sure I'm going to simplify her reasoning, but let me set it out as I understand it. Rini began:

> One of the first goals in any introductory ethics class is to disabuse students of an idea called naive relativism. This is the claim that every culture has its own morality and no one can legitimately criticise moral beliefs outside their own community. It's a popular and remarkably deep-rooted belief among young people, who are perhaps drawn by its suggestion of tolerance and inclusivity.

'Naive relativism' was, if you like, the Official FIFA Ethic of the 2022 World Cup. Rini took it apart. 'Just to start,' she wrote, 'there's the challenge of what to say about Nazi "culture".' Was every 'culture' beyond criticism just because it called itself a 'culture'? If so, then surely colonisation was fine, too? After all, it was presumably authentic western 'culture'.

Rini granted that there was a kernel of truth in naive relativism: 'People in rich, powerful societies ought to have some humility about their ability to judge the practices of others, since power leads to sloppy thinking.' That's mostly because the powerful receive little feedback. They can use their power to repress or ignore criticism, and keep doing bad things.

But by the 2020s, Qatar had become rich and mighty itself. Rini concluded: 'We shouldn't accept naively relativist arguments from the elites of increasingly powerful places such as Qatar and China. They owe a specific, positive argument for their moral claims, in just the same way westerners do.'

Indian restaurant, Doha, 17 December 2022

My housemate Josh and I went for dinner with two other English journalists in a relatively upscale Indian restaurant – about £15 a head for everything we could stress-eat. The other customers all seemed to be middle-class Indians.

During the meal, one of our party received a WhatsApp from a source, who was, shall we say, very close to Gareth Southgate. The source confirmed that Southgate had decided to stay on as England manager. It was a scoop, sort of: admittedly, another newspaper had already published the news, but it had buried the lede, and it was hard to work out from its article that Southgate had agreed to extend his contract.

Even the FA didn't know yet. So the journalist apologised to us, pulled out his laptop, and spent the next half an hour banging out his story amid the debris of our Afghan mixed grill. The adrenaline was pumping through his body as if he were a trader trying to break the Bank of England. The rest of us understood.

We'd been there. It didn't occur to any of us to sneak out and send the scoop to our news desks. (Admittedly, the *Financial Times* wouldn't have cared.) By the end of dinner, his story was up on his paper's homepage, billed 'Exclusive'. In our job, that was a big win. We were happy for him.

Al Mansoura, Doha, 18 December 2022

On the morning of the final, Josh came 'home' to our apartment and reported that he had found the perfect hipster coffee place just a short walk away. It even had a little patio shielded from the sun. Josh had enjoyed a flat white, a poached egg and 'real vegetables' (which I hadn't seen in a month). This was terrible news – we were leaving Qatar at 5.15 the next morning.

By this point, our building had almost emptied out. Most of the journalist residents had left when their national teams were knocked out. The Filipino building manager told Josh: 'Look for yourself, there is nobody here. There is never anybody here. This place is free money for no work for people like me.' And that was on the day of the final. Imagine what Doha would be like in a couple of weeks, when there was no more football and nothing left to build.

Our building was being returned by Qatar's Supreme Committee to its owner, who would presumably try to rent it out to 'executive bachelors'. The building's staff would be out of work in a fortnight. The ones I asked said that they hoped to find new jobs in Qatar, though they were open to going almost anywhere on earth. Many had globetrotting careers in the service industry. I saw that for people doomed to migrant labour, Qatar might be one of the better options.

France-Argentina, World Cup final, Doha, 18 December 2022

There's only one game in this book that calls for a – truncated – match report: the most breathtaking World Cup final anyone had ever seen.

Messi's companion since teenage years, thirty-four-year-old Ángel Di María, had been brought into Argentina's starting line-up, in a surprisingly attacking reorganisation to probe France's right flank. It worked. Di María proved too tricky a dribbler for Ousmane Dembélé, usually a winger himself but here continually needed to fill in at right-back. Di María was frolicking through the French penalty area when the panicked Dembélé gave him what was probably an unnecessary shove in the back. On twenty-three minutes, Messi netted his fourth penalty of the tournament.

Then a magnificent Argentine counter-attack, featuring a visionary flick by Messi, ended with Di María netting alone in front of Hugo Lloris. The scorer, overcome after so many disappointments in his years in blue and white, wept. The game already seemed over.

France at this point hadn't shown up. In the first half they barely constructed a passing move, and they didn't register a shot. Their starting line-up included five men who had won the previous World Cup final, yet they played as if paralysed with nerves, and surely weakened by the virus epidemic in their camp.

A tranquil Argentina, playing in its compact formation, stayed

2-0 up for eighty minutes. They relied on their go-to defensive tactic of the tournament, fouling the instant their opponents started building an attack. Messi operated mostly at inside right, passing both imaginatively and near faultlessly, whereas Kylian Mbappé barely touched a ball.

But Argentina probably grew complacent. After eighty minutes, Mbappé materialised from nothingness to score two goals in ninety-seven seconds, the first a penalty, the second a gorgeous long-range volley into Emiliano Martínez's far corner.

The madness continued in extra time, with chance after chance on both sides. It was exhausting just watching. Messi seemed to have won the trophy after 108 minutes when he stabbed home a rebound from point-blank range, his seventh goal of the tournament. But then Gonzalo Montiel stopped a drive from Mbappé with his arm, and the Polish referee Szymon Marciniak, who got very little wrong in the match, gave France the night's third penalty. Mbappé struck it, apparently nervelessly, into the same right-hand corner as before, for the first hat-trick in a World Cup final since 1966. After 120 minutes, the score was 3-3.

The penalty shoot-out was held in front of the stand filled with Argentinian fans, who had been singing most of the match but were now silenced by tension. Mbappé took a third penalty within an hour against the same keeper. Again he went for Martínez's right-hand corner and, though the keeper dived the right way and got a glove to it, he could not stop it. Messi rolled his penalty just past Lloris's outstretched hand. But France's Kingsley Coman and Aurélien Tchouaméni couldn't score, Montiel netted Argentina's winning kick, and Messi was draped by Qatar's emir in an Arab ceremonial robe before he lifted the FIFA World Cup trophy.

Teammates carried their little captain around the field as he waved and kissed the cup. A photograph of him holding it above his head garnered a record seventy-four million likes on Instagram. (The site's previous record had been held by a photo of an egg.)

Amid the frenzy, two FIFA officials went up to Di María, who was celebrating with a different trophy, and told him not to let anyone else touch it. Di María was baffled. 'What's that then?' he asked, pointing at Messi's cup. Messi's was a fake, thrown onto the field by Argentinian fans. Di María was holding the real thing.

The stadium's metro station afterwards was impassable. Hordes of Argentinians dressed in Messi shirts and chanting 'Messi!' were trying to get in, while hordes of Bangladeshi and Indian migrant workers wearing Messi shirts and chanting 'Messi!' were arriving at the station and piling out, desperate to share in football's biggest day.

Doha, 19 December 2022, 5.15 a.m.

I got about two hours sleep. When Josh and I checked out of our executive apartment, he asked, jokingly, if I would 'miss home'. We took an Uber to the airport. It was our goodbye to Doha, its motorways and office towers. The road at this hour was full of exhausted Uber drivers in small cars. Our Pakistani chauffeur said he was looking forward to getting some sleep after a sixteen-hour shift.

He explained that driving in Doha was stressful, because the 'citizens', Qataris, recognisable by their four-by-four cars, assumed they had a right to cut in front of non-citizens. They got angry with Uber drivers who didn't comply. I wasn't going to miss Doha.

A little later, I sat slumped at an airport gate packed with French journalists and fans, waiting for the flight to Paris. There was silence except for one Argentinian extrovert, who was strutting around, bawling out his team's songs. This was Omar da Fonseca, an ex-footballer who had worked in France forever as a TV pundit. He was only teasing. The French passengers grinned feebly. None of them minded much. Everyone liked Omar. But imagine the converse: a Frenchman doing this to a group of shattered Argentinians who had just lost the World Cup on penalties.

Paris and Buenos Aires, 19 December

We landed at a placid Charles de Gaulle airport, where it was as if the World Cup had never happened. That night, my sons went to the Place de la Concorde to welcome back the French team. The square was packed with tens of thousands of people, not all of them teenage boys. My sons came home euphoric: they had had a distant side view of their heroes waving from the balcony of the Hôtel de Crillon.

A few days later, the rapper Vegedream released his song for the team, titled '*Merci les Bleus*'. The French were fine with having got to within penalties of winning a second straight World Cup while missing nearly half their starting eleven through injury. Like Holland, this country didn't need the trophy.

Meanwhile, in Buenos Aires, where hunger was on the rise amid an economic crisis, four million people came out to greet the winning team. The victory parade was abandoned in chaos. You could understand the euphoria: in what other global ranking would Argentina come first? The World Cup is a vision of an alternative international hierarchy, in which the US is an also-ran and China doesn't even figure.

Postscript

The day the world closed the door on Qatar, the spotlight went off. NGOs had been demanding that FIFA and Qatar create a compensation fund for migrant workers killed or hurt while building the infrastructure. But after the World Cup, the media lost interest, the pressure relented, and FIFA and Qatar never set up the fund.

Qatar also stopped reforming its kafala system. Women and LGBT+ people remained second-class citizens. The legacy of the World Cup, wrote the NGO Human Rights Watch in 2025, amounted to 'widespread migrant labour abuses, including thousands of unexplained deaths, rampant wage theft, and exorbitant recruitment fees'.

In other words, Qatar and FIFA got through the tournament

almost unscathed. All their flaws combined couldn't do lasting damage to the World Cup. A month of joyous football overshadowed a few western whines. In fact, FIFA's president Gianni Infantino concluded that the tournament had been a successful test-drive for a World Cup in a still-more-brutal Gulf monarchy. In 2024, FIFA named Saudi Arabia as host for 2034. Only the usual suspects complained.

Saudi's kafala system is worse than Qatar's. Migrant workers will build stadiums in fifty-degree heat with almost no safety rules. No country will boycott the tournament.

*

Paris Olympics, July–August 2024

My family bought a bunch of cheap Olympic tickets and we went to events as fans, which felt weird. I had forgotten how to watch sports without working. I was also flummoxed by most Olympic sports. How to appreciate archery, or pole-vaulting? I ended up spending a lot of time watching other spectators. I noticed that few of them knew much about the sports we were watching either. What most people seemed to get out of the Olympic experience was simply being at the Olympics. The ambiance was relaxed, cheery and uninformed.

The only times you felt something of the intensity of a World Cup was when French athletes were in action, and especially against Argentina. Just over a week before the Games began, a video had leaked from the Argentinian football team's bus showing Enzo Fernández, a world champion of 2022, singing a racist song about *les Bleus*:

> They play in France but they're all from Angola
> It's good that they run, they're like transvestites, like that
>   bitch Mbappé
> His mum's Nigerian, his old man's Cameroonian
> But his papers say his nationality is French

There had been no particular needle between France and Argentina before, not even during the 2022 World Cup final. Now, suddenly, there was. At the rugby sevens in the Stade de France, the crowd shrugged off the ecumenical Olympic atmosphere to boo the Argentinian team. The France-Argentina men's Olympic football match (1-0 to the good guys) ended in a mass brawl between the players.

I have to admit I was pleased. Over the decades, France had lost Germany as a football enemy. Finally, the World Cup had a new top-class rivalry.

Lunch at Les Résistants, rue du Chateau d'Eau, Paris, 10 February 2025

Morocco had been bidding to host the World Cup since 1998. At last, in 2024, it got the nod to co-host the 2030 tournament with Spain and Portugal. It decided to build the biggest football stadium on earth outside North Korea: the Grand Stade Hassan II, set in a forest in Casablanca. The hope was that FIFA would choose the stadium over Madrid's Bernabéu to stage the final.

But which architect would get to build the stadium? Morocco held a competition. The winner was a small Parisian firm run by a husband and wife, the Moroccan Tarik Oualalou and the Korean-American Linna Choi. As it happened, they were neighbourhood friends of ours in Paris. 'We never thought we would win,' said Tarik.

I asked them to lunch to talk about the stadium they planned to build. Tarik did most of the talking, being a big football fan. ('"Big" is an understatement', said Linna). When I asked which grounds they were using as their role models, he explained that the typology of stadiums had changed so much that older ones were no longer very relevant. He said, 'Stadiums in the last thirty years have become places where it's more important how it's televised than how it's lived. They have become movie sets.'

Compare today's grounds with a stadium built before the

TV era, like Anfield, he said. The spectators there were right up against the field. But in a modern, movie-set stadium, the stands were set further back. The priority went to accommodating broadcast facilities, VIP lounges and restaurants.

Then there was the new kind of segregation of fans. In the past, fans of the opposing teams had been separated to prevent violence. Nowadays spectators are segregated by income. They no longer all arrive at the stadium the same way. Most ordinary folk come by public transport, while the VIPs arrive in limousines. The latter have to be kept apart from the former. To accommodate all these demands, stadium architects have hit on a new shape. Tarik said, 'Most stadiums, wherever you go, look like a Coke can that has been squished. They have a bowl, and a facade around it.'

Tarik and Linna wanted to build something more human in Casablanca, a football-mad city with two giant clubs. Tarik said, 'Their fans make the fans in the Bombonera [in Buenos Aires] look like Swiss citizens. The stadium has to work for the clubs before it works for the World Cup, because we are spending a huge amount of money.'

How to create a movie-set stadium that had something of the democratic warmth of Anfield? Tarik and Linna designed a tent-like white roof that extended far beyond the stadium itself. All year round, the roof would shelter markets, children's playgrounds, amateur sports and more. On match days, Moroccan fans often turned up eight or ten hours before kick-off, and they too could hang out under the roof. The Stade Hassan II would be a gathering place.

Tarik said, 'As a football fan building the stadium that might host the final, if Morocco goes to the final and beats France, my work on earth is done.'

20

The Planetary Feast

What is it about World Cups? It's not the quality of football, which has worsened as the tournament has grown from sixteen teams in the 1970s to thirty-two in 1998, and will balloon to forty-eight in 2026. As I write in 2025, FIFA is trailing the idea of sixty-four teams for the 2030 edition. But if you really want to maximise TV income, why not have 200 teams, each playing every other home and away, like in a league?

The magic of World Cups isn't the host-country ambiance, either. FIFA's vote on 2 December 2010 ushered in a new era of autocratic hosts: first Russia and Qatar, and, as a direct consequence of that epochal decision, Qatar's jealous neighbour Saudi Arabia in 2034. Before then, the chief host in 2026 will be Donald Trump. Asked about having to share the tournament with his country's new enemies, Canada and Mexico, he said, 'Oh, I think it's going to make it much more exciting.' Jules Rimet, the tournament's founder, who gave Mussolini a World Cup, would probably have smiled benevolently. For Rimet, even the nastiest among us could be a brother in football.

I struggled to articulate what's special about World Cups until I sat down one weekday morning in a parish church just north of Marble Arch in London with the vicar Father Lincoln Harvey. A lifelong Arsenal fan, he's the author of *A Brief Theology of Sport*; I quoted him earlier in the book. He explained to me that the World Cup is a bit like a religious feast – comparable to Easter, the Muslim Eid, or Hindu Diwali, but rarer, happening only once every four years, and shared by every country on earth.

A religious feast offers respite from life's drudgery and toil.

The World Cup, said Father Harvey, is a celebration of many things: football; great individuals, but also the team; our own nation, but also every participating nation in its uniqueness. During World Cups, people honour the differences – increasingly imagined – between Brazil, England, Cameroon and the rest. Nations compete, but joyously, knowing that football is only the most important of unimportant things. The victories and defeats are a pageant of life and death, full of contingency. Father Harvey said, 'You could see the horror of war as a fallen, corrupted sporting competition.'

As for the players, the World Cup is their pilgrimage. Every man, from goalkeeper to outside left, has his own vocation. The training camp is their monastery. Their reward for sacrifice is victory. Father Harvey said, 'For any footballer, the World Cup must feel transcendent – beautiful.'

The tournament, he concluded, 'is about as good as it gets. I don't think anything else comes close, to allow unity and distinction, togetherness and otherness.'

This is why I'll keep going to World Cups as long as I can. Part of the joy of the tournament is that it accompanies us all our lives. We change more than it does. I marvel now that as a young man in 1998 I wasn't sure that I wanted an imperfect *Oranje* to win the World Cup. Writing this aged fifty-five, with a diminishing number of World Cups ahead of me, I'd be happy with any *Oranje* winning just once – although I know it doesn't really matter.

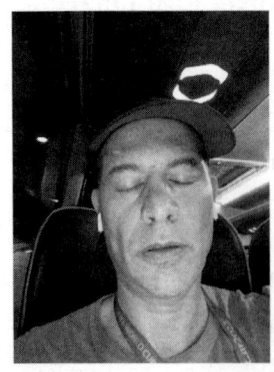

Paris, 16 June 2025

Acknowledgements

With thanks to Wilson Aquino, Henry Atmore, Mayur Bhanji, Matthijs Bolsius, Bryn Bowden, John Carlin, Andrew Dipela, Mark Gevisser, Mark Gleeson, Constantine Gonticas, Corinna Huber, Bjørn Johansson, Mehreen Khan, Lungile Madywabe, Achille Mbembe, Rupert Naylor, Frans Oosterwijk, Ignacio Palacios-Huerta, Alex Phillips, Danyel Reiche, Thomas Renggli, David Roberts, Derk and Ellen Sauer and their sons, Ronnie Schloss, Rutger Slagter, Khaya Thwala, Natasha Tsichlas, John Turnbull, Yiğiter Uluğ, Bruno Ziauddin and all the interviewees quoted in the book.

A shout-out to some of the colleagues with whom I made it through World Cups: Peter Aspden, Patrick Barclay, Alex Bellos, Christoph Biermann, Roger Blitz, Hugo Borst, François Colin, Simon Evans, Matt Garrahan, Olivier Guez, Ian Harrington, Patrick Harverson, David de Jong, Simeon Kerr, Richard Lapper, James Montague, Marcela Mora y Araujo, Hiroyuki Morita, Paul Myers, Josh Noble, Paul Onkenhout, David Owen, Harry Pearson, Tommaso Pellizzari, David Pilling, Jerome Pugmire, Gideon Rachman, Eliot Rothwell, Santiago Segurola, Philipp Selldorf, Lynne Truss, Darren Tulett, Peter Unfried, Jorge Valdano, Leo Verheul, Willem Vissers, Michael Walker and Jonathan Wilson.

I want to thank my longstanding agents Gordon Wise, Liz Dennis and Elliot Prior, and Andrew Franklin, Rebecca Gray, Nick Humphrey, Penny Daniel, Valentina Zanca and everyone else at my British publisher, Profile, who ensured that this book finally got written.

My daughter Leila Kuper photographed most of the accreditation badges and match tickets in the book, as well as the picture of me on the jacket. She's not a big fan of men's football, but my sons Leo and Joey make up for it, and have already won one World Cup more than their dad. My wife Pamela Druckerman has learned to care with them. Thanks, all of you, for your forbearance while I wrote five books in five years. It wasn't healthy and I promise I won't do it again.

Bibliography

On Jules Rimet

Carpentier, Florence, 'Le conflit entre le C.I.O. et la F.I.F.A. dans l'entre-deux-guerres. Les Jeux olympiques contre la Coupe du Monde de football', *Staps*, 68(2) , 2005, 25–39 (paper available at https://doi.org/10.3917/sta.068.0025)

Guillain, Jean-Yves, *La Coupe du Monde de Football: l'œuvre de Jules Rimet* (Amphora, Paris, 1998)

Heinrich, Arthur, 'Eine saubere Geschichte', *Die Zeit*, 16 March 2006

Lasne, Laurent, *Jules Rimet: la foi dans le football* (Le Tiers Livre, Montpellier, 2008)

Rimet, Jules, with Renaud Leblond and Yves Rimet (eds), *Le Journal de Jules Rimet: le récit rare du fondateur de la Coupe du monde de football* (First, Paris, 2014)

Veyssière, Laurent (ed.), *Le foot, une affaire d'État* (Archives Nationales, Pierrefitte-sur-Seine, 2016)

Vonnard, Philippe, and Grégory Quin, 'Jules Rimet: FIFA's Missionary President', in *Global Sports Leaders: A Biographical Analysis of International Sport Management*, Emmanuel Bayle and Patrick Clastres (eds) (Palgrave Macmillan, Cham, Switzerland, 2018)

On the World Cup 1954

Neukircher, Manuel, *Deutschland, dein Fußball! Eine Kulturgeschichte in 44 Objekten* (Edel Sports, Hamburg, 2022)

Smit, Barbara, *Pitch Invasion: Three Stripes, Two Brothers, One Feud – Adidas, Puma and the Making of Modern Sport* (Allen Lane, London, 2006)

Chapter 5: Early Forays, 1988–1996

Burns, Jimmy, *Hand of God: The Life of Diego Maradona* (Bloomsbury, London, 1996)

World Cup 1998

Brimicombe, Allan, and Rebecca Cafe, 'Beware, win or lose: Domestic violence and the World Cup', *Significance*, 9(5), October 2012, 32–35

Carroll, Douglas, Shah Ebrahim, Kate Tilling, John Macleod, George Davey Smith, 'Admissions for myocardial infarction and World Cup football: database survey', *BMJ* 325(7378), 21 December 2002, 1439–42

Wang, Huajun, Lunchang Liang, Ping Cai, Jianli Zhao, Lan Guo, Huan Ma, 'Associations of cardiovascular disease morbidity and mortality in the populations watching major football tournaments: A systematic review and meta-analysis of observational studies', *Medicine* (Baltimore), 99(12), March 2020, e19534

On Geoff Hurst

Hamilton, Duncan, *Answered Prayers: England and the 1966 World Cup* (riverrun, London, 2023)

Hurst, Geoff, with Jasper Rees, *Last Boy of '66: My Story of England's World Cup Winning Team* (Ebury Spotlight, London, 2024)

On match fixing

Hill, Declan, *The Fix: Football and Organized Crime* (McLelland & Stewart, Toronto, 2008)

On Zidane

Baudrillard, Jean, *Carnaval et cannibale* (Editions de l'Herne, Paris, 2008)

Domenech, Raymond, *Tout seul: souvenirs* (Flammarion, Paris, 2012)

On South Africa

Alegi, Peter, *Laduma! Soccer, Politics and Society in South Africa* (University of Kwazulu-Natal Press, Scottsville, 2004)

Alegi, Peter, *African Soccerscapes: How a Continent Changed the World's Game* (C. Hurst, London, 2010)

Archer, Robert, and Antoine Bouillon, *The South African Game: Sport and Racism* (Zed Press, London, 1982)

Auf der Heyde, Peter, *Has Anybody Got a Whistle? A Football Reporter in Africa* (Parrs Wood Press, Manchester, 2002)

Bloomfield, Steve, *Africa United: How Football Explains Africa* (Canongate, London, 2010)

Carlin, John, *Playing the Enemy: Nelson Mandela and the Game that Made a Nation* (Atlantic Books, London, 2008)

Gevisser, Mark, *Thabo Mbeki: The Dream Deferred* (Jonathan Ball Publishers, Jeppestown, 2007)

Humphrey, Luke, and Gavin Fraser, '2010 FIFA World Cup stadium investment: Does the post-event usage justify the expenditure?', *African Review of Economics and Finance,* | 8(20), December 2016

Kuper, Leo, *An African Bourgeoisie: Race, Class, and Politics in South Africa* (Yale University Press, New Haven and London, 1965)

Mandela, Nelson, *Long Walk to Freedom* (Abacus, London, 1996)

Mbeki, Moeletsi, *Architects of Poverty: Why Africa's Capitalism Needs Changing* (Picador Africa, Johannesburg, 2009)

Niehaus, Isak, 'Biographical lessons: Life stories, sex, and culture in Bushbuckridge, South Africa', in *Cahiers d'Etudes Africaines,* 46(181), 2006, 51–73

North, James, *Freedom Rising* (New American Library, New York, 1986)

Perlman, John 'The Lost Boys', in *Back Home: How the World Watched France 98*, Mike Ticher and Andy Lyons (eds) (WSC Books, London 1998)

Ross, Robert, *A Concise History of South Africa* (Cambridge University Press, Cambridge, 1999)

Russell, Alec, *After Mandela: The Battle for the Soul of South Africa* (Hutchinson, London, 2009)

Schoon, Edwin, *De macht van de bal* (L.J. Veen, Amsterdam, 2010)

Thabe, G.A.L. (ed.), *It's a Goal! 50 Years of Sweat, Tears and Drama in Black Soccer* (Skotaville Publishers, Johannesburg, 1983)

Vladislavic, Ivan, *Portrait with Keys: The City of Johannesburg Unlocked* (Portobello Books, London, 2006)

On FIFA

Bensinger, Ken, *Red Card: FIFA and the Fall of the Most Powerful Men in Sports* (Profile, London, 2018)

Conn, David, *The Fall of the House of FIFA* (Nation Books, New York, 2017)

Yallop, David, *De voetbal maffia: De corrupte spelletjes van de FIFA* (Van Gennep, Amsterdam, 1999)